Insuring Inequality

Administrative Leadership in
Social Security, 1935–54

Jerry R. Cates

Ann Arbor   The University of Michigan Press

6 5 4 3 2 1   1986 1985 1984 1983

Library of Congress Cataloging in Publication Data

Cates, Jerry R. (Jerry Ray), 1946–
   Insuring inequality.

   Bibliography: p.
   Includes index.
   1. Social security—United States—History.
2. United States. Social Security Administration—
History. 3. United States. Social Security Board—
History. 4. Income distribution—United States—
History. 5. Public welfare—United States—History.
I. Title.
HD7125.C35   1982   353.0082'56   82-13517
ISBN 0-472-10026-2

For my son Ashok Cates

Acknowledgments

I gratefully acknowledge the guidance and support of Rosemary Sarri, Mayer Zald, William Birdsall, Charles Tilly, David Street, and Joseph Sanders. Rosemary Sarri's dynamism and commitment to social welfare have been of special importance beyond this particular project. To Philip Booth, my former policy professor, I owe most of what I know about American social insurance. Others whose support directly contributed to the completion of this work include Dale Watermulder, Bogart Leashore, Roger Nooe, Wilhelmina Simmons, and Cindy Reynolds.

This research was supported in part by a grant from the Administration on Aging, Department of Health and Human Services. Researchers undertaking such projects are encouraged to express freely their professional judgments. Therefore, points of view or opinions stated in this document do not necessarily represent the official position or policy of the Department of Health and Human Services.

Additional financial support was provided by the faculty research funds of the School of Social Work, University of Tennessee, Knoxville, for which I thank Roger Nooe and Ben Granger.

Contents

Introduction

By the late 1970s social security had emerged as a commanding public issue, fed by fears for the fiscal soundness of the system. By this time it had also become clearer than ever how social security's operations were biased against the poor. Certainly it has been known from the beginning that the payroll tax is a regressive one and that wage-related benefits provide less for poorer workers. Yet by the late 1970s there were available increasingly fine-tuned analyses of the full extent to which the system works against the lowest income classes. In the political arena, however, better treatment of the poor has not emerged as a major issue; in fact, major proposals for shoring up the system have called for escalating the antipoor bias.

All this is an immensely curious situation. What is the largest antipoverty program in American history doing with such an antipoor bias? Certainly the fact that a major American institution is twisted in favor of the middle and upper income classes is no surprise in itself; only the most naive of observers would find that fact startling. However, a knowledge in fine detail of the process through which the bias has been institutionalized would be fascinating in itself, could shed light on the nature of American redistributive policy making, and conceivably could contribute to current debate over the future of social security.

Several factors shaped this study. From my background in organizational sociology came a curiosity about the evolution of a fundamentally important organization, the Social Security Administration (SSA) and its predecessor, the Social Security Board (SSB). This was supplemented by an awareness of the virtually untapped social security materials found in the National Archives and National Records Center. These collections offer, in at times bewildering detail, huge deposits of policy and organizational records—agency files containing everything from requisition forms for office furniture to the most confidential of political strategy documents—all available to the scholar. The most important factor shaping this study, however, is my curiosity about the treatment of the poor in American social security. These curiosities coalesced into the present volume, a case study of the early years of the SSB/SSA, utilizing archival holdings to study the evolution of policy as seen through the eyes of agency leadership.

The investigation was designed to focus on choice points at which agency leaders balanced the needs of the poor against other factors in making policy decisions. This focus on leadership is one way of getting at the process questions that are so intriguing. First, we need to identify leaders who, because of their positions, have had great influence over the character of policy; this is certainly true of SSB/SSA leadership. Then we can try to position ourselves to watch these leaders (retroactively in this case) as they are confronted with policy choices regarding the poor; listen to them as they define the issues and options; tap their perceptions of long- and short-range consequences; consider the values against which they weigh the various courses, and then watch them as they select an option and pursue its implementation. If we can do all this we can learn a great deal about redistributional policy making. The richness of the archival holdings, I believe, carries us a long way toward these objectives, allowing us, in effect, to look over their shoulders as these leaders were in the act of decision making.[1] (See the appendix for a listing of data sources.)

In studying policy formation, the decision was made at the beginning to accept as an object of study, rather than as given fact, the traditional SSA explanation and defense of policy. Much time in this work has been spent examining alternatives to conservative social insurance and studying the extent to which policy leaders, over the years, were aware of those alternatives and felt it necessary to oppose them.

This traditional rationale, including the explanation for the treatment of the lowest income classes, has until recent years dominated most writings about social security. Voluminous material is available to the reader interested in its fine details.[2] My interest focuses on illuminating that traditional rationale by holding it up against the light of competing understandings of social security. The entrenchment of social security has produced a situation in which certain policy concepts have achieved virtually the status of givens. For example, the SSB/SSA has been successful in cultivating the notion that the phrase *social insurance* has only one meaning, that embodied in traditional American social security. These givens have not been automatically accepted here: rather, this is a study of the actions taken by policy leaders to establish these givens as policy parameters.

The goals and intentions of these leaders, as well as their strategies and perceptions, play a large part in this work. Any such attempt to describe strategy and to distinguish intended from unintended consequences runs the danger of inappropriate attribution of intention. This danger is at its height if intention is inferred from apparent patterns in decision making. Frequently, however, it has been possible in this study to have direct access to staff intentions and goals as expressed in their own words in agency records. A prime example of this is found in the informal minutes of the SSB meetings. These minutes constitute detailed accounts of policy discussions preceding the formal decisions of the SSB. These highly informal discussions, originally intended for use only by SSB members but now available to the public, contain vivid, candid expressions of long- and short-range goals held by leadership. Some staff, such as Chief Actuary Williamson, were in the habit of dictating lengthy, diarylike memoranda to the office files describing personal preferences for policy and analyzing the ways in which these preferences meshed with other leaders' wishes.

Another potential difficulty is mistaking short-run tactics for long-range strategy. Mitigating this threat are two factors: (1) the long time span studied permits the discernment of enduring themes over a twenty-year period and (2) this work's multiplicity of approaches reduces the chances of an inappropriate characterization of leadership's goals regarding redistribution's place in social security. When their redistributional inclinations have been characterized, this has been based on an examination of a large number of redistributionally relevant policy issues.

Yet another potential limitation of this study stems from the great importance attached to agency leadership's perceptions of environmental opportunities and constraints. Throughout this time period leadership constantly monitored its political environment, keeping track of policy competitors that threatened their preferred programs. The question of the accuracy of these environmental assessments can be raised. Were the environmental threats actually as potent as they appeared to leaders? To some extent, this issue has been dealt with by turning to others who have studied those environmental threats (such as Piven and Cloward's study of Depression-era social movements and Messinger's study of the Townsend organization) for a check on the accuracy of these perceptions.[3] By and large, however, I have taken leadership at its word when it has labeled the Townsend movement and its own public assistance system as genuine threats to the existence of conservative social insurance. In any event, whether or not the leadership's assessments of threats were *accurate*, it is clear that they *mattered*; they were fundamentally important in shaping policy positions. These perceptions and policies are studied for the 1935 to 1954 period, a time span that encompasses the creation and institutionalization of a major policy organization.

The reader already familiar with social security history will have noticed that the time period encompassed by this work coincides with that covered in the memoirs of Arthur J. Altmeyer.[4] Altmeyer was the dominant social security leader for the first two decades of the system, and his memoirs, until recently, have dominated contemporary understanding of the origins of social security. In many respects the present work constitutes a more detailed telling of events only touched upon, or left untreated, in his memoirs. His is the principal shoulder over which I have looked to observe social security policy in the making. Altmeyer, as his memoirs testify, was a private person; his memoirs are often oblique and tantalizing in their allusions to important issues that are then never developed. I am sure that if he could read this work, he would resent the intrusion and strongly disagree with many of my conclusions. I can only defend my accuracy by pointing to the extent to which the argument is grounded in primary source material and justify the intrusion by the hope that this will contribute to a better, richer understanding of such an important program.

CHAPTER 1

Social Security and Income Redistribution

One of the most prestigious voices to have critiqued the redistributional limitations of social security was that of President Johnson's Commission on Income Maintenance Programs. The points established in its 1969 report are still valid.

> Regressive social insurance taxes in effect exempt high income people and those with property income from participation in income redistribution through social insurance and raise a question about the continued support by ordinary working people for the scheme. . . . Social insurance has not been effective in correcting long-term chronic poverty. The contribution/benefit orientation of a social insurance system automatically leaves uncovered those who cannot contribute and pays small benefits to low contributors. The ones who benefit from a contributory program are those who were more fortunate in the past. A social insurance system does not alter the basic principle of income distribution. . . . For this reason, social insurance programs can do little to alleviate existing poverty, however effective they may be in preventing households from falling into poverty if their normal flow is interrupted.[1]

Though the social security system does not fundamentally alter the distribution of income between classes, clearly there is the potential for significant reduction of distributional inequality in the massive flows of social security taxes and benefits. By 1977, $83.8 billion were flowing out in benefits (exclusive of Medicare), an amount which constituted one-fifth of the national budget. The social security payroll tax is the second-largest source of federal revenue and has been the fastest growing tax in recent history.[2]

Brookings Institution economist John Brittain has been able to specify the impact of the payroll tax on income inequality. According to Brittain, the 1969 regressive impact is shown on after-tax shares of income. For example, prior to the payroll tax, the 4 percent of earners who were in the highest income class (incomes over $15,000) received 18.4 percent of total pretax earnings. The regressive effect of the tax was to increase their share to 19.3 percent. The lowest income class ($7,800 and below) received 9 percent of total pretax earnings and 8.8 percent after the tax.[3]

According to Brittain: "The payroll tax directly and symmetrically counteracts the progressive income tax by hitting the poor the hardest and by virtually sparing the rich. . . . The payroll tax is highest in poverty-income ranges where the income tax rate is zero and then approaches zero for high incomes as the income tax rate approaches its maximum."[4]

Given that the social security tax has grown faster than the income tax, Brittain argues there has been an increasing amount of inequality injected into the total income distribution, a trend that will continue as long as the system continues to rely on the regressive payroll tax financing.

Given the severity of Brittain's critique, it is important to make clear the three major assumptions of his analysis: (1) Although, nominally, the employee's social security tax is matched by an equal amount by the employer, Brittain assumes the employer tax is in reality a reduction in labor's earnings—an assumption of 100 percent worker incidence. This incidence assumption is now accepted by most economists; even a defender of the payroll tax and an opponent of increasing redistribution in social security such as Alicia Munnell accepts that assumption.[5] (2) Redistributional effects of the tax are computed on the basis of factor income; transfer income is excluded. (3) It is useful to consider the redistributional effects of social security taxes independently of the effects of benefits.

The third assumption is an extremely significant one. Brittain argues that it is essential to analyze the impact of the taxes independently of benefits because of the long time lag between payment of taxes and receipt of benefits. The tax-paying earner of today is contributing to the current support of today's beneficiaries. A person in poverty can be driven deeper into poverty because of the compulsory payroll tax. Yet, because as much as fifty years later that same person may finally receive benefits that are moderately weighted to favor the low wage earners, the combined tax-benefit impact can be termed progressive over the lifetime of the worker.

In examining this net progressive impact we can look at the lifetime rates of return for earners (the dollars of benefits received compared to the taxes paid). Brittain has calculated future rates of return for today's taxpayers, deriving his findings from a simulation model built on a series of assumptions about the rates of growth of average earnings, modes of social security financing, and so on. He has demonstrated that the lifetime rates of return are such that the average participant gets back the value of his/her taxes with an increase in value, with low income taxpayers receiving slightly higher percentage rates of return. Brittain characterizes this progressivity as modest and says:

Although there is a modest degree of progressivity in the yield-earnings relationships, the yields at the low end of the income scale are highly unattractive to the poor. Low-income families frequently must borrow at very high interest rates. It is therefore difficult to justify forcing them to save, even at a real interest rate of 7 percent under social security; they may at the same time (and in part as a consequence) be borrowing at 36 percent or more. . . . families found to be in poverty should not be forced to contribute substantially. . . .[6]

Arguing that the insurance and savings imagery of the social security system is a misleading myth that has served to obscure the regressive burden of the tax, Brittain asserts that the system should be stripped of its insurance imagery and seen as a system of taxes and benefits, two elements which should be evaluated independently.

Opposing Brittain is another Brookings Institution economist, Alicia Munnell, who argues that redistribution has proceeded too far in social security, and that the system is best seen as a compulsory savings mechanism rather than a welfare arrangement of taxes and benefits. If further modification of the income distribution is desired, she argues, let it take place through systems other than social security. For Munnell, the conceptualization of social security as a system for transferring income from the current working population to those currently withdrawn from the work force (Brittain's view): ". . . seems at variance with the existing structure of the social security program. The social security system is inappropriate as an annual redistributive scheme. The present system can best be understood when considered in a lifetime compulsory saving framework."[7]

For Munnell, progressive redistribution has already reached, or even exceeded, an appropriate limit in social security. She bases this conclusion on an examination of the current benefit structure, with its minimum benefit guarantee and its benefit formula weighted in favor of low income earners. The benefit structure is designed to favor the low wage earner, and thus promote redistribution, she argues, because of the weighted formula which awards low income retirees a benefit that represents a larger proportion of previous average earnings than for a higher wage earner (see table 1). As one goes up the earnings scale, average benefits expressed as a percentage of average earnings *decline*; however, it is important to note that the absolute size of the average benefit *increases* as one goes up the wage scale. Thus, even though the lowest wage earner receives a benefit that represents 75 percent of those low wages; his/her benefit is still only 43 percent as large as the benefit of the highest wage earner.

Munnell has been one of the most articulate critics of the minimum benefit provision of social security (that policy guaranteeing all those who qualified for any benefit at all a benefit that would not drop below a stated level).

TABLE 1.   Old Age, Survivors', Disability, and Health Insurance Benefits: Single
            Beneficiary, 65 and Over, 1971, Average Monthly Benefits

Average Monthly Earnings	Average Benefits Paid	Average Benefits as Percentage of Earnings
$150	$112.50	75%
250	145.00	58
350	178.00	51
450	189.00	42
550	242.00	44
650	263.00	41

Source: Philip Booth, *Social Security in America* (Ann Arbor: University of Michigan–Wayne State University Institute of Labor and Industrial Relations, 1973), p. 42.

Arguing that the minimum benefit should be phased out (as is now being done), she says it is an inefficient way of transferring money to the poor. The goal of guaranteeing a minimum benefit to the poor could be achieved much more directly through public assistance programs. For Munnell, such a welfare concept is in conflict with the wage-related principle upon which the social security system has been built.

Munnell's criticisms are in agreement with the antiredistributional stance of the 1974 Subcommittee on Fiscal Policy of the Joint Economic Committee chaired by Congresswoman Martha W. Griffiths. The subcommittee's report argues that social security has gone as far as it can in redistributing income in favor of the poor. This redistribution has been achieved through the previously discussed minimum benefit policy but also because of the fact that low wage earners tend to have more children and thus, as a group, receive a disproportionate share of dependents' benefits. Any attempt to further redistribution in favor of the poor should take place outside the social security system, the Griffiths report argues.[8]

Rebutting both Munnell and the Griffiths subcommittee is policy analyst Martha Ozawa who argues that, despite its appearances, the social security system in all probability has a regressively redistributive net impact; that is, it redistributes income from the poor to the rich. Her first piece of evidence is her study in which she compared rates of return for hypothetical workers with varying tax payment records. She found that:

a worker retiring in 1973 at age sixty-five who paid maximum contributions since social security started collecting contributions, could expect, on the average, subsidies from the working population in the amount of $26,000, discounted to the 1973 value, in his lifetime. This contrasted with $18,000 in subsidies, discounted to the 1973 value, for a worker with the same employment and demographic backgrounds except that he contributed one-half the maximum every year for the same period of time. Thus . . . calculating amounts of income redistributed from one generation to another, convince[s] us that the direction of income redistribution through social security is opposite to what is believed by the members of the Subcommittee on Fiscal Policy; that is, the high-wage retiree receives a larger amount of subsidy from the working population than does the low-wage retiree.[9]

Ozawa, further developing her rebuttal, considers the dependents' benefits argument of the Griffiths subcommittee. This argument simply is erroneous, she says, for

the social security benefit structure is mostly insensitive to family size due to the provision of a maximum family benefit [the policy of setting an absolute maximum which benefits cannot exceed no matter how many dependents are present]. Worse still, a beneficiary family of a low-wage earner must settle for a maximum family benefit that is smaller in amount relative to the PIA [primary insurance amount, the benefit for the wage earner] than is the case for the beneficiary family of a high-wage earner.[10]

Ozawa points to other factors that obstruct downward income redistribution in social security. For instance:

There is the question of how different numbers of years of life expectancy at birth among various racial groups influence redistribution through social security. At birth white men have life expectancies of 7 more years than black men; there is a difference of 6 years between white and black women. The difference is even greater between whites and American Indians . . . many blacks and American Indians may contribute to the social security funds for a longer period of time than do whites since they have less chance to go to college and thus start working earlier.[11]

In summarizing her position, Ozawa concludes: "It may well be that income redistribution is taking place in the opposite direction from what is generally believed; that is, beneficiary families of a high-wage earner receive a larger amount of subsidy from the working population than do those of a low-wage earner, although it is difficult to quantify the magnitude of income redistribution."[12]

The preceding discussion shows that one's assessment of redistribution in social security depends on: (1) whether one views the system as an annual arrangement for transferring income from current workers to those currently withdrawn from the work force or as a compulsory lifetime insurance or savings mechanism; (2) whether one evaluates taxes and benefits separately or jointly; (3) whether one considers just the tax and benefit structures as written in the legislation or whether one considers variables such as high interest paid by the poor for loans and differential life expectancies on the actual impact of this social policy. Despite the conflicting views about both the desirability of and the precise extent of redistribution, it is clear that there have been forces at work that have placed strong limits on the extent of progressive redistribution in social security.

Administrative Leadership and Redistribution

What has been the SSB/SSA's role in giving this limited redistributional cast to social insurance? Has organizational leadership fought for or opposed redistribution? What has been its perceptions of the sources and consequences of the antipoor bias? We know from memoirs and previous studies that in the organization's early days, these leaders predicted that social insurance would expand over the coming years in such a way that it would greatly reduce, if not eliminate, the need for the highly redistributive public assistance program.[13] But these writings do not tell us if leadership expected and worked toward a line of development in which social insurance would broaden to incorporate public assistance's direct redistributional function or if leadership's expectations and goals were the virtual elimination of this redistributive component.

In considering these questions, an obviously relevant factor has been the insurance imagery of social security, an imagery at the heart of the ideology used by the SSB/SSA to defend its program. Drawing an analogy between private insurance and social security has been the principal means of legitimating this social welfare program. This private insurance analogy was used especially during the first twenty years while the organization was pursuing political institutionalization. What role has this insurance ideology played in limiting the redistributional character of social security? A critic such as Brittain argues that the insurance imagery has been a powerful roadblock to redistribution.

> This strenuously promoted insurance analogy has proved extremely powerful; it has been used explicitly to stave off criticism of the payroll tax and such suggested reforms as the introduction of [tax] exemptions. . . . The implication of the insurance analogy is that the poor must pay for their federal social security as they would under private insurance programs. . . . The celebration of the "insurance principle" has been a key factor in the headlong growth of payroll taxation in the United States.[14]

On the other hand, others argue that the insurance imagery has been an essential protective device, both making it possible to sustain whatever redistribution does take place and protecting the rights and dignity of beneficiaries—a position taken by Wilbur J. Cohen. "Payroll taxes despite their regressivity, and despite all the other criticisms . . . are valuable. They safeguard the . . . benefit as a matter of right. I don't justify this as a method of taxation. I only justify it as a moral and compassionate method of giving security to people so they don't have to go through the humiliation of a means test." [15]

Cohen, former secretary of the Department of Health, Education and Welfare (HEW) and longtime policy leader in social security, sums up his analysis of the insurance rhetoric and its relation to minimal or negative redistribution in a debate with economist Milton Friedman:

> People do live by rhetoric. You can't understand what goes on in the United States if you don't understand something about rhetoric. . . . Finally, Mr. Friedman attacks the idea that social security is primarily a system of redistribution of income to middle income people. Actually I think he is probably right about that. But, that is part of the system's political sagacity . . . to the extent that . . . there is a transfer of money from low income people to middle income people, the situation could be improved by certain changes in the financing. . . . But let me emphasize that the reason why the Office of Economic Opportunity and other such programs don't get the appropriations, don't get support from the taxpayer, is that they do not appeal to the middle class, middle income person. [16]

In considering the variables of policy, administrative leadership, and organizational ideology, a question emerges: Is the history of the SSB/SSA one that parallels that of the Tennessee Valley Authority (TVA) as described by Philip Selznick? [17] Is the history of the SSB/SSA insofar as the limited redistributional focus of the program is concerned that of an organization trapped by the unanticipated consequences of its own protective ideology and strategy? The question emerges when one considers that the insurance ideology, in addition to being a source of organizational and policy legitimation, has also provided the base from which critics can launch arguments against its redistributional elements.

The history of the TVA as described in Selznick's classic work is that of an organization co-opted by means of its own protective ideology. A centerpiece of New Deal social planning, the TVA was established with a broad range of goals: flood control, power production, environmental conservation, and agricultural development. This new agency was situated in a politically conservative environment that was suspicious and frequently hostile. Neutralization of the environmental threats was a prerequisite for organizational success and, in Selznick's view, this neutralization was achieved through the elaboration and institutionalization of a protective ideology that served to ex-

plain and justify the organization to the environment. This protective ideology, the doctrine of grass roots involvement, called for decentralization in
agency decision making and the involvement of local citizens in the policy
making of this major federal agency. This direct invitation to potential local
opponents constitutes the classic example of co-opting the opposition, a process which Selznick tells us consists of "absorbing new elements into the
leadership or policy-determining structure of an organization as a means of
averting threats to its stability or existence." [18] Co-optation achieved its anticipated effect of managing potentially harmful local opposition; however, co-
optation turned out to be a two-way process and the TVA itself was unexpectedly co-opted as well. The agency suffered a dilution or displacement of
original policy goals. The local elements the TVA most needed to contain
were, unsurprisingly, the more powerful ones in the political environment; the
less powerful ones posed little threat to the agency. Involvement of these
powerful elements, however, had the unanticipated consequence of distorting
the TVA's goals in their favor. Thus, the American Farm Bureau, a powerful
and politically conservative organization, was co-opted but, in turn, it caused
TVA to exclude non–Farm Bureau (and frequently more liberal) organizations from the benefits of TVA. Similarly, co-optation of the local power
structure meant appealing to the white organizations: thus white land-grant
colleges benefited from the TVA's agricultural assistance projects, but local
black colleges were excluded. As these events developed, the TVA found itself opposing fellow New Deal agencies that one would have expected the
TVA to support. Selznick has traced the TVA's often-criticized environmental
conservation record, in particular its support of strip mining, back to the involvement of local interests in the agency.

Goal displacement, or organizational drift, as described above is, in
Selznick's view, almost inevitable to some degree for all organizations. Organizational leadership, typically, is committed to original policy goals and
seeks ways to nurture and sustain them, to defend them from opposition. At
times, however, the very protective devices established for the sake of the
goals, devices which typically are the expression of some attempt at political
accommodation with opponents, can have the unanticipated consequence of
eroding those very goals they were designed to protect. The sacrifice of some
aspects of an organization's goal structure is, in Selznick's analysis, a necessary price to pay for survival in an unfriendly environment; and at times that
sacrifice, as with the TVA, is accomplished in an unplanned, unwitting manner.

Is there a similar history of drift and displacement in the SSB/SSA regarding the redistributional character of policy? Does the insurance analogy
occupy a position parallel to the grass roots ideology? Or is the comparison a
misleading one? Was there actually no goal drift or displacement in the SSB/

SSA? Perhaps significant redistributional goals were never seriously entertained by leadership. Going even further, has the SSB/SSA, in fact, used the insurance ideology to ward off redistributional pressures from the environment? Or, to complicate matters, does the answer lie somewhere between these two positions? Did SSB/SSA leadership perhaps entertain no significant redistributional goals at first, later embrace them, but then find themselves handicapped in their pursuit by the entanglements of the well-established insurance defense?

With these yet-to-be-answered questions we have come a considerable way in refining our initial curiosities; but before proceeding further it is necessary to take a closer look at the organizational ideology in question—the social security ideology.

Social Security Ideology

Ideology as defined by Selznick, Strauss, and Bendix and used here in the same sense, is a set of shared ideas espoused by organizational personnel to explain and justify policy.[19] This set of shared ideas constitutes a system; that is, they are a coherent, interrelated whole rather than a collection of disjointed elements. Typically, ideologies contain statements both about the way the world is and the way it ought to be. As used here, the concept does not "imply the truth or falsity of those ideas but [is used] only to denote the ideas themselves."[20] The following description of the social security ideology is drawn from Eveline Burns's classic analysis of American social insurance programs, Alvin Schorr's writings, and the published writings of Committee on Economic Security and Social Security Administration personnel, many of whom were principal architects of the Social Security Act and its amendments.[21]

The phrase *social security*, when it was coined more than forty years ago, meant both social insurance and public assistance. Over the years, however, the phrase has come to mean, for most people, only the federal social insurances: retirement, survivors', disability, and health insurance. It is in the original sense that the phrase is used here. The social security ideology is a set of statements about the nature of social insurance and public assistance, as well as the proper relationship between these two programs. In this ideology social insurance is seen as the rightfully dominant program.

Social insurance, as it is described in this ideology, can be understood as a reaction to the perceived inequities of the Elizabethan Poor Laws which were based on the principle that economic support should be provided only after individual means tests had been administered. The Elizabethan Poor Laws were hated by reformers for the economic segregation they promoted:

poor people were isolated and programs designed exclusively for them were then administered. The means test was the instrument of segregation. An impulse of the social insurance reform movement was to avoid, as much as possible, the isolation of the poor, to include them in a program that encompassed the middle and upper classes as well. Eliminating the isolation of the poor, it is believed, will greatly reduce their stigmatization. Unfortunately, it is argued, not all the poor can be saved since social insurance cannot take care of the poorest of the poor, those with marginal or nonexistent attachment to the work force who have been unable to earn social insurance coverage. So it is necessary to tolerate the means test for these residual poor, but it is hoped these programs will be small. Thus, the social insurance movement has not eliminated the economic segregation of the Elizabethan Poor Laws and admits the impossibility of completely doing so.

The stigma and social controls accompanying the Elizabethan Poor Laws gave reformers a distaste for and fear of the means test which has persisted to the present day. The desire to avoid the means test was a strong impulse behind the development of social insurance: if workers qualify for benefits under social insurance, then benefits are administered without individual means tests. Benefits automatically flow when the specified contingency, such as retirement or disability, occurs to a covered worker or dependent, regardless of the worker's wealth or lack of it. This ideology asserts that social insurance cannot do the entire job of eliminating poverty, but it is believed that social insurance can and should take care of almost all economic needs not met in the marketplace.

The social security ideology under examination here asserts a particular version of social insurance. It is important to remember that social insurance is an imprecise term that could be used to describe any of a wide range of programs from highly redistributive to minimally or regressively redistributive, from ones that cover only those people with substantial work force attachment to those with little or no such attachment. It has been characteristic of the Social Security Administration to speak of social insurance without making it clear that only one particular version is under discussion. Proponents of the American social security ideology have spoken as if their preferred version of social insurance is the one and only version. For example, we find SSA Administrator Arthur J. Altmeyer in 1941 announcing that it is a "fundamental principle" of social insurance that benefits shall not exceed former wages.[22] (This would hold even if former wages and benefits were both subpoverty level.) This particular principle is by no means an inevitable element of a social insurance program, although it has been an element of the social security ideology under consideration here. To highlight the fact that the American social insurance system being studied here is only one possible model of social insurance, it will generally be referred to from this point on as *conservative social insurance* to distinguish it from other social insurance models with much greater redistributional impact.

At the heart of the social insurance ideology is a set of three principles that govern financing and benefit decisions: the principle of risk selection, the contributory principle, and the wage-related principle.

The Principle of Risk Selection

The social insurance approach is not addressed directly to economic need; it is directly addressed to the occurrence of carefully specified contingencies such as loss of earned income springing from retirement, disability, or loss of working spouse or parent. This principle is invoked to avoid a repetition of the stigmatization and social control of beneficiaries present under the Elizabethan Poor Laws. This principle calls for the payment of benefits on the occurrence of the specified event regardless of need. It is essential to avoid a needs assessment, it is felt, because such an assessment would require a potentially abusive and degrading means-testing investigation. Thus, we may find someone quite wealthy, with considerable property income, still qualifying for social security benefits.

The Contributory Principle

Workers should contribute toward the payment of their own benefits because this will have a beneficial disciplinary effect, preventing them from voting in unreasonably large benefits since they realize they must pay for these benefits out of their own wages. The fear of what would happen if the contributory principle is weakened is illustrated in the following assertion. "When the something-for-nothing principle enters it may give impetus to the notion that the government is a bottomless well of funds supplied by someone else, to which anyone in need of money has a constitutional right by mere virtue of being alive and present." [23]

Other phrasings of the disciplinary argument broaden it to include the inculcation in workers of a sense of responsibility for efficient public administration. "The citizens as insured persons should realize that they cannot get more than certain benefits for certain contributions, should have a motive to support measures for economic administration, should not be taught to regard the State as the dispenser of gifts for which no one need pay." [24]

Another justification for the contributory principle is that workers, having paid for their benefits, will look upon benefits as a right rather than as charity. Individuals, it is argued, want to feel self-supporting and this feeling will be promoted by the contributory principle. Public assistance is degrading to beneficiaries because it thwarts this natural desire and encourages a dependent attitude. In addition to improving self-image, this principle will foster a more respectful attitude on the part of society as a whole toward beneficiaries; others will see beneficiaries as merely collecting what is rightfully theirs.

Another elaboration of the contributory principle is that it is a reliable source of funding. The earmarked payroll taxes flow automatically into social insurance accounts; the social security system is basically self-supporting. Thus, there is no need for the social insurance program to compete with other demands on general revenues. Abandonment of the contributory principle, through general revenue financing, would threaten the stability of the program.

In the American social insurance system, employee payroll taxes are matched by employer taxes. The social security ideology has, at times, justified the employer contribution with an argument that draws a parallel between the depreciation of workers and the depreciation of machines. "Just as the employer regards what he has to set aside for depreciation and obsolescence of his plant as part of the costs of doing business, so too, it is argued, should he provide, as part of business costs, against the obsolescence of his working force." [25]

The Wage-Related Principle

Social insurance benefit levels should be keyed to past wage levels: workers with a history of higher levels should receive higher benefits. Although benefit formulae may be weighted so that poor workers may receive benefits that represent a higher percentage of previous wage levels, still the size of their benefits should be lower than those of higher income workers. This principle has been justified with general philosophical statements that in a free enterprise system an income support system should embody incentive principles. "The higher income secured by the higher paid (and presumably therefore more enterprising) workers should be reflected in higher social security benefits." [26] At times the above general position is broken down into more specific statements about the need for and effectiveness of social controls on labor's behavior with the argument that elimination of the penalty for idleness and reward for productivity will have adverse effects. At the individual worker level, benefits should not exceed former wages, it is argued, for incentives to work will be damaged if people see another person (or anticipate they themselves can) receive more in social insurance benefits for not working than they can receive in earned income. (In the disability insurance program this is expressed as fear that high benefit levels will encourage malingering.) The wage-relatedness principle at times has been defended with statements of its administrative simplicity. In a heterogeneous country such as the United States, it would be a costly and time-consuming task to set benefit levels according to individual analyses, case-by-case, or to establish benefit levels that varied according to geographical location or occupational grouping. By applying the wage-related principle (setting benefits as a specified percentage of former wages) it is possible to "apply a uniform principle regardless of residency and at the same time maintain any desired differential between benefit and normal earnings as well as occupational differentials."[27] Still another argument is that the wage-related principle, like the contributory principle, helps to depoliticize the program. If benefit levels are set automatically by this principle, then the involvement of politicians in the process is reduced and stability is enhanced.

The imprint of these three principles can be found throughout American social security. Frequently compressed into the often-used insurance analogy, these principles constitute the core of the ideological system used by SSB/SSA leaders to explain policy goals and to defend those goals from competitors. In addition to being an ideology of *policy* these statements are a prime example of an *organizational* ideology. The SSB/SSA has been the ideology's home base; that agency's administrators have taken the lead in articulating the fine details of ideology, and they have served as arbiters of the ideological correctness of discrete policy choices. It is by looking within this organizational home base to observe the intermingling of administrative leadership, organizational ideology, and policy choices that we can learn a considerable amount about the origins and institutionalization of social security's antipoor bias.

Organizational Sources of the Antipoor Bias: Drift or Tool View?

This study's focus on the SSB/SSA means that only part of the total policy-making system is studied directly. Other elements of that system include, among others, the president and other executive branch offices, Congress, and program constituencies. These other elements are not ignored in this work, rather they are primarily dealt with *as they have been perceived by SSB/SSA leadership*. We lose something in breadth of focus by this, but we gain something in return: such concentration allows us a richer, deeper understanding of policy decision making and allows us space to scrutinize and reflect upon the SSB/SSA's role. Such an intense examination of a single agency is justified by that agency's strategic location in the total policy-making system.

The SSB/SSA has had two major areas of responsibility: (1) the administrative interpretation and implementation of existing legislation and (2) the production of (and unofficial lobbying for) new policy initiatives. While this agency's actions obviously have not been the sole determinants of policy, they have been sufficiently important to warrant detailed examination in their own right. Thus, a partializing, disaggregating inquiry is undertaken, an approach based on a view of government policy making described by Marmor and Allison. "The actions of government—the sum of the 'behavior of representatives of a government' involved in a policy issue—'is rarely intended by any individual or group' . . . what the government does is a collage of individual acts, outcomes of minor and major [bargaining] games and foul-ups. The understanding of that cumulative process requires piece-by-piece disaggregation of the policy-making." [28]

In studying the SSB/SSA's contribution to the antipoor bias of social security, I wanted to test the adequacy of the goal drift explanation derived from Selznick's work and discussed earlier. It is no surprise that the outline of such an explanation should suggest itself, given the extraordinary impact that Selznick's work has had on the study of organizations. His conceptual framework has been remarkable both for the influence it has exerted and the degree of criticism and debate it has precipitated. One of the most trenchant criticisms is Charles Perrow's; he warns against too quick an assumption of goal drift processes. Such unintentional drifting may occur, but "it is also possible that we cannot freely assume goodwill on the part of [organizational] leaders. What some sociologists like to see as 'goal displacement' may refer only to goals never entertained by the leaders. The outputs may be just what they planned." [29] This alternate explanation, goal achievement rather than goal drift, is called a *tool view* by Perrow to emphasize the organization's possible role as an instrument in the hand of its leaders, an instrument through which leaders can at times marshal resources to reach out to change, influence, or dominate the environment rather than simply responding to and adapting to the environment.

Crucial to deciding the adequacy of a drift or tool explanation of the SSB/SSA's role in giving the antipoor bias to social security is the question of intention. Is that bias an unintended consequence flowing from the use of an adaptive mechanism or is the bias actually an intended consequence? At this point we have come full circle, back to the original desire to study SSB/SSA leaders in the act of decision making, for it is in those acts, mirrored by the agency's archival holdings, that we can discern intention. The records pertaining to highest level decision making in both social insurance and public assistance were thus examined for the 1935–54 period.

Three top-level units relevant to the shaping of SSB/SSA policy positions in social insurance have been: (1) The Office of the Chairman/Commissioner, which included the head of the agency and support staff such as special assistants for legislative affairs; (2) The Office of the Actuary, led by actuaries with private insurance backgrounds who had the task of determining the actuarial soundness of the system and providing tax and benefit estimates; (3) The

Bureau of Research and Statistics, which had responsibility for investigating the extent of economic need in the country and developing policy proposals for its alleviation.

Prior to my study of the agency records, I had expected, in a common sense way, to find variations across these units in two things: allegiance to the social security ideology and corresponding positions on the desirability of income redistribution in social insurance. I had expected to find the chairman/commissioner mediating between an ideologically purist (and thus antiredistribution) actuarial department on the one hand and an ideologically much freer (and proredistribution) research staff on the other hand. It was by examining in fine detail this hypothesized mediation process, with an eye to perceptions of redistributionally relevant threats and opportunities in the environment, that I hoped to assess the adequacy of drift and tool explanations of the institutionalization of the antipoor bias.

The records have provided much material that directly addresses the goal versus drift question, but that common sense expectation of a mediation process proved to be inadequate—too simplistic and simply wrong. Any value this study has lies primarily in its explication of how and why that nicely balanced scenario proved to be so far off the mark. It was an appealing scenario, grounded in a consideration of each department's functions. The actuarial staff were keepers of the system's symbols of legitimation: the private insurance imagery. Surely this would have given them great leverage in the organization, and they would have used that influence base to oppose departures from a private insurance model. This would have made the actuarial staff a strong antiredistributional pressure point. Research staff, on the other hand, with their mandate to measure and respond to economic need, would have been most sensitive to the ways in which the social security ideology turned its back on the greatest need and, stemming from this sensitivity, theirs would have been a strongly proredistribution stance. A major function of the chairman/commissioner has been that of representing the organization in the external political bargaining game with other executive branch departments when competing for the president's support and when dealing with opponents and supporters in Congress. The agency head had essentially a political task, balancing responsiveness to economic need and actuarial soundness against what could be successfully maneuvered through Congress. Under direct pressure to temper need considerations with political strategizing, it was thought the head of the agency would emerge from this study as roughly mid-way between research and actuarial staff in his allegiance to social security ideology and as a mediator between proredistribution and antiredistribution pressures.

The actual picture that emerges here is vastly different: the chairman/commissioner appears in the following chapters, not mediating, but firmly im-

posing on both actuaries and researchers a strict, redistribution-limiting version of the social security ideology. The actuaries, surprisingly, at times are
seen as exceeding both the chairman and the researchers in their willingness to
abandon private insurance concepts to make the social insurance system more
responsive to lower income classes. The picture of top administrative leadership painted here shows consistent fear of strong proredistributional forces in
society and use of insurance imagery and organizational resources to ward off
those pressures. This study concludes that a tool view, goal achievement interpretation of social security's antipoor bias is most appropriate along the following lines:

1. The SSB/SSA was a powerful tool in the hands of leadership bent
on blunting the thrust of redistributional movements arising out of the
Depression-era need.

2. The minimally redistributive character of social insurance was no
unintended consequence flowing from the adoption of a protective device
but, rather, the intended consequence of the device.

3. The same organizational ideology which helped leaders put a cap on
redistributional pressures in the 1930s and 1940s also helped them to
protect their essentially conservative goals from policy opponents of the
1950s who were even more antiredistribution than they.

4. The negative consequences for the aged flowing from redistributional inadequacies in both social insurance and public assistance were
consequences both foreseen and intended by SSB/SSA leadership.

The fourth point's reference to public assistance inadequacies refers to a
policy area that was surprisingly important in understanding social security's
development. During the 1935–54 period studied here, the SSB/SSA had administrative responsibility for public assistance as well as social insurance.
My original intention was to study only social insurance, but as the investigation proceeded, I encountered frequent statements by staff that public assistance policy was a factor that had to be taken into account in formulating
social insurance positions. It soon was apparent that public assistance, especially old-age assistance, was seen as a prime policy competitor with social
insurance. Agency leadership found itself in the position of having to administer a program that was seen as a direct threat to its preferred policy. It soon
became obvious that a conflict of interest existed, with leadership intentionally constraining the development of an adequate public assistance system so
as to protect social insurance.

The presentation of material leading to the above conclusions begins
with the following chapter's description of the newly created SSB and the
background of its leadership. Then an introduction is given to the efforts of
the SSB to translate the elements of the social security ideology into a firm

organizational character, to create a clear image of itself, and to defend itself against policy competitors. The relationship between policy content on the one hand and imagery and political strategy on the other is discussed. This material is preceded by a brief presentation of the historical antecedents of the 1935 Social Security Act, contextual material necessary for the subsequent discussion.

CHAPTER 2

Defining the Terms of Competition

The economic disaster of the great American Depression with its acute suffering and consequent political turmoil opened the doors of possibility to social change. Very little was predetermined, however, about who or what would come through those doors. Political unrest demanded social policy response, but the nature of the response appeared to be up for grabs. Policy competitors vied for access to that opening. One who shouldered his way through the crowd, Franklin Roosevelt, saw the competition as fierce and threatening. "I am fighting Communism, Coughlinism, Townsendism . . . I want to save our system, the capitalistic system; to save it is to give some heed to world thought of today. I want to equalize the distribution of wealth." [1] One competitor, Louisiana's Huey Long with his Share Our Wealth plan to soak the rich and establish a federally guaranteed income, grew strong enough to endanger Roosevelt's reelection in 1936 by threatening to garner a full 10 percent of the Democratic vote around the country. Another competitor, Dr. Francis E. Townsend, mobilized the nation's elderly into a system of local Townsend clubs. This Townsend movement demanded a universal, flat-rate pension for citizens sixty years of age and older, and brought considerable pressure to bear on Congress through such devices as a petition bearing twenty-five million signatures. The Social Security Act of 1935 surpassed the Townsend plan in this particular aspect of the Depression policy competition, but the Townsend plan and other flat-rate pension plans remained powerful threats to the new social insurance system for several decades. [2]

Policy competition was nothing new to the social insurance system: its origins lay in competition. The 1935 act can be understood as the culmination of a struggle between competing schools of social insurance in the United States. Lubove's analysis of this struggle portrays it as a battle over the place of redistribution in social insurance. [3] In the 1900–1935 period, at the state level, there was considerable experimentation with social insurance: workmen's compensation, health insurance, and unemployment insurance. Political battles were waged between proponents and opponents of social insurance and within the social insurance camp itself over leadership of that movement.

The two competing models of social insurance have been characterized by Lubove as the Wisconsin (conservative or antiredistributional) model versus the Ohio (liberal or proredistributional model). The Wisconsin school of thought developed around the work of institutional economist John Commons and reform leader John Andrews. The Ohio school of thought was led by Abraham Epstein and Isaac Rubinow. Rubinow had helped shape the Ohio unemployment compensation system and Epstein had been a leader in the fight for the Pennsylvania old-age pension system. The differences between these competitors can be illustrated by contrasting their approaches to state unemployment compensation policy.

The Andrews-Commons model envisioned a social insurance system that reflected what they saw as the dominant American values of individual initiative, competition, and thrift. Their philosophical stance called for using "capitalist methods—competition and the profit motive—to achieve collective security."[4] Translated into policy specifics, this ideological base produced an unemployment compensation system built on the concept of prevention. The paramount goal of such a system was to prevent unemployment rather than deal with unemployment after it occurred. Thus, the social adequacy of unemployment benefit levels was downplayed. Prevention was to be obtained as follows: benefits were financed (in the case of the 1932 Wisconsin plan) through employer taxes that were collected by the state in individual employer accounts. Employers paid for benefits only for their former employees. These individual employer reserves had to be maintained at a specified level, and the employer tax rate (expressed as a percentage of payroll) fluctuated between zero and 2 percent as needed to maintain the reserve. Thus, the theory went, employers had a financial incentive to stabilize employment: individual tax rates varied directly with individual unemployment experience. The profit motive could be harnessed to mitigate unemployment.

The Ohio approach to unemployment compensation rejected the concept of prevention as unrealistic, asserting that the forces producing unemployment rates were beyond the control of individual employers. The focus on prevention, it was argued, diverted attention from the real purpose of such systems: providing adequate financial support for the unemployed. The Ohio school of thought pressed for pooled employer reserves instead of individual ones, higher benefit levels, and the use of a governmental contribution out of general revenues in the financing of benefits. Rhetorical attacks and counterattacks were vigorous. The Wisconsin advocates defended their model as "extraordinarily individualistic and capitalistic." It was truly an "American approach" with "possibilities of stabilization of employment and not merely a program of relief."[5] Abraham Epstein dismissed the Wisconsin model as the "most stupid undertaking that has ever been suggested," scoffing at the notion that individual employers could contain unemployment.[6]

In summarizing the differences between these two models, Lubove focuses on the role of redistribution; regarding the Wisconsin plan: "If income maintenance is subordinated to prevention and employer incentives, it follows that a social insurance will have little or no redistributive function."[7] On the other hand, "Together with Rubinow, Epstein personified a social insurance tradition which stressed social adequacy as the ultimate test of an insurance or assistance program. They insisted that social adequacy and strict adherence to the equity principles of private insurance were incompatible, favored government contributions . . . favored the use of social insurances to . . . divert wealth into the secondary system of income distribution."[8]

The social insurance principles embodied in the 1935 Social Security Act represent a high point in the influence of the Wisconsin antiredistributional approach. The retirement system of this act was financed entirely from regressive payroll taxation with no government contribution. An annuity system with benefits only for the worker was created, with no survivors' or dependents' benefits. Benefit levels were low: the original act called for monthly retirement checks ranging from $10.00 to a high of $51.25, the latter payable only to a worker retiring at sixty-five after forty years of covered employment with a history of high average earnings. The act was presented by its supporters as meshing with the values of a capitalistic society. "Only to a very minor degree does it modify the distribution of wealth and it does not alter at all the fundamentals of our capitalistic and individualistic economy. Nor does it relieve the individual of primary responsibility for his own support and that of his dependents. . . ."[9]

The extreme conservatism of the 1935 Act's provisions in the face of the great need among the Depression-era aged has prompted a variety of responses from scholars. Lubove refers to the act as displaying an "equity obsession" with private insurance principles.[10] Leuchtenberg refers to it as "an astonishingly inept and conservative piece of legislation."[11] Booth, on the other hand, describes it as a "reasonable and workable foundation" upon which "the program could expand."[12] Widespread unrest with the conservatism of the 1935 Act—in particular labor criticism—prompted the addition of dependents' and survivors' benefits in 1939 and a modest increase in benefit levels.

The influence of the Wisconsin model on the 1935 Social Security Act is not surprising when one considers the background of those given responsibility for drafting the legislation. Roosevelt appointed Secretary of Labor Frances Perkins to chair the drafting committee, the Committee on Economic Security (CES). Perkins, in turn, called upon labor economist Edwin E. Witte, of the University of Wisconsin, to take a leave from his academic post to become executive director of the CES, in charge of directing the research and technical writing. Witte had been a student of Wisconsin labor economist John Commons, whose work provided the intellectual and philosophical foundation for the conservative Wisconsin model of social insurance. (Writing in 1945, Witte commented "I owe to Commons my entire outlook on life and a great many of my ideas.")[13] Witte was given "general direction of all the work of the Committee on Economic Security," and the parameters of the emerging legislation were largely a reflection of his leadership.[14]

Edwin Witte brought with him from Wisconsin a former student of his, Wilbur J. Cohen, as his personal research assistant. Cohen wrote a variety of research papers for Witte and established himself as Witte's representative at all the congressional hearings held for the social security bill. At Witte's instructions, Cohen also attended all executive sessions of the congressional committees and aided in the actual drafting of the Social Security Act.

Working closely with Witte was Arthur J. Altmeyer, a University of Wisconsin labor economist and a former student of both Witte and Commons. Like Witte, Altmeyer had been active in shaping much of Wisconsin's social insurance program. Altmeyer was appointed chairman of the CES Technical Board, a committee composed of representatives from various federal government agencies to provide consultation to the outside experts called in for the drafting of the legislation.

With the authority to establish lines of research, to select staff, and to direct the actual writing of the legislative drafts, representatives of the Wisconsin tradition wielded considerable influence on the emerging act. This influence was carried over into the administration of the act once it had become law. While Witte returned to his academic post, Altmeyer, in 1935, became a member of the three-person Social Security Board created to implement the act. In the following year he became chairman of that board. By 1946 the board structure had been replaced with a single-executive structure and Altmeyer headed the agency as commissioner for social security, a position he retained until leaving government service in 1953 after the return of the Republicans to the White House. Cohen, too, remained in Washington, working out of Chairman Altmeyer's office and quickly emerging as one of the organization's leading political strategists. Cohen remained with the organization even longer than Altmeyer. He left the agency for a time while it was controlled by the Republicans, but he returned to government service under the Kennedy administration and eventually became President Johnson's secretary of health, education, and welfare.

The Social Security Act of 1935 was an omnibus act establishing a wide variety of programs which were subsequently administered by several different federal agencies. Under the act, the United States Public Health Service and the Children's Bureau were given responsibility for programs concerning expanded public health research, special aid to crippled and disadvantaged children, health work with mothers and children, and improvement of public health staffs at the state level. The Social Security Board was created and given responsibility for a federal-state unemployment insurance system, a national system of retirement annuities, and a federal-state system of financial public assistance for needy aged, the blind, and children deprived of parental support.

The original members of the board were Arthur J. Altmeyer, Vincent M. Miles, and John G. Winant. Winant was the first board chairman, but was succeeded in that position by Altmeyer in 1936. The board itself was responsible for formulating general policy, coordinating federal-state relations, and reporting to Congress on the administration of its programs. Reporting to the board were three operating bureaus (unemployment compensation, federal old-age benefits, and public assistance) and five staff bureaus (general counsel, research and statistics, accounts and audits, business management, and informational service). Twelve regional offices were established, each with eight subunits corresponding to the operating and staff bureaus.[15]

From 1935 to 1939 the board was an independent agency, reporting directly to the president. The 1939 President's Reorganization Plan placed the board under the supervision of the newly created Federal Security Administration (FSA), which was also given responsibility for the United States Public Health Service, the Civilian Conservation Corps, the National Youth Administration, and the United States Office of Education. The Federal Security Administration, in turn, was renamed the Department of Health, Education and Welfare and raised to cabinet status in 1953.

Throughout the 1935–54 period studied in this work, the SSB/SSA was an organization characterized by great stability of leadership. There had been continuity as well between the leadership of the newly formed SSB and its predecessor, the Committee on Economic Security. Chairman Altmeyer had been a leader in the CES deliberations and a nucleus of approximately twenty key staff members was carried over from the CES to the SSB, including legal counsel Thomas Eliot, special assistant Wilbur Cohen, Bureau of Public Assistance Chief Jane Hoey, Bureau of Research and Statistics Chief Walter Hamilton, and the first director of the Bureau of Old-Age Benefits. As McKinley and Frase describe it, the administrative agency created to implement the new social welfare legislation "had access, at the beginning of its career, to the accumulated information and thought of the group responsible for its conception."[16] One of the most important tasks facing the new agency was that of defending the new social insurance retirement system from policy competitors.

Overview of Competitors

Policy competitors of social insurance had been dealt a serious blow by the 1935 Act, but some remained on the scene as genuine threats to the new system. The advocates of conservative social insurance faced three types of policy competitors: (1) liberal social insurance, (2) flat plan proposals, and (3) public assistance or "welfare" proposals. A definitional campaign was launched by leaders of the new agency, a campaign to structure terms of the policy debates by setting forth definitions of issues and policies that would place conservative social insurance in the best possible light.

Liberal social insurance, as represented by the Rubinow-Epstein tradition, was eclipsed by the passage of the 1935 Act with its embodiment of conservative social insurance principles. Ohio-school representatives had been excluded from CES deliberations, prompting Rubinow to complain that his colleague Epstein had been "treated shabbily by Miss Perkins and all her lieutenants."[17] Wisconsin thought dominated the 1935 Act and Wisconsinites dominated the new organization. The twenty-year hold on the White House by the Democrats gave organizational leaders a period in which to press for their policy preferences and to consolidate the organizational character of the new agency. During these decades the liberal school declined, leaving the field to the conservative school of social insurance. This enabled the conservatives to write and speak as if there were only one model of social insurance, the Wisconsin one.

The other policy competitors remained vigorous foes and were perceived by SSB leadership as genuine threats to the establishment of conservative social insurance. Public rhetoric of SSB leaders asserted that conservative social insurance uniquely meshed with dominant American values and thus represented the only social welfare approach that could thrive in this society. Privately, however, this same leadership was not so sanguine about the triumph of conservative social insurance and expressed fears that policy competitors had excellent chances of supplanting it.

Flat plan competitors were a mixed group, some liberal, some conservative. A *flat system* referred to one which either (a) granted an identical benefit to all people in a certain category (such as Minnesota's 1936 plan to issue a monthly assistance check of $30 to every blind person in the state with a yearly income below $365 per year), or (b) called for raising all beneficiaries to an established combined income-assistance level (for example, Colorado's 1937 plan for granting whatever assistance was needed to bring every aged person's combined income-assistance total to a minimum of $45 per month). The latter type of flat plan represented a forerunner of the guaranteed annual income proposals that dominated welfare reform debate in the 1960s and 1970s. While there are extremely important policy differences between the two types of flat plans, the SSB, in combating them, lumped them together, portraying them simply as versions of the Townsend plan. Flat plan competitors represented either liberal or more conservative alternatives to conservative social insurance depending on the level at which the benefit or benefit-income lines were drawn. From 1935 through the middle 1940s, highly redistributive, liberal versions of flat plans were the dominant threats to conservative social insurance. By the late 1940s and early 1950s, however, the flat rate competition was led by conservative opponents of social welfare who wanted to replace both assistance and insurance with a very low flat rate grant to the aged which would have represented a cutback in levels of support.

Both conservative and liberal flat plan proposals were subject to rhetorical fusillades by conservative social insurance advocates in which *flat* became a catch word embodying political, social, economic, and moral evils. Equality itself came to be identified with flatness. Thus, liberal flat plans to alleviate income inequality were branded as attempts to weaken America by, in effect, flattening it. J. Douglas Brown, former member of the CES and leading social security advocate, warned Congress that a proposed flat plan–social insurance compromise would threaten the very foundations of the nation: "This country is on the brink of a long and steady descent into a condition of flattened differentials. . . ." One of America's "greatest dangers" was embodied in "flat insurance benefits, flat assistance grants, flat rates of pay, flat levels of education, and a tragic averaging toward a single norm in scores of aspects of life. . . . We have begun to confuse equal political rights with equal economic attainment. . . ."[18]

Public assistance (or welfare competition) was, ironically, given to the SSB to administer. Publicly, the SSB spoke of its public assistance system, particularly the old-age assistance system, as a safety net to deal with need not yet addressed by the developing social insurance system, with the need for this safety net to decline and the program eventually to wither away as social insurance matured. Privately, SSB leadership, within six months of the Social Security Act's passage, was speaking of a growing race between conservative social insurance and assistance as to which one would be embraced by the nation as the primary income-support model.

The early years of the SSB were taken up with definitional imperatives: clearly articulating a public image of conservative social insurance and distinguishing it from its competitors in the sharpest possible terms. This was an important task facing the new organization, one made difficult by the 1935 Act's limitations. Under the 1935 legislation, the first social insurance benefits were not to be paid until 1942, although payroll tax collection began in 1937. Public assistance payments, on the other hand, began within a year of the act's passage. Much of the work force was not covered under the social insurance provisions, there were no dependents' allowances, and retirement benefits were small. The SSB was confronted with the task of selling a conservative program that would take seven years for the first benefits to get off the ground, of relying on a prime policy competitor, assistance, to deal with need until insurance matured, and yet making sure that the stopgap assistance competitor did not usurp insurance's place. In their struggle to achieve these ends, SSB leadership articulated ideological themes in the first five years of the agency's life that were to be elaborated and institutionalized over the coming decades.

It was necessary, the leadership felt, to make sure the public distinguished between insurance and assistance, and the most direct route to cultivating this awareness was to emphasize the themes of right and dignity. Social insurance benefits, it was argued, went to recipients as a matter of right, while assistance was a gratuity. SSB Chairman Altmeyer, speaking to the National Conference of Catholic Charities in 1938, argued that the public assistance approach was symbolized by the old-fashioned poorhouse. Inevitably, he asserted, a public assistance program meant detailed, individual investigations into income and resources by a caseworker that were bound to be "distasteful and demoralizing." The "exhaustion of resources" principle was supposedly another inevitable element of public assistance; that is, the approach would grant aid only after people had been "required to exhaust their own resources and many times the resources of friends, relatives, and creditors. . . . The demoralizing effect of spiraling downward to a level of destitution and the difficulty of spiraling upward again from that level is well known." [19]

This theme of public assistance as degrading and less than a right was sounded over and over again by SSB personnel in the early years. Minutes of a 1936 meeting of the Social Security Board show top agency executives reviewing the script of a short public relations film to be used in movie theaters. The film was to feature actors portraying recipients of old-age public assistance and old-age social insurance. Altmeyer instructed the scriptwriter to dramatize vividly the distinction between these two classes of recipients, requesting a much "sharper differentiation" than the writer had offered. Convey the message, he instructed, that social insurance is a "matter of right" and that, unlike public assistance, it is a sign of personal thrift and initiative on the part of recipients. In referring to the characters of the two insurance recipients, he instructed: "Show the superior advantages of this spinster lady and self-respecting man getting checks as a matter of right, which perhaps will enable them to go to the seashore or have a hunting lodge, or something like that. Emphasize that it is not necessary for them to be 'down and out' in order to get this fixed income." [20] Other Board members agreed, urging that when portraying the insurance recipients, the dominant phrases be *self-support*, *self-respect*, and *self-confidence*, to distinguish them from the public assistance recipients. The incongruity of an agency so sharply condemning one of its own programs was not lost on some of the SSB's lower level staff who occasionally protested the discrediting of public assistance. For example,

Robert Huse, associate director of the SSB's Informational Service, in commenting on a draft of the agency's 1936 annual report asked: "The phrase 'humiliation of public relief' is a pretty strong condemnation of the public assistance provisions of the Act. Does the Board want to condemn these provisions so strongly in its own report?"[21]

While the SSB never abandoned its position that public assistance was inevitably flawed and inferior to social insurance, it did, over the years, moderate its rhetoric to the point of acknowledging that assistance recipients did indeed have a right to their benefits once their eligibility was established. Consider a typical, early (1938) Altmeyer statement comparing social insurance and public assistance in which the concept of right is associated with social insurance but conspicuously missing in relation to assistance:

> The benefits paid under the Federal old-age insurance system will be paid as a matter of right irrespective of need, whereas the benefits paid under the State old-age assistance laws will be paid only in accordance with proven need.[22]

Compare the above with the following statements by Altmeyer made in the mid-1940s:

> In the one [public assistance] rights are conditioned on needs; in the other, on wage loss. Yet they are of the same kind, although people sometimes hold that those arising out of contributions paid by a person, or on his behalf, are more valid. I do not believe that such a distinction can be made.[23]

Again, in a statement from 1946:

> Public assistance is paid as a matter of right even though it is based on a showing of need.[24]

In attacking the various flat plan proposals, the SSB leadership painted a picture of those proposals as embodying values and assumptions in conflict with American society. SSB Chairman Altmeyer in 1936 argued that liberal flat benefit approaches, as illustrated by the Townsend plan,

> proceed upon the assumption that society owes an obligation to persons in various categories such as the unemployed, aged, widows, and orphans to pay them a flat minimum sum sufficient to maintain them. . . . Collateral notions are that certain of these categories such as the aged . . . have rendered a service to society which entitles them to a reward. . . . This notion is particularly prominent in the case of the aged.[25]

In contrast to the above assumptions, conservative social insurance, Altmeyer argued, was an expression of American initiative and free enterprise.

Because, by and large, Americans believe that each man ought, insofar as possible, to do *his* part for his *own* security, social insurance has a strong appeal. Since these benefits . . . are in proportion to the individual worker's past earnings and are payable as a matter of right, they may truly be said to represent self-earned security.[26]

The social insurance approach stimulates individual initiative and thrift. . . . The social insurance approach proceeds upon the assumption that it is desirable to retain as far as possible the advantages of a competitive society. . . . [which] brings about an automatic adjustment between the individual's interest and the common interest.[27]

Adoption of Insurance Imagery

The Social Security Board's efforts to monopolize the language of social insurance and to create sharp, even exaggerated, distinctions between conservative social insurance and its policy competitors was from 1935 to 1937 complicated and constrained by a fundamental paradox. The language of the 1935 Social Security Act did not characterize the program as "insurance"—social or otherwise—nor were there any references to contributions or premiums. The 1935 Act spoke simply of taxes and benefits. This carefully chosen terminology was an expression of a defensive political strategy on the part of the act's authors.

Social insurance language was avoided in the 1935 Act as part of a strategy to deal with a perceived threat from the Supreme Court: the fear that the Court would declare a national social insurance scheme unconstitutional. After decades of exposure to social insurance imagery, it may be difficult for a contemporary audience to realize, but is nevertheless true, that the 1935 Social Security Act avoided any mention of a social insurance system. One title of the act was used to establish a payroll tax to be collected by the Treasury Department; another title established a system of old-age benefits to be distributed by another agency, the Social Security Board. The constitutional defense was then based on the long-established separate powers of Congress to enact taxes and to appropriate funds. These two elements were designed to be two separate congressional actions that just happened to be in the same social security bill. J. Douglas Brown, a member of the Committee on Economic Security that drafted the act, comments on this strategy.

In the . . . battle, to assure constitutionality, we got the advice of some of the best professors of constitutional law in the country to help us design a double-barreled law: one barrel covering the contributions, based on the taxing power; the other barrel covering the benefit payment, based on the appropriation power. The only link was the wage records, a sort of coincidental hyphen between the two titles of the Act . . . the device worked![28]

Former Secretary of Labor Frances Perkins relates the origins of this strategy in her memoirs. As chairperson of the CES, Perkins had been much concerned about the constitutionality threat. One afternoon at a Washington social occasion she expressed this concern to another guest, Supreme Court Justice Stone, whereupon Stone whispered in her ear: "The taxing power of the Federal Government, my dear; the taxing power is sufficient for everything you want and need." [29] Perkins promptly instructed CES staff to begin work on the "double-barreled" strategy.

The Social Security Act was passed by Congress in this form, although the separation of titles ploy was a transparent device that Republican critics in Congress did not fail to attack. "The best legal talent that the Attorney General's office could marshal has for weeks applied itself to the task of trying to bring these titles within Constitutional limitations. Their best effort is only a plain circumvention. . . ." [30]

Two years were to pass before the Supreme Court declared the Social Security Act constitutional and, in the interim, the SSB's efforts to establish a clear public identity for conservative social insurance were complicated, but not stalled. Agency personnel continued to speak of the virtues of social insurance in speeches, radio presentations, and newspaper articles, but avoided characterizing their own program as social insurance in official publications. In 1937 the Supreme Court ruled in favor of the act; this favorable response was probably less a consequence of the double-barreled strategy than the Court's own defensive reaction to President Roosevelt's threats to pack the Supreme Court. In any event, the SSB took the favorable ruling as a signal to embrace insurance imagery officially. The agency felt free to do this even though the Court had been silent on whether or not the old-age benefit system constituted a system of social insurance. Within hours of the Court decision, SSB Chairman Altmeyer was announcing to the press that "The decision . . . validated the Federal old-age insurance program contained in the Social Security Act." [31]

The speedy adoption of insurance imagery is also illustrated in the public information pamphlets produced by the SSB. Pamphlets prior to the Court decision avoided insurance imagery while postdecision pamphlets spoke of payroll taxes as premiums paid on an insurance policy with the government. The following are excerpts from pamphlets produced prior to the Supreme Court decision.

[1937 pamphlet, "Security in Your Old Age"] The U.S. Government will send checks every month to retired workers . . . under the old-age benefit plan. . . . The same law that provides these old-age benefits for you and other workers sets up certain new taxes to be paid to the United States Government. . . . [32]

[1937 pamphlet, "The Social Security Act, Who Gets the Benefits?"]

[workers] . . . will be earning benefits which will come to them in the form of monthly payments from the United States Government. . . . All payments will come out of an "Old-Age Reserve Account" set aside in the United States Treasury. . . . Meanwhile, the law provides that employers and workers will pay a tax on the worker's wages. . . .[33]

Pamphlets produced after the Supreme Court replace talk of taxes and benefits with imagery of premiums and insurance policies.

[1938 pamphlet, "Old-Age Insurance, Safe as the USA"] More than 40,000,000 American wage earners have applied for accounts under the Federal old-age insurance plan established by the Social Security Act.[34]
   [1940 pamphlet, "Your Social Security Card: Why You Have It—What You Do With It"] Your . . . card shows that you have an insurance account with the U.S. Government—Federal old-age and survivors insurance. This is a national insurance plan for all workers in commerce and industry . . . taxes are like the premium on any other kind of insurance. . . .[35]

Another expression of the drive for insurance imagery in the months following the Court's decision was the SSB's decision to change the name of the Bureau of Old-Age Benefits to the Bureau of Federal Old-Age Insurance. Staff members throughout the SSB reacted to the name change. The director of Informational Services welcomed the insurance terminology as another means of clearly segregating the retirement program from the welfare or relief programs.

The head-line in this morning's *Washington Post*: "Social Security Board has 29,954,821 on Pension List" is another bit of evidence of the desirability of using the term "old-age insurance." I think the sooner we get away from the conception of beneficiaries under Title II as "pensioners" the better. Referring to these benefits as "insurance" will speed the day when Title II will be regarded in its proper light rather than as a part of a relief program.[36]

SSB's actuary (the agency's private insurance expert) was wary of the insurance terminology, supporting its adoption only if it indicated the development of a program that would be more truly insurance-oriented than that set up by the 1935 Act.

I do think that such a change does call for a clearer definition of the word "insurance" than is present to date. . . . the use of the word may be awkward. . . . until there is more common ground for terminology. It surely needs clear definition.[37]

The legal staff warned of difficulties:

From a legal standpoint I question the accuracy of the word "insurance." . . . In the absence of contractual or other vested rights, it appears to me that the statutory word "benefits" is more accurate than the word "insurance." Use of the latter word might, by suggesting rights as fixed as those under an insurance policy, embarrass future revisions of the benefit rate structure.[38]

However, if leadership insisted on the name change, the legal counsel felt it would probably raise no new constitutional issues.

I am unable to see any Constitutional reason for objecting. . . . While [the Supreme Court] opinion . . . does not discuss the question whether Titles II and VIII constitute a system of insurance, I think the Court has necessarily overruled any contention that such a characterization of these two titles would render them unconstitutional. . . . If the purpose of the proposed change is to accentuate the distinction between old-age benefits and old-age assistance, I suggest that possible alternatives would be to refer to Title II payments as old-age retirement benefits.[39]

The strongest objection to the name change came from the SSB's Office of Research and Statistics. Acting Director Ewan Clague warned against embracing the commercial insurance analogy as this would run the danger of permanently locking the system into regressive payroll financing. The insurance imagery, with its language of contributions and premiums, would close the door to future progressive, general revenue financing.

The opportunity for the use of progressive taxation as a means of financing social security—attained as an incident in solving a constitutional problem—holds great promise for the future of social security. The terminology now in use supports this opportunity and cultivates its acceptance by the public. A shift to insurance nomenclature might operate as a step backward. . . . The separation of contributions in Title VIII from benefits in Title II . . . [is one of several] important elements which deserves careful attention by all who look forward to the development and strengthening of the program. They are precisely the elements which free a growing American social security program from . . . restraints inherited from precedent voluntary insurance or borrowed from actuarial theory and commercial insurance.[40]

Clague acknowledged that insurance imagery would build on the "insurance-mindedness" of the American people, but there would be a price to pay for this political advantage. "To replace our current terminology with that of insurance may tend to create a new set of misunderstandings and fallacies by analogy with the forms of insurance with which workers in general are familiar."[41]

As Clague spelled out in his memo to Chairman Altmeyer, much more than sheer imagery and public relations was involved in the adoption of insurance language: choices about fundamental policy orientations were being made. It has been tempting to see the conservative Supreme Court as a major reason for the minimally redistributive nature of the new retirement system on the hypothesis that CES drafters curtailed their goals in the face of this powerfully conservative threat, thus casting the new system in an antiredistributive mold that was difficult to break in later years. However, the material presented here argues that, paradoxically, this conservative threat precipitated major redistributional opportunities for the system. The defensive tactic of avoiding an insurance model by separating the tax and benefit titles, as Clague pointed out, had the effect of loosening the relationship between the three policy variables of wages, taxes, and benefit levels. The looser this relationship (in other words, the weaker the contributory and wage-related principles), the greater the possibility for redistributional policy choices such as the use of general revenue financing. While Clague saw the opening of this redistributional door as an opportunity, Chairman Altmeyer and other agency leaders saw it as a powerful threat and moved quickly to shut the door by an exercise of administrative discretion: the adoption of insurance imagery which implied a close, minimally redistributive relationship between wages, taxes, and benefits.

Further evidence of the potentially liberalizing pressure of the Supreme Court threat is found in an examination of the options that SSB leaders weighed in anticipation of the Court's striking down the 1935 Act. Under consideration were substitute plans that were vastly more redistributive. Evidence of this is found in a 1937 document written three weeks before the Supreme Court gave its decision. The document, entitled "Alternate Security Plans If the Present Plan Is Declared Unconstitutional," was compiled by the SSB chairman's office and circulated by Technical Assistant Wilbur Cohen. Staff members were sent the document with these comments: "I regret very much having to send this to you for study over the weekend but the possibility of the Supreme Court decision on Monday necessitates our having ideas fairly well in mind in case an emergency should arise."[42] In case both the tax and benefit titles were struck down, the memo proposed to substitute a federal old-age benefit system financed by progressive general income taxation. Such a system would be coupled with a completely federalized old-age public assistance system. This dual program, modeled after the Swedish system, would have made the federal government exclusively responsible for the financial security of the aged. Should the Court completely exclude the federal government from administering any old-age benefit system, it was suggested that funds could be raised through progressive income taxes and then turned over to the states for their use in approved old-age benefit systems.

Staff responses to the proposals varied; research staff objected to any substantial increases in the income tax for the poor, arguing for significant tax exemptions at the lower end of the income scale. Actuary Williamson argued for abandoning the wage-related principle in benefits. "I should like to stress both the greater simplicity and the greater logic of uniformity of benefits divorced very largely from past service."[43] Legal staff proposed that the best strategy would be simply to apply for reargument of the original plan, such a strategy being compatible with Roosevelt's plan for packing the Supreme Court. "The resignation of Mr. Justice Van Devanter makes certain that a new Court will consider the application for reargument. Furthermore, such procedure might conform more readily to administrative tactics on the proposal to reorganize the Supreme Court."[44]

These policy options were shelved upon receipt of the Court's decision; their inclusion here is to illustrate how a perceived conservative threat forced essentially conservative policy leaders to seriously consider embracing liberal, more redistributional, policies. The antiredistribution decision of adopting insurance imagery in 1937 is impressive when one considers that it was an exercise in administrative discretion on the part of the SSB leaders. Not until the 1939 amendments to the Social Security Act was there any statutory characterization of the system as social insurance. The introduction of insurance terminology into the social security law at that point illustrates congressional ratification of an earlier bureau decision, a process which emphasized the active role of agency leaders, the exercise of choice, in the adoption of the imagery.

This process provides an interesting parallel at the policy level to an organizational phenomenon studied by Kaufman. In his analysis of federal bureaucracies, Kaufman distinguishes between bureaus established by statute and bureaus accorded statutory recognition. The latter class of bureaus represent those that "were originally set in motion by action by a department head, later to acquire statutory underpinning by mention in an appropriation act, and only much later in their lifetime to be recognized in a piece of substantive legislation." This pattern is distinguishable from one in which bureaus request congressional prior approval for the creation of a new agency. "The distinction between the two is not trivial: for they represent differences in the locus of decision-making initiative." The incorporation of insurance imagery in social security, it is argued here, represents a similar locus of decision-making initiative in the SSB.[45]

The congressional use of insurance terminology in the 1939 amendments proved to be a touchstone for SSB spokespersons in later years. The SSB's use of insurance imagery, and the conservatizing policy implications of this imagery, could be justified by pointing to congressional use of the terminology and downplaying the SSB's own leadership role in originally adopting the imagery. With the decline of the liberal social insurance school of thought in the United States, it was a fairly easy matter for the organization to monopolize social insurance language and to speak as if that term had only one meaning—conservative social insurance—and to argue that congressional use of the phrase implied a congressional mandate to keep the system within conservative boundaries. This enabled the SSB to deflect criticism of its policies by pointing to Congress and downplaying the considerable extent to which SSB administrative interpretations and SSB lobbying efforts were responsible for the conservative features of the system. The reliance on congressional use of the term *insurance* is well illustrated in a 1971 debate between economist Milton Friedman and long-time social security policy leader Wilbur Cohen.

> *Cohen:* Mr. Friedman also attacks the insurance aspects of social security and his criticisms suggest he doesn't know what insurance is. He gives us a Friedman definition, but not the right definition. . . . If he wants to have his definition, let him have it. It is not mine, and it is not the definition that the Congress of the United States has given. Congress has called social security insurance. . . .

> *Friedman:* As many of you probably know, there are quite a number of state legislatures that at one time or another have passed a law saying that the value of Pi should be three. . . . According to Mr. Cohen's meaning of insurance, that means that Pi is now three.[46]

The reliance on insurance imagery in defending the agency's opposition to policy liberalizations is well illustrated in the SSB's long-term fight against blanketing-in proposals. These called for bringing into the benefit structure those workers who were too old at the time of the act's passage ever to have time to earn sufficient work credits to qualify for social security benefits. The SSB opposed these proposals as dilutions of the contributory and wage-related principles. One line of argument was to assert that any such action would be a violation of social insurance principles (when, in fact, such actions would have been compatible with the liberal social insurance principles of Rubinow and Epstein). Arthur J. Altmeyer, representing the SSA in 1953 testimony before Congress, opposed a blanketing-in proposal with this reasoning.

> The very fact that this is an insurance program means that benefits must bear some relation to contributions and that some contributions must have been made before the benefits are due, and that in turn means that it takes time to feel the full beneficial effects of this protection. To expect anything else is about as reasonable as it would be to expect to pick a crop of apples the day after the sapling had been set out in the orchard. . . .[47]

The absence of insurance terminology from both the original act and the Supreme Court decision left a residue of ambiguity in the SSB's imagery which invited attack. Between the 1937 SSB unilateral adoption of insurance imagery and the 1971 Friedman-Cohen debate, the appropriateness of social security's insurance imagery was frequently questioned by external critics of the system. Internal dissatisfactions cropped up as well; for instance, in 1944 Jack Tate, agency legal counsel, complained to Wilbur Cohen: "I have never been enthusiastic . . . about pretending that compulsory contributions are something different from taxes. In a constitutional sense they are taxes or they are nothing. . . . We persuaded the Supreme Court . . . that the levies are taxes and I should dislike to seem to repudiate that decision."[48] Internal criticism of insurance imagery was strongest from the actuarial department, a source of internal policy dissension discussed at length later in this work.

Policy Implications of Imagery: Benefits

Conservative social insurance ideology was not mere window dressing; these principles had important policy consequences as illustrated in decisions during the first fifteen years of the system regarding the design of the benefit structure. The following is a brief discussion of the impact of a strict application of the contributory and wage-related principles to three elements of the social security benefit structure: the minimum benefit, the maximum family benefit, and the weighting of benefits. These elements have been chosen for examination because of their importance to the redistributive character of the benefit structure. The retirement benefits in effect between 1939 and 1949 ranged from a monthly minimum of $10 for a single worker to a monthly family maximum of $85. Within these limits, benefit levels varied according to previous wage levels, determined by the following formula, which expressed the primary insurance amount as a function of average monthly wage: 40 percent of the first $50 plus 10 percent of the next $200 plus an increase of the total by 1 percent for each year of coverage.[49] The heavier weighting of the first $50 of average earnings allowed the SSB to speak of the benefit structure as being "weighted in favor of the poor worker" even though poorly paid workers still received benefit checks that were smaller in size than those of better paid workers. Dependents' benefits were added to the worker's benefits in proportion to the number of dependents, but a ceiling was placed on maximum family benefits such that in no case would the total benefit check exceed 80 percent of the former average earnings (even if this meant 80 percent of former wages that were subpoverty level) or $85, whichever was smaller.

All three of these benefit elements had important redistributional and antipoverty implications. The minimum benefit level was important, for this was the benefit the most poorly paid, most sporadically employed workers would receive. The point at which the maximum family benefit ceiling was placed had important implications for adequacy of benefits for poorly paid workers. (Consider the widow and children of a marginally employed worker with subpoverty wages whose total benefit check could not exceed 80 percent of former average earnings.) Obviously, the extent of the weighting had important implications for the social adequacy of the benefit levels for poor people.

The strict application of the social security ideology (in particular the contributory and wage-related principles) produced what can be described as a benefit squeeze which oriented the system against the poor. The goal in designing the benefit structure was to establish both minimum and maximum benefit levels that were sufficiently low so as not to impair work incentive, yet to have these two benefit levels sufficiently far apart so there was ample room for a wide variation in benefit levels between them, for full expression of the wage-related principle. Consider the maximum benefit level: Chairman Altmeyer enunciated as a "fundamental principle" of social insurance that benefits should never exceed 80 percent of former wages.[50] (This "fundamental principle" was by no means inherent in social insurance; the liberal social insurance tradition in the United States, for instance, would not have agreed with this statement.) The 80 percent level was established on the theory that work incentive would be damaged if nonworkers received public benefits close to or higher than what had been earned, even if earnings had been subpoverty level. Once this upper cap was established, there was downward pressure placed on the minimum benefit level so as to provide sufficient room between it and the maximum for significant variations in benefit levels. Benefit variations were very important to SSB leaders for both ideological and strategic reasons. Strategically, it was felt that anything that flattened the benefit structure, such as the crowding that would result by raising the minimum benefit, would play into the hands of the Townsendites and other flat plan advocates. It was feared that policy moves such as increasing the minimum which caused the social insurance system to incorporate resemblances, however faint, to flat plans would encourage policy opponents who wanted either to replace conservative social insurance with a flat plan or to force an insurance–flat plan compromise. Similar strategic reasoning lay behind the SSB's opposition to weight benefits more heavily in favor of the poor, for such downward weighting would tend to flatten benefit amounts, thus inciting further efforts by flat plan advocates.

The above decisions, products of ideological commitment and political strategy, are reflected in SSB responses to suggestions that the benefit structure be made more responsive to the needs of the poorly paid worker. We find Chairman Altmeyer, in 1949, confronted with this criticism of the wage-related principle: "It's unsocial to pay the highest benefit to the higher paid worker because he is the one who should have been able to lay aside the most to supplement his social security benefit. . . ."[51] Altmeyer, responding with a statement of ideological commitment, praised a strict expression of the wage-related principle as a method: "to reward individual thrift and incentive. . . . It is consistent with the American principle of individualism that those who have established a higher level of living through their efforts during their working years should also have a higher level when they retire."[52] In response to a proposal to weight benefits more heavily in favor of the poor, Altmeyer argued this would be undesirable because: "A formula which would give greater weight to lower wages . . . would tend to level benefits. . . . It seems preferable not to flatten the benefit structure further by heavier weighting of benefits in favor of the low-paid worker."[53] The political danger in flattening the benefit structure was discussed by SSB staff writing a position paper in 1948 against a congressional bill to raise the minimum benefit level; such a move would reduce benefit variation (dilute the wage-related principle) and "encourage the activities of those pressing for a system of flat benefits."[54] One way to ameliorate the benefit squeeze on the poor would have been to remove the arbitrary 80 percent ceiling on maximum family benefits. This was opposed, at least in the time period studied here (1935–49), by the SSB, however, as expressed in the following position paper:

> We are strongly opposed to the removal of the maximum of 80% of the average monthly wage for total family benefit. A program of social insurance should attempt only to replace a part of the wages on which the beneficiary family was accustomed to live. It should not operate to leave the family in a better financial position. . . .[55]

Thus, with the maximum cap in place for work incentive reasons, the minimum kept low to allow room for benefit variations, and weighting limited to minimize flattening, the benefit structure was kept within minimal redistributive boundaries.

Policy Implications of Imagery: Financing

We have looked briefly at some important benefit variables that have restricted the redistributive impact of the system. On the financing side of the picture, the absence of general revenues has had similar consequences. The regressive effects of the payroll tax were discussed earlier. Introduction of general revenues into the financing of benefits would have served to mitigate those effects since a relatively more progressive source of funds would be utilized. Prior to examining the SSB's position on general revenue financing of social security benefits, it is helpful to consider two drastically different models for financing a retirement system. With this context in place, explanation of the SSB's general revenue stance will be easier. Drawing upon Schlabach's lucid account, we can refer to one as the full reserve model and the other as a pay-as-you-go model.[56] Consider a purist full reserve approach to retirement annuities. Under such a system, payroll taxes (employer and employee) would be collected in trust funds composed of interest-bearing United States securities. Upon retirement, an individual worker would receive only such benefits as his taxes earned actuarially. There would be no dependents' allowances, and the whole approach would be based upon a severe application of the individual equity principle. Under this model, people retiring when the system was still new would receive extremely low retirement annuities since they would not have had time to contribute much, and a strict individual equity approach would forbid granting them gratuitous, unearned benefit supple ments. In addition to extremely low initial benefits, it would be necessary to have a benefit lag, that is, an interval of several years between onset of payroll taxation and the paying out of the first benefits to allow funds to accumulate. Reserves would grow to tremendous size under this system. The Committee on Economic Security, when considering a full reserve approach to social security, forecast that a full reserve model would accumulate federal annuity reserves between $50 billion and $60 billion.

At the opposite extreme, consider a purist pay-as-you-go system: the only reserve would be a minimal one to smooth out fluctuations in tax receipt; most taxes paid into such a system would be expended almost immediately on benefits. Strict individual equity would be abandoned and general revenue supplementation of payroll taxes would be provided. This general revenue subsidy would allow several things: the payment of immediate benefits with no tax-benefit lag, the payment of much larger benefits for the first retirees, including dependents' allowances, and regressive payroll taxes could be held at a much lower level, though, of course, income taxes would be increased. The full reserve model is an extremely individualistic approach while the pay-as-you-go approach can be described as a much more social approach. Under the full reserve approach, the economic risk of old age would be "the responsibility of the individual, to be carried forward, through time."[57] The other model views the risk "as one to be socialized, to be spread laterally throughout society."[58]

The Committee on Economic Security debated the merits of the two models outlined above and recommended a modified reserve approach to President Roosevelt. Under the CES proposal, an annuity system would be established, with no dependents' allowances, to be financed from payroll taxes by both employer and employee. It was felt that to make the program salable to the public, two things would be necessary: (1) a moderate beginning to payroll taxes with gradual escalation as the system gained acceptance, and (2) higher initial annuity benefits than a strict application of private insurance actuarial principles would dictate. The CES proposed to:

> give some extra insurance credits gratuitously to older workers to increase initial annuities. Their plan was to introduce payroll taxes slowly to soften the shock . . . and after five years gradually to begin paying annuities. Young workers would eventually receive benefits calculated as if the system operated fully on actuarial principles . . . however, the system would accumulate not a full actuarial reserve, but only a partial contingency reserve of about ten billion dollars.[59]

Under this modified reserve proposal, a general revenue subsidy was projected—but not until forty to fifty years had elapsed. This eventual subsidy would be needed to handle the deficit effects of the early liberalized annuities and to replace the interest that would have been earned by the enormous trust funds under a full reserve model. An eventual general revenue subsidy to be introduced, perhaps half a century later, was acceptable to the CES Wisconsinites for several reasons. By that time, it was felt, universal occupational coverage would be achieved. Since all workers would be participating, a general revenue subsidy would simply be a universally based contribution or premium; thus, the projected subsidy could be rationalized in terms of contributory ideology. Secondly, such a long-range event would allow increased annuities to recipients at the beginning of the system, an important point in selling the program to the public. Additionally, under the withering away theory held by CES and SSB leaders, by the time the subsidy point was reached, the maturing social insurance system would have reduced the need for old-age public assistance to virtually zero. The general revenue funds that had gone to finance these public assistance payments would thus be available to provide the insurance subsidy.

President Roosevelt at first gave approval to the CES proposal although, apparently, there is some doubt as to whether he fully understood the projected subsidy provision at the time he gave his approval.[60] Treasury Secretary Morgenthau, an opponent of deficit spending in social security, was aware of the projected deficit, however, and urged Roosevelt to retract his support, which Roosevelt did. The result was the famous Morgenthau amendment to the Social Security Act which instituted full reserve features with high initial payroll taxes, lowered initial benefits, and a projected federal reserve fund of $50 billion.

The incorporation of these features in the act proved to be a political liability for Roosevelt, prompting both Roosevelt and Morgenthau to reverse their policy positions within the next four years. The very low benefit levels were attacked as an inadequate response to the needs of the aged. Both business and labor attacked the payroll tax mechanism. Organized labor called for the payroll tax's replacement by progressive financing, and business leaders were concerned that high payroll taxes and the accumulating reserves were siphoning off money that properly should be circulating throughout the economy. Prominent economists such as Marriner Eccles, chairman of the Federal Reserve Board of Governors, pointed to this drain as a major cause of the 1937–38 recession. By 1939, Secretary Morgenthau had completely reversed himself, testifying in favor of a reduction in payroll taxes, reserves limited to the equivalent of five years of benefit payments, and even the use of a general revenue subsidy. Roosevelt, too, by 1939 supported abandonment of the strict full reserve model. The president supported the 1939 amendments which: (1) postponed a scheduled increase in payroll taxes for three years, (2) removed the full reserve feature by requiring reserve fund trustees to "report annually on the prospective financial status of the system for only five years in advance," (3) added dependents' benefits, and (4) advanced the payment of benefits by two years.[61] The 1939 amendments, however, did not address the subject of a general revenue subsidy.

In the 1939 hearings, Chairman Altmeyer had pointed out that going off the full reserve model would necessitate a general revenue supplementation to the system some forty or fifty years later. This far distant supplementation was acceptable to Altmeyer, but he was opposed to any earlier general revenue contribution as an ideological threat. (This was a major reason for his opposition to blanketing-in; the blanketing-in benefits would have been financed out of general revenues.) General revenues were permissible only after the system had become firmly established, and policy competitors such as the Townsendites had been defeated. The incorporation of general revenue financing prior to these events, however, would constitute an ideological threat to the system. By 1980 or 1990 the force of events (the aging of the population and the resulting escalation of payroll taxes for the work force) would compel Congress to turn to general revenue supplementation, Altmeyer predicted, but by then the social security system would be universal, its ideological character would be established, and policy competitors would be gone from the scene. In summary, the long-range general revenue SSB strategy regarding supplementation was to soft-pedal the need for it in the interests of consolidating the image of social security as a self-supporting insurance system, and to allow population pressures to bring it about after the improved political-ideological situation made it tolerable.

Despite the long-range strategy just described, Altmeyer and the SSB kept a low profile in 1944 when Congress enacted legislation calling for the appropriation from general revenues of any amount needed to fully finance social security benefits should there be trust fund insufficiencies. Altmeyer was not worried by this authorization because Congress, at the time of enactment, said, in effect, that such insufficiencies would not happen. This situation stemmed from an error the SSB had made in its technical work for the 1939 amendments. Those amendments carried provisions for future payroll tax increases based on the agency's projections of benefit outgo. The agency had miscalculated and by 1942, payroll taxes were accumulating at a much faster rate than expected and benefits were flowing out at a much slower rate. Reserves were unexpectedly large in 1942. Congress, seeing an opportunity to reap the political advantages of holding the line on taxes without curtailing benefits, promptly postponed for one year the scheduled payroll tax increase. This yearly postponement was repeated in each year between 1943 and 1949 due to the continuing reserve surpluses. The SSB was very upset by the postponements, fearing their 1939 error was permitting Congress to erode the contributory principle; Chairman Altmeyer repeatedly testified against tax increase postponement.

The leader of the tax postponement movement was Senator Vandenberg, who had no intention of undermining the fiscal status of social security or of precipitating general revenue financing. He simply wanted to correct the SSB's error by holding the line on taxes until the reserve excesses were gone. The general revenue authorization had been proposed by SSB supporters, who also had no intention of forcing early general revenue financing. Senator Murray, who proposed the authorization, hoped that by thus raising the specter of weakened trust funds needing a general revenue bailout, he could force Vandenberg to retreat. Vandenberg did not drop his postponement initiative, but to emphasize his support for the fiscal soundness of social security, he supported the general revenue authorization as well, explaining that it "carried with it no implication that any additional sums are necessary now or in the foreseeable future."[62] The authorization remained in effect until the tax postponements stopped. The last postponement was in 1949 and the general revenue authorization was removed in the 1950 amendments. Chairman Altmeyer and the SSB again retained a low profile on the removal of the authorization. Such an authorization would be needed in the distant future, but Altmeyer was in no hurry to get it on the books because of its dangerous implications for a still-maturing conservative social insurance system whose ideological character was not securely established. General revenues remained, in Altmeyer's eyes, a long-range necessity but a short-range threat.

Financing: Defending Regressivity

In the meantime, the regressivity of payroll taxation remained a politically sensitive issue and the SSB sought to protect itself in a variety of ways, including outright denial that the payroll deductions were taxes, suppressing staff studies of the regressivity's effect, and developing elaborate ideological justifications for the levies. While the regressivity of the payroll tax has always been a point of attack for external critics, SSB staff felt free to criticize it only in the first few years of the agency's life. Quickly, however, staff learned such criticism was not tolerated by agency leadership. As discussed earlier, Clague, the head of the research department, supported the early use of progressive general revenue financing. E. J. McCormack, special assistant to the SSB, in 1936 urged the SSB to support a payroll tax exemption for the lowest paid workers to take some of the sting out of that regressive tax.

> I definitely feel that there should be some exemptions made for those wage earners whose income is so small as to make the tax an immediate hardship. For instance, there are hundreds of thousands of wage earners whose income is inadequate to provide for the actual necessities of life for themselves and their dependents. The Scotch philosophy to save a part of every dollar one earns may be ennobling to the spirit but is rather undernourishing when applied realistically to a family of four or five eking out an existence on ten or twelve dollars a week. Fifty cents a month is equivalent to four plus quarts of milk and that much milk during the month to an infant might prove a better investment in human values than the same amount put away over a period of years to provide for the old age of that infant's father.[63]

To other staff members the regressivity posed no problem, and, in fact, to some it was a virtue. For example, Head Actuary Rulon Williamson opposed proposals to build in a tax exemption for poor workers by saying: "I am still sufficiently insurance-minded to believe that all citizens must pay for all the benefits they receive. These taxes, since they are contributions toward an insurance program, should be regressive. They should bear with some weight upon those who are providing for themselves."[64] In fact, to the actuary, the downward reach of the payroll tax served the admirable purpose of highlighting the large number of poor people who were not paying enough in the federal income tax system.

> The spread of the tax base has developed in Social Security into one of the most rational recognitions that our present income tax base has been altogether too narrow. We already have a very sizable income tax applicable to the higher incomes. Through the contributions under the old-age and survivors program we have pretty well extended that tax rate to the lower incomes among the covered individuals.[65]

Effective as he felt the payroll tax was, however, there were still citizens escaping its reach: those in uncovered occupations such as farm workers and domestic laborers or those citizens not working because of retirement or disability. This prospect of some element of the population escaping social se-

curity cost-sharing prompted Williamson to flirt with the idea of a universal
social security poll tax: making the right to vote conditional on the payment of
a social security tax. In his proposal entitled "Taxes for Democracy—Poll
Taxes," circulated within the SSB in 1940, he argued that such a poll tax
would once and for all establish the principle that "all are contributing toward
the costs of protection." While such a tax might have to be geared at a low
rate, it would be useful for "It does underline the desirability of over-all sharing of costs under the social security programs."[66]

While Williamson's poll tax proposal never got off the ground, SSB leadership remained firmly committed to payroll tax financing and was faced with
the task of fashioning defenses for its use, a process in which Altmeyer took
the lead. Perhaps the most common tactic for defending regressive payroll
financing was to assert that the payroll deductions were not taxes at all, but
insurance premiums or a form of compulsory savings. Thus, there was an
attempt to sidestep the whole issue by arguing that the regressivity concept
was simply inappropriate. This tactic failed to stop criticisms; for example,
Dorothy Thompson, a Washington, D.C., newspaper columnist, attacked the
payroll tax as "an intolerable burden on the backs of the very people whom it
is theoretically designed to assist."[67] Responding to this charge, Altmeyer said
that, in fact, the ultimate incidence of the tax was unknown and it could not be
said for certain that the deductions were a burden on the workers. Perhaps the
deductions were being shifted forward to consumers in the form of higher
prices: "The question of whether the employees, the employers, or the con-
suming public pays these taxes cannot be answered except in the light of specific situations."[68]

The argument of uncertain incidence was only one of several elaborations of payroll tax incidence doctrine that the SSB formulated in these early
years. Sensitive to the charge of regressivity, the SSB leadership adopted and
discarded several defense tactics before settling on a reliable one. The original
defense had been the fifty-fifty incidence theory: the argument that worker
contributions came out of wages and represented contributions or premiums;
these contributions were then matched by an equal employer contribution
which came out of profits. This original defense was supplemented by the un-
certainty of incidence position discussed previously. Another early approach
to handling this issue was fashioned by Altmeyer, drawing on his Wisconsin
social insurance background. He developed a cost of production rationale for
the payroll tax, arguing that the employee tax would be shifted forward to
consumers.

> Regardless of what the eventual incidence of payroll taxes may be, there is no
> question that the original incidence is upon the payroll which enters into the cost
> of production so that under competitive conditions there is a strong probability

. . . that the consumer will pay . . . in the price of the product. . . . . Gearing the costs to the payroll brings about a truer equality between the costs of production and the price of the product.[69]

An interesting development is the eventual abandonment of the cost of production, forward-shifting incidence theory by Altmeyer in favor of a return to the fifty-fifty incidence theory couched in terms of personal thrift rhetoric. This doctrinal shifting is due to tax incidence studies conducted by the SSB's own staff who concluded that in all probability the whole payroll tax was not shifted forward to consumers and, in fact, the employer's share was probably shifted backward to workers in the form of reduced wages, thus aggravating the perceived regressivity of the payroll tax. This study, completed in 1936, was conducted by Bureau of Research and Statistics member H. P. Mulford and entitled *Incidence and Effects of the Pay-Roll Tax.*[70]

Mulford analyzed the impact of the payroll tax on industrial profits, theorizing that the employer share feature would have an unequal impact on various classes of industries in accordance with their labor costs. Mulford's detailed analysis concluded that "there is a basis for the claim of inequality in the pay-roll taxes . . . between major industries." However, industry profits would not be significantly impacted since "ultimately it is believed the employer's share will be practically entirely passed in some manner either to the consumer in the form of higher prices or back to labor in the form of suppressed wages." In considering the shift-to-labor possibility, Mulford felt this was so probable that payroll tax policy should be modified to relieve workers of this additional regressive impact. In a cautiously worded conclusion to his report, Mulford said, "The burden, especially where it is shifted largely to labor, will undoubtedly prove of sufficient weight that any moderation which may be compatible with the actual necessities of the security program is desirable. . . ."[71] Fully aware of the ideological commitment to payroll tax on the part of his superiors, Mulford was quick to point out that he was not suggesting abandonment of the payroll tax or the introduction of general revenue financing, leaving open the possibility of modifications in the form of tax exemptions at the lower income levels.

Despite the caution with which he framed his conclusions, Mulford's statements were threatening to the policy position of Chairman Altmeyer. The conclusion that regressivity was in all probability even more severe than the fifty-fifty theory suggested would provide ammunition to the system's critics. Altmeyer's uneasiness was not relieved by SSB Actuary Williamson's comments on the Mulford report. Williamson announced himself delighted that Mulford "starts with the assumption that the employer's payment is a tax rather than a contribution." Further, Williamson endorsed the view that the employer tax actually came out of wages. Still further, Williamson added, the

Mulford analysis laid the basis for arguing for a general revenue subsidy to finance benefits.[72]

Altmeyer responded to Mulford's report by suppressing its publication, at least temporarily.

> I do not think that conclusions should be expressed at this time based upon deductive reasoning such as is largely the case in this report. Thus, I do not think we are prepared to make statements such as the following "It is unlikely, however, that such absorbtion of the tax by the original payer [employer] will take place to any great degree. . . ."[73]

Altmeyer particularly objected to Mulford's statement that the burden of the employer tax would be shifted to "labor through depression of wages or reduction of employment."[74]

The repercussions of the Mulford incidence study were several. The study prompted the SSB to embrace even more firmly the fifty-fifty incidence theory and to downplay any possibility of employer tax being shifted forward or backward. This meant an abandonment of the Wisconsin cost of production argument, an abandonment of the tactic of saying incidence is really unknown (as in response to the previously discussed Thompson criticism), and an escalation of the use of contribution and premium terminology along with increased use of the personal thrift rhetoric—all to divert attention away from tax incidence theories. Regressivity was such a politically dangerous issue that the notion of regressivity had to be contained and camouflaged with system imagery. Eventually the Mulford report was published as part of the SSB's technical report series, but with circulation restricted to the SSB. Such regressivity studies were not undertaken again by SSB staff, and it remained for external researchers such as Brookings Institution economist John Brittain to do detailed research on payroll tax incidence.[75]

Despite the sensitivity of the regressivity issue for their own policies, SSB leaders, knowing a politically potent charge when they saw one, incongruously at times used the charge of regressivity against policy competitors when it suited their purposes. For example, we find Chairman Altmeyer in 1940 writing to Congressman McKeough, attacking the Townsend Plan's financing plan as being regressive. "It should be noted that the gross income tax bears most heavily on the low-income groups, being an even more extensive form of the very regressive sales tax."[76]

An important SSB strategy for dealing with the sensitive regressivity issue is revealed in early attempts to influence the way in which the social insurance funds would be presented in the national budget. In November, 1936, Altmeyer's technical assistant, Wilbur J. Cohen, posed the issue in a memo showing the distribution of federal revenue sources in terms of progressive versus regressive tax sources. "Should the 'income tax levied upon employees' [social security payroll tax] be considered as progressive or regressive taxation? Revenue for these social security purposes are going to loom large in the national budget. Perhaps a separate system of accounts will be set up for these taxes in order to distinguish them from other general governmental revenues."[77] This, in fact, is what occurred. Until the 1960s, social insurance revenues and expenditures were treated as separate elements of the federal budget, not taken into account in computing national deficits or surpluses. The important point here is that for the first thirty years of the program's existence, the budgetary reporting format lent support to the image of social security as an insurance system, serving to buffer the system from questions about the regressivity of its taxes. This has provided other political benefits as pointed out by Marmor.

> Social security programs were financed out of separate trust funds that were not categorized as executive expenditures; the billions of dollars spent by the SSA were until 1967 not included in the annual budget the president presented to Congress, a political advantage not likely to be lost on Democratic presidents worried about the perennial charge of reckless federal spending.[78]

The preceding pages have traced how the fifty-fifty tax incidence doctrine was promoted as a defense against regressivity charges. This became increasingly difficult in the following decades as a 100 percent worker incidence theory became commonly accepted among economists outside the SSA. In 1971, Wilbur Cohen, prime defender of the social security ideology, and at this time out of government service, felt secure enough about the system's future to abandon the fifty-fifty incidence theory in a debate with economist Milton Friedman.

> *Friedman:* I want to ask you a . . . very simple question. Do you agree that the division of the total tax between a tax on the employer and a tax on the employee has little or no effect on who actually pays it?
>
> *Cohen:* That is correct; so what?
>
> *Friedman:* I regard this as an historic moment because I have never seen that admission in any social security document or in any document written by you.[79]

CHAPTER 3

Fighting the Flat Plan Threat

The vigor and inventiveness SSB leadership poured into their conceptual and rhetorical efforts were fully matched by the vigor and strategic skill of the more tangible political steps taken against policy competitors. In this chapter we will survey such actions taken against flat plan opponents. Two periods stand out: a pre–World War II one in which liberal, highly redistributive competition predominated, and a postwar era marked by a conservative flat plan threat. As we will see, the anti–flat plan rhetoric developed by leadership proved remarkably adaptable to both liberal and conservative opposition. Another feature was shared by both types of competition: those needy aged who stood outside the circle of protection offered by conservative social insurance proved to be political capital for the opposition. By pointing to them, the competitors could highlight the shortcomings of the existing program. Leadership was acutely aware of this and, in the course of events, the unprotected aged came to embody threat as well.

The Liberal Flat Plan Threat

The leading liberal flat plan competitor was the Townsend Plan, a proposal for a $200 monthly pension for all citizens over sixty years of age. Recipients would be required to be both completely unemployed and to spend the entire pension within the month to stimulate business.[1]

In fighting flat plan policy competitors such as the Townsend Plan, the SSB sought to maintain an outward appearance of being apolitical; thus, while it felt free to use official SSB publications to criticize the general principles purported to underlie flat plan proposals, it was reluctant to attack openly specific advocates, such as Townsend, by name. Such attacks were therefore launched by the SSB in an indirect manner. One avenue of this indirect strategy was to encourage friends in nongovernmental organizations to publish critical studies of the Townsend Plan; for example, the SSB requested and received a report from a private research organization, the Social Science Research Council, that was highly critical of the Townsend Plan.[2] Other indirect tactics included planting anti-Townsend attacks with friendly newspaper contacts; press correspondents useful for this purpose were "Louis Stark, who was used most frequently; Max Stern; Zon of the Federated Press, and Hodges of Labor."[3] Similar planting tactics were used in the Congress with SSB staff preparing anti-Townsend attacks for use by sympathetic Representatives and Senators. At times Edwin E. Witte (former director of technical studies for the Committee on Economic Security and at that time returned to his academic post at the University of Wisconsin) helped the SSB in fashioning these broadsides. In 1935 Leonard Calhoun, of the SSB's legal office, described the personnel needed to develop the anti-Townsend campaign: "In collecting Townsend Plan data and preparing congressional memoranda, I suggest: (1) an economist, (2) a statistician, (3) a newspaper man." This attack should cast the Townsend Plan in the following light: "(1) as a 'racket' for enrichment of its higher ups, (2) as economically impossible, (3) as administratively impossible, (4) as morally dangerous."[4]

A vivid illustration of an anti-Townsend salvo from this campaign is found in a 1937 speech draft sent by SSB Chairman Altmeyer to Congressman Doughton, chairman of the House Ways and Means Committee, with a copy passed along to newspaperman Max Stern. The attack characterized the Townsend Plan and all other flat rate plans as crackpot, dangerous schemes used by politicians to buy the votes of America's aged, turning "our old folks into catspaws for politico-economic manipulation."

> With State elections in the offing this fall throughout the country, a bumper crop of pension-panaceas is being ripened for the harvest—their growth sedulously cultivated for their vote-luring value. . . . The first seeds were sown late in 1933 with the Townsend movement until today nearly every State in the Union has bred its own peculiar hybrid old age pension plan.[5]

Much of this attack is taken up with characterizing uniform, universal pension schemes as systems of "wildcat money" or "financial ledgerdemain," based on regressive taxation that would be a burden on labor (an ironical charge considering the regressivity of the social security payroll tax), while simultaneously stimulating "bankruptcies and business failures on a large scale." Rather than pursue these "will o' the wisps that hover over the quick-sands of economic chaos," the nation should support the 1935 Social Security Act.

> Let us not leave the path of progress that has been so clearly charted in the past few years. . . . During the past few years we have taken practical and effective steps in this direction and have made substantial advances toward security, both for the aged and for the nation as a whole. But these advances, real and measurable though they are, have been too slow for impractical visionaries and impatient promoters, who prefer high speed spurts of fancy to the steady pace of gen-

uine accomplishment. . . . The pity and the danger is that their rosy dreams seem so tempting. . . .[6]

Elsewhere in this same attack a different theme is sounded—that of the aged as menace. "The fact that these grandiose old-age pension plans won't work, is only one of the arguments against them. There is the further question of whether—in all justice to and respect for the aged—we would really wish to put them into operation if we could."[7] The danger, it was argued, was clear: the aged would drain away all available social welfare funds for themselves, leaving orphans, the blind, and other needy citizens to starve. This document makes exactly that claim by pointing to the state of Colorado where citizens had passed a state constitutional amendment promising all the aged a pension such that the benefit, when added to other income the person may have had, would amount to $45 a month. As a direct consequence of this benefit grab by the aged of Colorado, it was argued: "The state capital is in a turmoil . . . funds are running short for nearly every State activity . . . hundreds of State employees are being dismissed . . . children are fainting in the schools from hunger . . . homes are being broken up . . . relief in Denver averages less than half of the minimum for subsistence."[8] The image of school children fainting from hunger is a powerful one indeed. The attempt to blame this on the Depression-era aged's fight for survival is a measure of the occasional lengths to which conservative social insurance advocates, both inside and outside the SSB, would go to fight for their preferred policies. While the aged-as-menace theme was not a major one used in the anti–flat plan attacks, it did crop up again; in this the SSB reflected a theme that was latent in society at large. As late as 1949 in the course of SSA discussions of renewed flat plan efforts, staff inside the SSA circulated among themselves excerpts from a speech delivered by Agnes Myers (not an SSA staff member) to the American Public Welfare Association. "The organized pressure of the aged is already becoming ominous in California and Colorado. If the same old peoples' lobbies spring up in our eastern and middle-western States, the old folks will become a ghoulish nightmare that saps the vitality of the younger generation."[9]

Reminiscing in later years on the anti–Townsend Plan tactics of the SSB, Head Actuary Rulon Williamson (himself sympathetic to a conservative flat plan pension scheme as a substitute for conservative social insurance) alleged that the SSB deliberately supplied inaccurate cost estimates to Congress and the press which exaggerated the cost of flat plan proposals. In a memorandum entitled "The Exaggeration of Costs for the Townsend Plan," he claimed:

Almost steadily the figures given as representing the costs of a Townsend-like system have been exaggerated. Some years ago, when Sen. Downey was given information from our Bureau of Research and Statistics, I had some discussion on this point with Research and Statistics staff . . . as to why they had given these padded figures. . . . [The staff's] major admission was that they were giving figures so as to sufficiently exaggerate the costs to reduce the probability of this type of legislation.[10]

Williamson claimed this exaggeration was achieved in the following manner: when presenting costs for the existing federal program, the SSB allowed for postponed retirements beyond the minimum retirement age, but in cost estimates for the flat plans no such allowances were made, thus inflating the latter's cost and minimizing the former's.

Liberal Threats in the Federal Government

Within the Roosevelt administration itself were advocates of liberalized income support plans for the aged, critics who were impatient with the small benefits of the existing programs. One important group of critics included Marriner S. Eccles, Federal Reserve Board chairman; Leon Henderson, economist on the Securities and Exchange Commission; Isodor Lubin, commissioner of Labor Statistics; and Launchlin Currie, member of the Federal Reserve Board's research department. This group sought replacement of the social insurance system with one that would provide larger benefits for more aged at an earlier date. These critics wanted to address two objectives simultaneously: getting bigger benefits to the aged and strengthening consumer spending power. To do this they proposed taking money from the social security reserve funds and disbursing it immediately in benefits instead of allowing the reserves to accumulate until 1942, when the first social insurance benefits were scheduled to be paid. A 1939 newspaper account explained their rationale. "Delay in the expected business upturn has led New Dealers of the spending school to cast about for means of pouring more money into purchasing power to stimulate business, and this [immediate disbursement of payroll tax accumulations] has been considered by them the most logical formula since it does not call for new appropriations by Congress."[11] This group of critics sought abandonment of the wage-related and contributory payroll tax features, wanting benefits to be financed from general revenues. The concept of varying spending to counteract business cycles of inflation and depression underlay their proposals. This promised little stability for individual recipients who would have no assurance from year to year about the size of their retirement benefits, a point of attack for Altmeyer in his battle against these opponents.

Members of this group made the mistake of sharing their ideas with Jane Hoey, head of the SSB's public assistance bureau, who immediately reported to Altmeyer. He in turn complained to President Roosevelt and pressured Secretary of the Treasury Morgenthau to curtail the "dangerous" activities of those dissidents found in the Treasury Department. In his memoirs Altmeyer casts two of the dissident economists in a sinister light, informing us that: "A number of years later the two economists were accused before congressional committees of having been associated with a communist group. I have no reason to believe that was so. However, I do know from personal experience that they did have a great urge to manipulate and influence prominent officials in making decisions of considerable public importance." [12] In an attempt to forestall any future administration critics of conservative social insurance, Altmeyer engineered the creation of a cabinet-level committee on social security affairs, ostensibly for the purpose of generating recommendations for social security amendments, but, more importantly, to serve a watchdog function in containing administration critics of the established program. As Altmeyer euphemistically put the matter, a major function of this committee was "assuring that subordinate officials in the respective departments under the Cabinet secretaries would act in a responsible manner." [13] This tactic failed to stifle criticism in the Roosevelt administration, however, and the next major attack came from a particularly threatening source—Altmeyer's own superior.

In 1940 the continuing support within the Roosevelt administration itself for a heavily redistributive, uniform pension version of social insurance was brought home to the SSB in an incident involving the newly created office of the Federal Security Administrator. The FSA, forerunner of HEW, was created in 1939 to consolidate New Deal social welfare programs. No longer was the SSB an independent agency reporting directly to the president; now it was but one of several subordinate agencies in a large, consolidated agency. Throughout the following decade, however, the SSB was to prove itself adept at winning policy disputes with its superior agency.

The FSA was a threat to the SSB for more reasons than the simple cutting of the direct link to the president; the greater danger lay in the fact that its creation injected into social security policy formation a new layer of officials who did not come from the Wisconsin tradition of social insurance, officials who had not gone through the critical experience of the first few years of the SSB's life and were not carriers of the social security ideology. This meant the SSB had a superior agency that was willing to challenge the adequacy of the whole conservative social insurance approach.

The first head of the FSA was Paul McNutt, former governor of Indiana and a Democratic presidential aspirant in the days before Roosevelt announced his decision to run for a third term. McNutt, from his FSA position, began developing a political platform on which to run for the nomination. His social insurance position was part of his larger economic and social philosophy, which basically consisted of staking out positions that were more liberal than Roosevelt's. McNutt called for a more substantial attack on poverty than Roosevelt had launched. The continuing existence of large-scale American poverty, he argued, was preparing the ground for the emergence of an American form of fascism and dictatorship.

To forestall this threat and to launch a frontal attack on poverty required massive redistribution of income—more redistribution than could be accomplished through the Roosevelt programs of work relief, low level public assistance, and existing social insurance. McNutt was prepared to call for the replacement of the existing social insurance plan with a uniform pension for all aged, financed with progressive income taxes. "The necessity for . . . redistribution . . . suggests the elimination of the pay-roll taxes and the transfer of social security services to the general budget at the earliest moment possible." [14] This proposal was part of a speech McNutt prepared for delivery to the National Industrial Conference Board in Boston in 1940. The speech, however, was not delivered. Altmeyer, hearing of McNutt's proposals the day before the speech was to be delivered, went over his superior's head and appealed directly to the president, persuading Roosevelt to censor McNutt's speech and to require him to deliver an SSB-written substitute speech which praised existing social insurance. Though McNutt did not deliver his original speech, details of it did reach the press. In the censored speech he had argued for a social insurance approach to caring for the aged, but a social insurance based on progressive financing arrangements. He advocated not abandoning social insurance, but embracing a different, more redistributive version of it. McNutt developed his position by making use of several of the SSB's favorite ideological elements; however, he used them to reach a conclusion drastically different from that of the SSB. Like the SSB, McNutt clothed his social insurance proposal in American values, saying his proposal was a result of "thinking out the principles of public insurance in terms of American conditions and requirements" and that his plan was congruent with "American traditions." [15]

In his undelivered speech he contrasted social insurance with public assistance, arguing, as did the SSB, that public assistance was inevitably inferior, flawed with "the humiliating means test with its many opportunities for the recrudescence of the barbarities of the ancient poor law." Economic support, he argued, must be given as a right and

> not as charity. They must be regarded together with the services of schools, libraries, roads, milk inspection, or fire protection all of which are accepted by citizens of every class without humiliation or loss of self-respect. . . . The present social-security law provides for old-age annuities and unemployment insurance . . . with the definite implication that these benefits are given by right because the beneficiary or his employer has paid a part of the premium through the pay-roll tax. [16]

So far, in the eyes of the SSB, so good. McNutt had sounded what today would be called the residual-institutional policy distinction and had firmly placed public assistance in the residual category with all its negative implications.[17] If he had stopped at this point, leaving the implication that payment of payroll taxes conferred the status of right on social insurance benefits, he would have been safely within the confines of SSB ideology; however, he did not stop here and in succeeding paragraphs proceeded to attack the SSB program as one which, in fact, hampered the development of an institutional view of social insurance. The regressive payroll tax actually *hindered* the acceptance of benefits as a right, he argued. He approached this point by referring to the organizational resources needed to maintain the SSB's tax and wage records for American workers. This record-keeping machinery was at the heart of the system, for accurate records were needed to determine payment of taxes and benefit size. At that time, worker's records were kept on individual file cards.

> Why all these cards? Why these thousands of Government clerks and all this vast bureaucracy? . . . The reason for all this complexity is, in fact, a very good one. At present we Americans can't admit an old man's right to a pension unless we have a detailed record of his tax payments, although we know well enough that if he is poor he has paid his fair share of general taxes all his life. All this fuss is the expression of our desire to do justice by every man, according to our lights. As we get more experienced, I trust our lights will grow brighter, and we shall be no more concerned with the actuarial records on a small pension than on similar records that would entitle a man to walk in Central Park. . . .[18]

This argument was immensely threatening to the SSB leaders, constituting as it did a direct attack on one of their fundamental principles and, in fact, using some of their own favorite concepts to frame the attack. As Altmeyer put it in his complaint to Roosevelt: "Needless to say, we in the Social Security Board are shocked at the casual way seven years of planning and progress are brushed aside. . . . The basic principles of contributory social insurance, which automatically relate benefits to wage loss, automatically protect benefit rights and automatically control costs, are completely rejected."[19]

In his censored speech, McNutt developed his argument that redistribution was needed to prevent the social disruption found in other countries of the world. "The Government cannot overlook the fact that incomes tend to be so distributed as to encourage centralized controls in business. This naturally leads to monopoly and in certain countries has overthrown democratic governments. A democracy has to protect itself by continuous redistribution of income."[20] A "practical instrument of redistribution" was needed; the existing social insurance system was insufficient, there weren't enough work relief projects to accomplish the task, and public assistance was inadequate. The proposed instrument of redistribution was a "modest flat-rate, universal pension, paid out of a graduated personal net-income tax, with a small reserve for contingencies."[21]

McNutt carefully dissociated his proposal from the Townsend movement, calling that movement's demands for benefits of $200 a month fantastic and asserting that the Townsend financing device, a form of sales tax, would be dangerous if implemented nationally. He regretted that the spectacular proposals of the Townsend movement were attracting so much publicity. "The insistence on such proposals by considerable groups stands as a real obstacle to any fruitful national understanding of the social-security problems, from which desirable amendments might be derived." [22] McNutt's plea was that not all uniform pension proposals were simple copies of the Townsend plan; there were more choices than the SSB conservative social insurance model on one hand and the Townsend model, easily attacked for its extremes, on the other hand. Between these two extremes there was room for a reasonable uniform pension plan that could be significantly redistributive, McNutt argued.

As previously mentioned, McNutt's speech was not delivered. On his way to the meeting hall, McNutt was met by a SSB staff member who handed him a substitute SSB-prepared speech with the president's order to deliver it. This speech, which McNutt did deliver, praised the SSB model of social insurance and saw as its principal problem simple extension of the existing model to as yet uncovered occupations. McNutt was forced into praising the "psychological value of purchased protection" which stemmed from the payroll tax and even into acknowledging the need for all those clerks and wage record cards, "It is of course of basic importance . . . that we should have reasonable and accurate evidence as to wages." Since advance notice of his censored speech's theme had been given to the press, a statement was issued claiming he had rewritten his own speech on the train ride to Boston. [23]

Altmeyer's successful appeal over the head of his superior was an impressive display of political infighting, as well as a measure of the entrenchment the SSB and its policies had achieved in four years of existence. In urging the president to suppress McNutt, Altmeyer blended arguments for the superiority of conservative social insurance with appeals to any reelection plans Roosevelt might have. Failure to suppress McNutt's speech would have handed Roosevelt's political opponents (both those in the Republican party and any Democratic rivals for FDR's third nomination, such as McNutt) an "explosive issue" in which the "outs will inevitably seize the opportunity to out-promise the ins," Altmeyer argued. Creeping Townsendism was another charge: despite McNutt's repudiation of the Townsend Plan, his proposal was essentially a "baby Townsend plan" which would fan the flames of that movement. There could be no such thing as a modest uniform pension benefit, for the pressure groups of the aged would inevitably distort any modest, general-revenue-financed system into an extravagant, nationally bankrupting scheme. The president should retain conservative social insurance, Altmeyer argued, for its basic principle of payroll tax financing would "automatically control costs." [24] This appeal to political strategy and fiscal conservatism prevailed for the moment with Roosevelt. However, political developments were to change Roosevelt's mind and cause him (to the dismay of SSB leadership) to endorse, at least temporarily, a national flat pension for all aged.

Emergence of Roosevelt as a Liberal Threat to the SSB

Roosevelt's endorsement of a flat, universal pension to supplement existing social insurance was stimulated by a variety of political pressures: the McNutt incident emphasized the political capital available to his opponents in a discussion of the existing system's inadequacies; in pre–World War II days, organized labor was vocal in its opposition to regressive payroll financing, low benefit levels, and incomplete coverage; in the Congress, a special Senate subcommittee to investigate the social security program focused national attention on the limitations of that system and injected new vigor into the liberal flat pension movement. Against SSB advice, Roosevelt, in the speech launching his campaign for a third term, endorsed the concept of a universal flat pension to supplement existing social security. This set of circumstances was shattered by the outbreak of World War II, however, and major social security reform was eclipsed by the war, not to reemerge until the late 1940s.

Altmeyer had warned Roosevelt in a 1937 memo about labor's unrest: "Both the A.F. of L. and the C.I.O. labor leaders and unions have publicly indicated dissatisfaction with the present provisions of the Social Security Act and particularly with the payroll tax provisions."[25] In fact, labor dissatisfaction with the 1935 Act had been one of the factors prompting the SSB and Roosevelt to support the 1939 amendments that introduced a degree of liberalization into the extremely conservative 1935 Act. The 1939 amendments had not gone far enough in labor's opinion, however, and in November, 1940, the Congress of Industrial Organizations (CIO) adopted a resolution calling for replacement of conservative social insurance and meager public assistance with a universal flat pension system.

> The Congress of Industrial Organizations endorses an old-age pension program in cooperation with all progressive and old-age groups based upon a flat pension of $60 per month with supplementary allowance to wives up to a maximum of $90 per month for each married couple with an age limit of 60 years and eligibility to all persons and administered through a single Federal system, and the additional funds for this program should be secured by taxes upon aggregate wealth and income. . . . Only 1 ½ percent of those people above the age of 65 are now being taken care of under the present program and they are being inadequately cared for, receiving only $15 to $25 a month. This amount is not sufficient to enable these old people to maintain a standard of living of health and decency. . . . It is the Congress of Industrial Organization's view that a substantial part of this increased social-security program should be financed by general

Federal income taxes which are levied according to ability to pay. . . . social security must be viewed as a measure for the redistribution of national income and the taxes therefore should come from progressive income taxes and not from regressive pay-roll taxes.[26]

This critical stance of the CIO is in dramatic contrast to organized labor's social security position in post–World War II years. Compare the 1940 CIO resolution above with a 1954 SSA presidential briefing document which summarizes labor's attitude toward social security. "Labor takes a very responsible view of the reserve [generated by payroll taxes] and guards it jealously . . . politically pressures from labor will increase only if the idea that it is 'their reserve' is destroyed [through proposed general revenue financing]."[27]

Derthick provides us with a fascinating overview of labor's transition.[28] Prior to World War II it is true that the CIO opposed social security as inadequate, but as time passed, the so-called deradicalization of that movement, stemming from a change in national leadership, produced a rightward shift that brought the CIO in closer alignment with the comparatively more conservative goals of the SSB. The other piece of the labor story, as Derthick tells us, is a corresponding leftward movement on the part of the American Federation of Labor (AFL). In pre–War World II years the labor movement was split between these two organizations, but whereas the CIO was an articulate opponent of the 1935 Social Security Act, the AFL acted in accordance with its traditionally apolitical stance. Historically the AFL preferred to achieve economic security through private sector collective bargaining rather than through governmental social welfare programs, and though it did go on record as supporting the 1935 Act, it was a relatively quiescent supporter. However, just as the CIO's character changed in post-Depression years, so did that of the AFL. The AFL's changing mass membership reflecting a shift from traditional craft unions to the industrial workforce, resulted in a more vigorous commitment to social security. Thus by the mid 1940s, Derthick paints a picture of convergence. "The two wings of the labor movement had finally converged regarding the social insurance program. They had converged with each other and also with the Social Security Board."[29] While the social security support of the total labor movement was not provided in lockstep fashion after this (Derthick notes some CIO wavering in the late 1940s and describes the strain on the SSA-labor political alliance stemming from the United Auto Workers defection from the AFL-CIO), labor by the end of World War II had emerged as a powerful political ally of conservative social insurance interests.[30]

But, to return to our consideration of prewar events, labor, on balance, was perceived by SSB leadership and Roosevelt as a liberal threat to social insurance. This pressure was supplemented, in 1940, by the emergence of another liberal pressure point, this time in Congress. A special subcommittee of the Senate Finance Committee was created to investigate the social security system, followed by full Senate Finance Committee hearings on a bill to establish a national, uniform pension for all aged, regardless of work history. News of the subcommittee's creation broke within weeks of the McNutt incident. Senator Downey of California, a well-known supporter of liberal flat plan pensions was appointed chairman; the fact that Senate Finance Committee Chairman LaFollette appointed Downey was taken as a sign of that powerful committee chairman's sympathy with some version of a universal flat pension. The subcommittee was specifically charged to produce legislative recommendations for "the early realization of a minimum pension for all who have reached the age of retirement and are not gainfully employed."[31]

These were important political signals to President Roosevelt, contemplating his third presidential campaign and aware of the need to be in a defensible position when confronted with the large numbers of aged left unprotected under existing policies. Consequently in May, 1940, Roosevelt requested and received a briefing from Arthur Altmeyer on the outlines of a possible compromise with the flat plan pension advocates. Altmeyer provided specifications for a two-layered retirement system (the double-decker proposal): A basic universal pension of $20 a week for all retired upon which the existing conservative social insurance system would be superimposed as a second benefit layer. Roosevelt was moving toward compromise despite Altmeyer's repeated warnings about the dangers to conservative social insurance in such a move. In September, 1940, Roosevelt formally opened his third presidential campaign with an address to the Teamsters Union convention in which he told organized labor of his support for a universal flat pension. "Our old-age pension ought to be improved and extended. . . . Yes it's my hope that soon the United States will have a national system under which no needy man or woman within our borders will lack a minimum old-age pension. . . . And I look forward to a system coupled with that, a system which in addition to this bare minimum will enable those who have faithfully toiled . . . to build up additional security."[32]

During the next year, Roosevelt provided no further specifics about a recommended benefit level or source of funding for the universal pension. Early in 1941, Senator Downey, preparing for his subcommittee's hearings which were to begin that summer, approached the president, lobbying for Roosevelt's support. Roosevelt referred Downey to Chairman Altmeyer for a briefing on the double-decker plan Roosevelt had alluded to in his Teamsters Union speech. Altmeyer, still opposed to any compromise with flat pension advocates, stalled Senator Downey with a discussion of the general concept of double-decker systems, but refrained from telling Downey of the series of technical reports his research staff had prepared on costs and implementation of a double-decker system, materials Downey could have put to good use in his hearings. In his memoirs, Altmeyer discusses his withholding of this information. "I avoided presenting a detailed plan to Senator Downey because this might have given the impression that the President and the Social Security Board were endorsing it."[33] The SSB's research staff conducted many technical studies of ways to merge conservative social insurance with flat pension systems over the coming decade, but not until the early 1950s were any of these papers shared with Congress or otherwise made public out of a fear that the studies would be ammunition in the hands of flat plan advocates.

The Downey subcommittee hearings were completed in the summer of 1941. The full Senate Finance Committee started hearings in December of 1941 on flat plan legislation; two days after the opening of the hearings, however, the United States entered World War II, removing social insurance reform as a priority issue and containing the flat plan threat until the end of the war.

Liberal Threats in Congress

The two sets of Senate hearings in 1941 provided a national platform for dramatizing the inadequacies of existing conservative social insurance. In his subcommittee hearings, Senator Downey made effective use of case examples to attack the principles of conservative social insurance. He illustrated the plight of the unprotected aged by reading from a series of letters from poor, aged California constituents, remarking to the committee: "One thing that sadly impresses me is the meek spirit in which these elderly people write these letters. Seldom is there any abuse of social conditions; nothing but most polite and considerate language used by these elderly people who are now slowly decaying and starving in this Nation." Then, quoting from a letter:

> All they [state public assistance program] give us [husband and wife] is $29.68 and $9.27 was taken out of that, so all I had left was $2.15 to buy food with after I paid my rent, which was $15 and gas and light was $3.27, and all they sent me was $20 from October 17; the check was due on the 15th. So you see, Mr. Downey, what I had left out of $20 rent, $15, gas and light, $3.27; total $18.27; only $2.15 to take care of my sick husband with, so I thought I would write you, Mr. Downey, because I knew you are over them at the relief office, and they have to do what you say. For I am really in need. I have no food in the house for almost 3 weeks and no money to buy food with. I thank you again, Senator Downey.[34]

Turning to another letter from an aged man whose California public assistance benefit (referred to as a pension) had been reduced, Senator Downey said, "I judge it a case in which the pension was cut off from the California amount of $40 to $25 or $20, probably because of unexpected support from children. . . ."

> My Dear Mr. Downey: Just a few lines this Thanksgiving Day. Most everyone around here seems to be gone to dinner somewhere, all but poor me. I am here alone out of money, out of everything to eat again. I pay my house rent, $15 a month, and water bill and gas bill and other little expenses. It doesn't leave me enough to live on until the first of next month.
>
> I am 72 years old. My right leg has been broken twice and almost every rib has been broken in a wreck. I am not able to work any. I make a loaf of bread do me a week. A small sack of potatoes a month. The last of the month, the last two weeks, I live on one meal a day. If I want to go to town I have to walk 2 miles as I haven't got the 10 cents to pay the bus fare. I am out of money, out of things to eat, and 10 more days to go.
>
> This morning I thought someone maybe would bring me something to eat, but haven't yet, and it is 2 o'clock. I worked hard to help elect you and Governor Olson. Now, will you give us old people a pension. I am satisfied there are thousands of old people all over this United States that need your help. In the Townsend plan. Give it a trial and see if it will work. . . ."[35]

The hearings included a blast from Dr. Townsend. "I think the social security law as it exists today is one of the greatest farces in the world, a ridiculous thing. It leaves out one-half of the population entirely and fixes a status of poverty for the rest beyond which they will not be able to go."[36] The hearings also included testimony from Congressman Marian Smith who argued that four-fifths of the aged were without a decent standard of living. Smith dramatized his testimony with a description of his visit to a Washington, D.C., poorhouse for the aged which was operated by the federal government. "Six or seven weeks ago I went out to Blue Plains, this monstrosity, this terrible hell hole—and that is all it is—conducted by our Government for the aged who live almost in the shadow of the dome of the Capitol of the United States. . . ." He then submitted a memorandum describing conditions at Blue Plains:

> Blue Plains Home for the Aged and Infirm: White men, 142; white women, 55; colored men, 238; colored women, 155; total inmates, 590. Per capita budget, 24 cents to 26 cents per day; clothing budget, $5,000 per year or $8 to $9 per capita; average age 64 years; equipment is that which has been cast off by other institutions as unfit for use, dishes are old and broken; kitchen appears dirty and filthy, all old cast-off equipment. The refrigerator is a "hole in the wall," unpainted, dirty and not a fit place for food. One doctor and one registered nurse on duty. Inmates housed in dormitories, separate buildings for men and women, couples are divided. Old iron beds, that were used during World War in a Government

hotel or dormitory now in use there. Location of home, odor of sewage treatment plant on the side of the river.[37]

The committee summoned SSB staff to hear the charges and respond.

In a confrontation with Chairman Altmeyer, Senator Downey bitterly attacked the contributory and wage-related principles of conservative social insurance, saying, "I hope the committee will excuse my vehemence . . . I am a partisan in this matter. . . ." Downey argued that a wage-related system of benefits was inequitable, for it gave benefits in inverse proportion to need.

> It has been my lot in life to practice law among the submerged and unfortunates of the world, and I know that 9 times out of 10 when the widow comes into my office to have her estate probated whose husband has had an average earning of $200 a month, $500 a month, or $1000 a month, 9 times out of 10 I say, that widow would probably own her own home, would have money in the bank, would have insurance, and would certainly have some well-to-do relatives. . . . If she had three children, that widow . . . would receive from your Uncle Sam $85 a month while the children were under age, and then she would receive a substantial allotment even after the children had reached maturity and she had passed 65. But the poor, desperate, forlorn widow whose husband made $25 a month, who came into my office with three children would not have money to buy groceries; that widow with her children would receive $20 a month.[38]

Chairman Altmeyer defended the treatment of the poor under conservative social insurance. "Now the formula, as I have explained, favors the low-wage earner, because it gives him 40 percent on the first $50 average earnings, and 10 percent on the average earnings above $50 . . . the formula is weighted in his favor."[39] This argument prompted an angry response from Downey.

> Well now, Dr. Altmeyer, let me say, with due respect to you, that your remarks do not at all meet the situation or the evil here involved, that they are entirely misleading and fallacious. They are the same sort of statements that have been made before other Congressional committees and I venture to say that no Senator or Representative has comprehended from the statements made by the Social Security expert, the terrible vice and injustice involved. . . . To the wealthy widow and her children we will give a generous gift monthly of $85; to the tragic widow of poverty, burdened by the task of supporting three children, we would pay $20 every 30 days—a sum totally insufficient for existence. And yet Dr. Altmeyer claims this system is weighted in favor of the miserables of the world . . . this plan is fictitiously and fabricatedly—if I may use the word—weighted in favor of the poor.[40]

Attention quickly focused on need among the sixty- to sixty-five-year-old age group; this was a particularly sensitive area for the SSB since both old-age public assistance and conservative social insurance were not payable until age sixty-five. The Townsend plan (and other flat plan proposals) called for benefits payable at age sixty. Need among the sixty- to sixty-five-year-old age group was discussed at the hearings by Dr. Marjorie Shearon who provided testimony of fundamental importance to critics of social security. Shearon was a former staff member of the SSB; while employed by the agency she had prepared the economic brief for the defense of the Social Security Act before the Supreme Court in 1937, an analysis which assessed economic need among those sixty-five and over. Justice Cardozo had cited her study, entitled "Economic Insecurity in Old Age," in writing the majority opinion upholding the act. Thus, when Dr. Shearon testified for Senator Downey's subcommittee and pointed out the limitations of existing social insurance, her opinions carried considerable weight. In her post–Supreme Court work for the SSB, Shearon had expanded on her original needs assessment and prepared an unpublished analysis of need among the sixty- to sixty-five-year-old age group entitled "Economic Status of the Aged." This second report had not been published by the SSB for fear that it would provide information useful to flat plan advocates, who needed solid evidence of the shortcomings of existing policies. In referring to this second Shearon study, Chairman Downey commented: "There has been some controversy over this material . . . for reasons of their own they did not want it published. I may state that one of the reasons for this was that Dr. Shearon . . . takes up the question of the age group between 60 and 75, and the Social Security Board . . . felt it would be a mistake to give out any information which would accelerate the public movement for pensions."[41]

The publicity generated by the Senate hearings forced Chairman Altmeyer to release the Shearon analysis, however, and Downey's subcommittee was supplied copies within two weeks of Shearon's testimony. Even Shearon's first analysis, used before the Supreme Court, had been suppressed by the SSB after the Supreme Court's favorable decision, Shearon reported, since the needs data in that analysis also highlighted shortcomings of existing public assistance and conservative social insurance. This original Shearon study had been published by the SSB in 1937 as part of its technical report series, but had a limited circulation within the SSB and was not released to the general public. After the favorable Supreme Court ruling, Shearon asserted that the SSB did not want the needs data (even for the over sixty-five age group) discussed publicly. "It was impossible for me, because of the Board's policy, to refer to this 1937 book in any way."[42] When it was suggested that this first Shearon study, along with her second needs analysis, be made part of the committee prints, Senator Green, the SSB's defender on the committee, objected: "If they were so careful not to have copies of the original volume published, perhaps the SSB may object to it being used. . . ."[43] The pressure generated by the hearings was sufficient, however, to get both of Shearon's analyses published in the committee hearings. Thus, needs data that once was a political resource for the SSB when arguing before the Supreme Court in defense of the 1935 Act had become a political liability for the agency due to its highlighting of the remaining deficiencies of the same act.

During her time with the Bureau of Research and Statistics, Shearon had come into frequent conflict with the bureau's director, I. S. Falk. Disagreements over Shearon's prerogatives and responsibilities as a staff researcher were common. From the beginning of her work on her second needs analysis, Shearon felt Falk had been nonsupportive, even obstructive of this project (which had originally been assigned to her by Wilbur Cohen). After more than a year's work, however, she completed it on January 10, 1941. Eleven days later, Ivan Tarnasky, statistican for the Townsend Legislative Bureau telephoned her, asking for a copy of the report. Shearon referred him to the chairman, saying she could not release it on her own. Well aware of the dangers involved in speaking with the opposing ideological camp, Shearon promptly informed Falk and Cohen of the contact, assuring them she had released no data. Within a week of Tarnasky's call, Dr. Townsend himself telephoned her with a luncheon invitation. Shearon shared this with Falk, who urged her "to avoid the meeting with Dr. Townsend, if she could gracefully. If she could not, to arrange to have someone attend with her. And to be cautious, careful, and as noncommittal as possible." [44] The luncheon meeting was held (apparently without a third party as witness) and, according to Shearon's written report to Falk: "He outlined his plans and the theory back of the Townsend Bill. I advised him to refer requests for specific information about my research findings . . . to the Board, since I was unable to release any of my material via unofficial channels." [45]

As events developed over the summer and it became ever clearer to SSB leadership what political leverage could be acquired from Shearon's needs analysis, an important issue became: Who had leaked news of Shearon's report to the competition? How had Tarnasky known within eleven days that Shearon's report was finished? Shearon told Altmeyer she didn't tell Tarnasky. "In about a week or ten days I received a telephone call from a man associated with the Townsend organization asking for a copy of the paper I had just turned in. . . . I stated that the document was a confidential one . . . that the Board alone could release it. I expressed surprise that anyone outside the Board should have heard about the paper, and was told that such things do get out." [46] Shearon pointed a finger at Falk: "I telephoned at once to Mr. Cohen over the 'leak' and stating that I did not see how such a thing was possible when, to my knowledge, Mr. Falk was the only one who knew about my paper. Mr. Cohen said Mr. Falk had gone to see Senator Downey a few days previously and had probably told him about my paper." [47] Falk objected:

"When I saw Senator Downey on January 13, 1941, . . . I had not told him anything about the manuscript; nor did our conversation on that day in any way touch on the subject of this or any similar or related manuscript. In short, neither Senator Downey not the Townsend organization learned about the manuscript from me." [48] Falk then threw the ball back in Shearon's court. "I asked her how they had learned she had turned in the manuscript. She said she didn't know. I had already skimmed through a copy of her manuscript, but no copy of the manuscript turned in to me had yet left my desk and I had not up to that time mentioned the document to anyone except to you [Cohen]." [49]

In the weeks and months following the luncheon with Dr. Townsend, tension between Falk and Shearon escalated and by mid-April she had left the SSB, transferring to the Public Health Service. The major item of contention from January to April had been Falk's handling of her needs analysis: she felt he had been suppressing it for political reasons and complained that he had selected prepublication reviewers who were guaranteed to give him the negative response he wanted. In February, Falk had sent the report to three other members of his staff in the Research and Statistics Bureau for a review as to publication possibilities. Shearon questioned their qualifications, later referring to their "profound ignorance of the subject of old-age dependency" and asked Falk to send her report to "some impartial academic people like Professors Edwin Witte and Douglas Brown" which Falk declined to do. [50]

The reviewers' report exacerbated the situation. His staff (Sanders, Woytinsky, and Schmitter) reported to Falk that the manuscript as it existed should not be published; with care perhaps one of her tables could be reworked to make it suitable for an issue of the agency's *Social Security Bulletin*, but as for the two-hundred-page document as a whole, it was marred by Shearon's obvious concern for the needy aged which gave it a less than "scholarly" air with a "sentimental tone in favor of the aged that prevails through the entire paper." Further: "In reading it one gets the impression that the economic status of the aged has been growing . . . worse . . . and that something drastic has to be done to avert the impending doom which is overtaking the aged. In view of the tremendous pressure already behind the pension movement for the aged, we doubt the necessity for the Board to add further to this pressure." [51] Beyond the political implications of the study, the reviewers raised technical issues including

> 1. The overlapping problem: The tables used by Shearon showed sources of income without taking into account the fact that the same person might have appeared in more than one table. The overlapping problem could work to deflate or inflate the picture of dependency.
>
> In one respect, people who have incomes from several sources may be economically independent despite the fact that the income from any one of these sources

. . . may in itself be insufficient for self-support. On the other hand, some of the people who are regarded as self-supporting because of earnings may also be the very people who have savings and insurance. . . . There is no discussion at all as to what extent these two opposing tendencies tend to offset one another. . . .[52]

2. Her definition of need: They complained she believed that "all aged persons who do not have incomes of their own should be eligible for some form of governmental pension regardless of whether they have spouses who are able to support them, or other relatives who are willing and able to care for these individuals. . . ."[53]

But the technical issues raised by the reviewers were secondary in Shearon's mind to their obvious concern with the political implications of a needs analysis. This, coupled with what she saw as Falk's foot-dragging in processing the report and his reluctance to go outside the agency for a review brought matters to a head, and she left the SSB.

When Senator Downey began his subcommittee hearings, he requested testimony from Shearon. Shearon, in turn, checked with her former superior, Altmeyer, about the advisability of her testifying. Given the fact that Downey could subpoena Shearon, Altmeyer could hardly do other than approve her testifying as long as she did not present her opinions as official positions of the SSB. Following this, one of the first things Downey wanted was a copy of her report. When Downey telephoned Falk on July 23, 1941, with a request for copies of Shearon's analysis, Falk said he could not comply with the request. Later, when challenged as to why he refused, Falk's disingenuous explanation was that he had not exactly refused to release the manuscript; it was just that he had only four copies of it and all four were out for review.[54] This caused an infuriated Shearon to complain to Altmeyer, "You know, as well as I, that those manuscripts could be recalled by Mr. Falk at any time he saw fit."[55] In any event, Shearon then supplied Downey with her personal copy of the report, causing Falk to complain angrily that she had no authority to remove the manuscript when she left the agency.[56]

In the course of Downey's hearings, Shearon's testimony precipitated debate between Altmeyer and Downey over the extent of need among the aged: Altmeyer seeking to downplay need to emphasize the adequacy of existing programs and Downey, using the data prepared by one of Altmeyer's former staff, portraying greater need as justification for his proposed flat plan. Marked differences between the Shearon-Downey analysis and that of Altmeyer in the interpretation of statistics were revealed—differences which accounted for the SSB's suppression of Shearon's post–Supreme Court work and her transfer out of the SSB to the Public Health department.

Altmeyer began his testimony by warning the Downey committee against exaggerating need among the aged. "While many of the aged still unprovided for are needy, it is frequently assumed that all aged persons are needy. As a matter of fact, many of those with the highest income and largest amount of wealth or savings are to be found in the higher-age groups. . . ." [57] Of the fourteen million two hundred thousand persons over the age of sixty in 1940, Altmeyer argued: "There are 8½ to 9½ million aged persons with independent means of support." [58] Upon questioning, Altmeyer explained he had arrived at this figure by simply totaling and adjusting for overlap:

1. The 20 to 25 percent of the aged who "have made some provision . . . through savings"
2. The number of aged possessing some form of private insurance
3. The number of aged with some form of pension from industry, the military, or state and federal pension other than social security
4. The 3,700,000 persons over sixty still in the labor force. [59]

Only after additional intensive questioning from committee members did Altmeyer acknowledge that his calculations of the number of aged "with independent means of support" did *not* mean aged with financial independence. That is, Altmeyer had not adjusted his figures to reflect the adequacy of the means of support he had inventoried. Here was the heart of the dispute between Shearon and her former supervisor, for Shearon, in her work for the SSB, had insisted on estimating the number of aged who indeed had financial independence. Shearon had devised estimates of those aged who had subsistence levels of support, a concept Altmeyer did not address in his testimony. Her figures showed that of Altmeyer's 8.5 to 9.5 million "with independent means of support" only 2.7 million could be counted as financially independent at a subsistence level.

This difference in viewpoints can be examined in more detail by looking at Altmeyer's and Shearon's respective interpretations of labor force statistics. Altmeyer pointed to the 1940 United States census which showed approximately two million of the nine million people over sixty-five as still in the labor force. These two million he had classified as having independent means of support and, by implication, these people could not be considered as needing a flat pension. Shearon, however, pointed out that those counted as being in the labor force included those seeking work as well as those working and, of those working, no distinction was made as to subsistence levels of earnings. Thus, Shearon adjusted the two million figure by excluding:

1. Those whose earnings were so small they could not live on them
2. Those seeking work
3. Those employed by public relief projects such as the WPA.

Of these two million, Shearon calculated that only one million could be considered as financially independent due to their labor force participation. [60]

Shearon was asked to provide illustrations of the types of workers she had excluded:

> For instance, we have great many old persons who take jobs as janitors, both the husband and wife, they are janitor and janitress, they get their rent, they never see any cash, and both would be counted in the census as having a gainful occupation. . . . Many women who are doing charwomen's jobs—and I might say of all women over 65 who are working half of them are in domestic service, regardless of what they may have been in the past. They may have been businesswomen, that is managers, and so on, but they are forced down into domestic service after the age of 65, and before that, as a matter of fact. Now these women earn $2 or $3 a week, $4 or $5 a week, not enough to live on, and I have excluded them, therefore, from the independent group as not being independent by reason of earnings.[61]

Fully a third of the two million people over sixty-five counted in the labor force were working on farms as farm laborers, tenant farmers, or farm owner-operators. Altmeyer and Shearon perceived this group in drastically different ways. Chairman Altmeyer, when challenged about his implication that all of the aged in the rural work force could be considered as not needing financial assistance, responded: "I assume if they live on a farm and are able to maintain themselves on the farm, they are classified as independent, just the same as a wage earner who is dependent on a weekly pay check. In fact, I think they may have a great deal more security than a wage earner who is completely without means of support when he is laid off. . . ."[62] Of particular importance for Altmeyer were census statistics showing that 98 percent of the rural males over sixty-five were working, suggesting a great deal of economic independence among this population. Shearon argued that this interpretation grossly exaggerated the degree of economic independence. "The explanation of that is that nearly all these are farm operators, so called. They are owners or tenants, and so long as they are on that farm they claim they are employed. . . . They do not relinquish their labor force status no matter if they were 100 years old."[63] Additionally, the census figures gave no indication of adequacy of farm income. Shearon made a deduction of one-third of the aged in agriculture as not being able to earn a living on farms. She based this deduction on a wide variety of published studies of the economic situation of rural Americans, such as one showing that "nearly one-half of the farm population is landless, and over 3,000,000 of those are both landless and propertyless. In other words, their little possessions can be put in the family car, and they can drive off. They have nothing at all."[64] Downey, in preparing the subcommittee's report, acknowledged the differences of view. "The picture painted by Dr. Altmeyer was somewhat more optimistic, but the committee is convinced that a deplorable situation exists. . . . If the opinion of Dr. Altmeyer is vindicated, it would happily mean that cost would simply be lower than estimated by the subcommittee."[65]

Contingency Planning: Double-deckers, Mythical Work, and Blanketing-In

Although World War II temporarily removed the threat of a social insurance–flat plan merger, throughout the 1940s and into the 1950s SSB leaders remained sensitive to flat plan competition. Leadership was acutely aware that its own program's limitations, in terms of benefit coverage and benefit levels, were prime arguing points for the opposition. Yet, leadership hesitated to redress these limitations, for such reform on their part would entail temporary dilutions of the wage-related and contributory principles and such tampering, it was felt, was dangerous. It would either: (1) simply encourage the flat planners in their efforts to replace social insurance with their proposed system, or (2) mark the beginning of subversion from within, the transformation of social insurance into a flat plan system. Thus, the existing program's vulnerabilities were tolerated by the SSB leadership out of strategic considerations.

One such vulnerability was the large number of people already too old when the act was passed in 1935 ever to work long enough to qualify for social insurance benefits. Officially, the SSB's position was that this was inevitable; as Altmeyer put it when advising Franklin Roosevelt on this issue, "No insurance system could provide assistance for those already old and in need anymore than a fire insurance policy could cover fire losses already sustained."[66] The continuing popularity of flat pension movements after the act's passage, however, caused the SSB to begin internal studies of ways to modify its stance and bring these unprotected aged into the system, but in such a manner as to dilute only minimally the contributory, wage-related character of the system. These internal studies, carried out by a group called the double-decker working group, began in the earliest days of the organization and continued throughout the 1940s and 1950s. In these discussions the concept of blanketing-in referred to the process of bringing all the currently aged into the system's benefit structure either on a temporary or permanent basis. Double-decker proposals were variations on this theme that envisioned a two-layered benefit structure: a lower, flat rate, noncontributory pension available to all aged, which would be supplemented by a second benefit of contributory, wage-related payments for those aged who qualified.

Throughout the 1940s and 1950s, however, the SSB's leadership could never bring itself to support any of these proposals generated by its own staff, and they also fought such proposals suggested by external critics. The internal double-decker working group's studies on blanketing-in were not passed on to Congress or subjected to public discussion in the 1940s, for the organization was fearful that publicizing this data would lend support to flat plan advocates. Not until 1950 was there public discussion of these studies. Throughout these internal deliberations, the organizational leadership balanced the economic need of the unprotected aged against leadership's political strategy for the maturation of conservative social insurance; the maturation strategy consistently emerged as the more important. The leadership felt that the social insurance system must be allowed to mature over the years in such a way that its contributory, wage-related character would not be seriously weakened. The best solution was to allow the current aged to rely on the admittedly inadequate state public assistance programs and wait for the day when most of the members of succeeding generations of aged would have had a chance to earn their social insurance benefits. Professor Arthur Larson, an academic supporter of the social security ideology, and subsequently undersecretary of labor for Eisenhower, put the matter bluntly in 1952. "If we wait even eight to ten years the problem of the large number of aged without pension rights . . . will have solved itself. Shall we wreck the fundamental principle because we cannot wait eight years more for it to get into operation?"[67] Larson's solution was to let the problem "solve itself" by simply waiting for the currently unprotected aged to die out. While the SSB never phrased the matter this crassly, its policy position was identical in effect: better a slowly maturing system— even if a chronically inadequate one—that maintained its ideological purity and minimally redistributive character than one which responded to need more quickly, but in so doing weakened its conformity to the contributory and wage-related principles. Former SSA Chairman Altmeyer was frank about his strategy when discussing in his memoirs his opposition to blanketing-in.

> We in the Social Security Administration were quite aware of the social need for protection of those already aged. . . . However, we were concerned that "blanketing in" the presently aged might weaken the incentive for uncovered groups to be covered under a contributory social insurance system. . . . We were even more concerned about the effect the payment of a uniform amount would have upon a system which paid differential benefits related to differentials in earnings. . . . It was because of all these considerations that the Social Security Administration never felt justified in actually advocating a "double-decker system." . . .[68]

The SSB was aware from its earliest days that the aged ineligible for social insurance benefits constituted a sizable population. In 1939 the research department was telling Chairman Altmeyer that in spite of advancements brought by the social security amendments of that year, a liberal estimate indicated that by 1940 a mere 6 percent of those 8.5 million citizens who were sixty-five and over would be eligible for social security benefits, either as primary beneficiaries or dependents of beneficiaries.[69] By 1941 this proportion would increase to 10 percent. Need among the ineligible was extreme, the research department reported: in 1939, 80 percent of those 8.5 million aged, in addition to having no social insurance protection, had no private insurance protection "nor have they substantial income." Nineteen years later, in 1958, the research department was reporting that still only 65 percent of those sixty-five and older were eligible for social security benefits; this figure was projected to rise to 81 percent by 1981.[70] By the early 1950s the working group had identified an especially needy subpopulation of the ineligible, those for whom blanketing-in was a critical issue. Attention was directed to a subgroup of 2.6 million who, in addition to being ineligible for social insurance, had no earnings and received no public assistance. Of this group, 80 percent were women and three-fourths of these were widows. Of these 2.6 million aged, over 60 percent were seventy-five or older; 60 to 70 percent had no money income of their own and a larger proportion lived with relatives or in institutions than for the aged population as a whole.[71] The need for blanketing-in was emphasized by a research department report pointing out the public assistance system's failure to care for these aged.

> Many aged persons who are in need because they are not covered . . . or because their benefits are not large enough to meet their needs, could turn to OAA [Old Age Assistance] for help. At present, however, many aged with little or no incomes are reluctant to apply for assistance; old-age assistance is not available to aged persons who fail to meet eligibility requirements; and in many states— particularly the low-income states—assistance payments are admittedly inadequate. Despite the existence of these two programs for income-maintenance for the aged, therefore, the needs of many aged still are not met adequately.[72]

The issue of the unprotected aged was not exclusively a matter of the current aged not having time enough to earn sufficient work credits; it was complicated by the original act's failure to cover all workers. As of 1939 only 55 percent of the civilian work force was covered, with those covered workers paying their taxes and "earning" their future retirement benefits. SSB leaders hoped to achieve universal occupational coverage by gradual expansion over the years to all the work force. For example, farm and domestic workers were brought under coverage in 1950. The blanketing-in problem, then, was to be a recurrent one: as coverage was extended to new occupational groups, each new group would have a number of aged workers who would not have time enough to earn sufficient work credits to qualify for benefits. Thus, this point of vulnerability was to be a repetitive fact of political life as long as needy aged were excluded from conservative social insurance benefits and public assistance for the aged was inadequate.

As late as 1950, Commissioner Altmeyer was shocked by the continuing large percentage of aged still ineligible for social insurance benefits, indicating that the organization had been overly optimistic about the speed with which universal occupational coverage would be achieved and overly reliant on mortality rates to remove the unprotected aged from the scene. Since 1935 the SSB had been defending its refusal to blanket-in the already aged by arguing that their lack of protection was a transitory feature, soon to disappear as the system matured. In 1950, while elaborating this rationale, Altmeyer wondered how many aged would still be ineligible for benefits in 1950 (after that year's amendments) if there had been universal occupational coverage from the beginning of the program. Research department studies found that even with original universal occupational coverage, by 1950 fully one-third of the aged would still have been ineligible for benefits. To Altmeyer this was an upsetting finding and he insisted on a recalculation. "I think this matter is of supreme importance. I must admit that it is incredible to me that such a large proportion of persons would still be unprotected under an insurance system with universal coverage . . . after a lapse of 13 years." The actuarial division confirmed the finding and Altmeyer admitted that "the survival factor is often a very surprising one" and that for over a decade the organization had not appreciated the "great persistence in longevity" among the unprotected aged.[73]

Nevertheless, Altmeyer's opposition to blanketing-in the unprotected aged went undiminished. Neither the discovery that the phenomenon of large numbers of unprotected aged was less transitory than organizational rhetoric had claimed nor the acknowledgment that the public assistance system was failing to care adequately for these same aged was sufficient to outweigh the perceived political and ideological threats posed by blanketing-in. Chapter 5 of this work argues that SSB leadership, acting upon similar strategic considerations, suppressed its own public assistance program that, nominally, was to act as the safety net for needy aged without social insurance benefits. There were efforts by states to liberalize old age assistance; many of these efforts were vigorously and successfully opposed by SSB leaders who saw their own public assistance system as a prime competitor with social insurance. Thus, for several decades, a large and vulnerable population of needy aged was caught in a pincers movement: caught between inadequate social insurance and inadequate public assistance, inadequacies which were, to a considerable extent, both tolerated and imposed by SSB leaders for strategic reasons.

One of the earliest blanketing-in proposals was delivered to Altmeyer in 1939 by I. S. Falk, then assistant director of the research department. Falk was concerned that the SSB's preoccupation with the long-range development of the social insurance system was slighting contemporary need among the aged, and such a gap, he felt, could raise serious political threats.

> The inadequacies of current provisions for those who are already aged, for those who are approaching old age without coverage, and for those who are discon-

tented with, or resentful of, old-age assistance provisions and practices, have played a prominent part in support of the extravagant old-age pension schemes which have recently been much in the public eye. . . . It is possible that experience under the act in the first year or two will bring about a deep feeling of disappointment and a widespread insistence that the act is not accomplishing its purposes. Steps must be taken to see that no serious reaction of public opinion sets in and that the interests of those who are now excluded are given the fullest possible satisfaction. . . . The existence of Title I [old-age public assistance] helps to some extent but it is unlikely that it can ever be the answer to the problem presented by the limited old-age protection which is a consequence of limited coverage. . . .[74]

To meet the needs of the current aged, Falk proposed a double-decker system consisting of a lower level of a uniform, noncontributory $15 per month pension for everyone sixty-five or over. Superimposed on this pension would be an upper level of contributory, wage-related social insurance benefits. The lower level would be financed from general revenues and could, if desired, have been limited to those with less than specified earnings, income, or capital.

Falk argued that such a plan would "meet the more acute needs of the current situation . . . while protecting the principle of contributory, wage-related insurance." Well aware of Altmeyer's aversion to universal, uniform pension proposals, Falk was quick to point out that he and his research staff were by no means committed to a double-decker plan and were merely drawing up specifications in case the flat pension advocates gained political strength sufficient to force a plan on the agency. "None of us is—because of this undertaking—committed at this time to a flat pension for all or most of the aged. . . . We have regarded the present study as primarily an inquiry to develop information against contingencies which we might face if a broadened program of old-age protection through flat pensions should become important in the legislative area."[75] It was estimated that financing this plan in the first year would require about one billion dollars above the amount raised by the federal insurance contributions, an amount that could be obtained through changes in the progressive tax levies. Further: "Preliminary explorations have been made as to the yields of diverse taxes which might be invoked to finance the plan. It appears that the lowering of the base exemptions under both estate and personal income taxes and the removal of the exemption of Governmental securities from income taxation would probably raise the required amounts of revenue."[76] The Falk proposal was rejected by Altmeyer who, however, permitted the research staff to continue work on draft specifications of variants of the double-decker approach, agreeing with Falk that the political environment might force them to accept, however reluctantly, such a proposal.

Over the next decade, the double-decker working group continued to submit blanketing-in proposals to Altmeyer, who rejected them all. There was never any real danger of the working group conducting basic research into income support policies that would challenge the dominance of conservative social insurance for "only those plans which utilize the framework of existing contributory insurance systems are considered," as one progress report put it.[77]

By 1949 the research group recommended another double-decker plan, calling it one which would encompass "the 2.5 million now on old-age assistance rolls, the 1.6 million receiving insurance benefits based on age, and other millions of aged persons who may be ineligible for assistance or insurance but who lack income sufficient to permit them to live in independence and comfort."[78] The double-decker proposal was built on the premise of complete withdrawal of federal grants for state old-age assistance and their replacement by a social insurance system with a lower level of benefits to all men over sixty-five and women over sixty with income below a specified amount. As in the 1939 Falk proposal, the upper level of benefits would include, in addition to the basic flat benefit for the uninsured, another layer of contributory, wage-related insurance benefits. Thus, the proposal, called for the merger of assistance and insurance plans into a single system.

The 1949 proposal constituted what analysts of a later day might term a guaranteed annual income plan since it proposed:

> a flat benefit of $40 a month to any noninsured individual whose income was not more than $20 a month, and a flat benefit of $60 a month to any noninsured couple with income of not more than $30 a month. For incomes above these amounts . . . there would be a dollar-for-dollar deduction from the benefit amount. In effect, then, an individual could have as much as $55 in income and a $5 benefit would be payable; a couple with income of $85 would receive a $5 benefit. If income exceeded $60 for an individual or $90 for a couple, no benefit would be paid.[79]

In a particularly significant recommendation, the group said the income test for the lower level of benefits could be administered in a dignified, non-stigmatizing manner with a "simple affidavit signed by the individual or the couple; there would not need to be any complex and subjective budgeting or any balancing of income against requirements."[80] This proposal is especially interesting since it foreshadowed the affidavit features, or declaration system of eligibility, of many of the negative income tax proposals of the 1960s. (It also represents an admission by SSA staff that means testing could be accomplished in a nonstigmatizing manner, a violation of an article of faith for conservative social insurance advocates who saw means testing as inevitably flawed and humiliating.) Abandoning the "complex and subjective budgeting or any balancing of income against requirements" would have meant abandoning the fourteen-year effort of the SSB's Bureau of Public Assistance to refine the individual casework approach to income support in public assistance. Since 1935 the Bureau of Public Assistance had been arguing that assistance levels could be determined only after a caseworker's investigation into individual life circumstances regarding resources and needs, including needs for social services in addition to cash. The presence of the affidavit or eligibility by declaration proposal in the 1949 working group's report is probably due to the fact that until 1949, the Bureau of Public Assistance had not been represented in the double-decker working group. Subsequently, the bureau was represented and the affidavit proposal did not appear again.

One effect of the proposed income testing by affidavit would have been that a much higher proportion of the aged population would qualify for the lower level of benefits than under existing public assistance programs. This, plus the fact that the federal payment to noninsured persons would be higher than the federal share of the federal-state assistance program, meant a proposed net increase in federal expenditures for noninsured aged. The upper level of benefits for the insured would be payable in addition to, not instead of, the lower flat benefit payment. While there would be no income test for the upper level of benefits, there would be an earnings or retirement test. The distinction between these two tests is that an income test is sensitive to income in any form, while an earnings test is sensitive only to wages and salaries, ignoring income in the form of dividends, rents, interest, and the like. The use of the income test for the lower level and the comparatively generous earnings test for the upper level was defended on the grounds that those people who had earned insured status deserved superior treatment. The benefit structure itself already guaranteed higher benefits for the upper level, and the more generous earnings test was an additional reward. This extreme differential in treatment between the two levels of benefits was defended on the grounds that it was necessary to reward the insured workers of the upper level "in recognition of the contributions they have made to the insurance programs." The staff estimated the cost of this double-decker system at $4.4 billion in 1950 with 9.8 million aged eligible for payments: 2.6 million insured and 7.2 noninsured.[81]

Prior to 1950 most blanketing-in or double-decker proposals generated by the study group spoke of a permanent arrangement such that any aged person in future years who had not earned coverage would receive a flat rate pension. By 1950, however, working group staff were responding to Altmeyer's worries that a permanent safety feature would also be a permanent, built-in threat to insurance principles. A permanent, unearned benefit, it was argued, would be subjected to increasing pressure for expansion and might even replace the upper level insurance benefits. Additionally, with this "free" permanent lower level, it was feared that uncovered workers, such as farmers, would resist being covered by social security since they could count on a free general-revenue-financed minimum flat pension. In response to these fears, the working group developed blanketing-in proposals that would "wash out" after a few years, thus giving the message to American workers that although current aged were to be blanketed-in, all future aged would have to earn their way into the social security system through payment of payroll taxes.

Such a transitional proposal built on the concept of granting temporary mythical work credits was developed in 1950. This system, dubbed the prior-service wage-credits approach, called for the granting of: "free wage credits . . . sufficient to ensure that persons who are already self-retired could qualify immediately for a benefit under the insurance system, with the level of the benefit predetermined through the hypothetical wage which has been credited."[82] These artificial wage credits would be transitional: "As soon as individuals have had an opportunity to earn their insured status, the prior-service wage credits should properly be ineffective."[83] Artificial wage credits effective for a five-year period were envisioned with a gradual washing out of their value, requiring workers to replace them with real credits in order to qualify for benefits. It was suggested that sufficient unearned credits be assigned to provide a benefit of $40 per month for individuals and $60 per month for couples. These unearned benefits would be financed from general revenues. As always, the proposal called for preserving the superior treatment for those who had earned real wage credits by proposing that "obviously, workers with actual wage credits should receive the full prior service credit too."[84]

Commissioner Altmeyer liked the mythical work-credit plan: it was transitory and, by preserving a simulacrum of the contributory and wage-related principles, it appeared to do the least damage to the system's ideological underpinnings of any proposal yet considered. His opinion was soon challenged, however, by Research Director Falk who argued that mythical work credits actually constituted a more severe ideological threat than a permanent double-decker system. An artificial work-credit plan, Falk argued: "introduced concepts that are in more serious conflict with fundamental principles of our insurance system and provides a stronger invitation to a flat pension system than in the case of a double-decker plan . . . [because it] uses a basic rationale that all persons contribute in one way or another to the productivity of our economy and it assigns a minimum wage value to that contribution."[85] This was a dangerous concept to introduce into the system: once it was asserted, even if on a temporary basis, that all people are valued contributors to the economy who should be supported in old age, then the whole notion of earned and wage-related benefits would be shaken. Why go through all the difficulty of keeping wage records and adjusting benefit size to those wage levels if we accept the notion that all are deserving of support? This was an ideological threat reminiscent of Federal Security Administrator McNutt's 1940 argument that society should be "no more concerned with the actuarial records on a small pension than on similar records that would entitle a man to walk in Central Park."[86] Rather than distorting the concept of wage credits, Falk argued, it was preferable to embrace frankly the notion of a means-testing, straightforward double-decker plan. This would clearly identify lower level benefits as unearned gratuities, not in any sense constituting a reward for being a productive member of society. General revenue financing of unearned insurance benefits to people with no work history "is defensible" as part of a double-decker system, Falk argued,

> on grounds which do not weaken the justification for the insurance system and its benefits. But a government contribution into the insurance system for prior wage credits to persons who have no work history and have not met an income test is a challenge to the whole system and an invitation to abandon the insurance system, its benefits based on earnings and given without a test of income, and to substitute a flat pension for all and complete general-revenue financing.[87]

Falk's warnings carried much weight with Altmeyer, but the mythical work-credit plan still had the virtue of being a temporary deviation from principles, while all other double-decker proposals had called for universal, perpetual blanketing-in. Actuary Robert Myers, who also disliked the artificial wage-credit proposal, provided Altmeyer a way out by drawing up specifications for a temporary version of a double-decker plan which bypassed artificial wage credits. The Myers proposal simply called for modifying the quarters-of-coverage requirement for older workers, but leaving it essentially intact for younger workers.[88] Thus, blanketing-in would wash out over the years.

Double-decker studies had taken on great importance by 1950 for by then, flat plan competition had reemerged with new vigor. Under the leadership of Republican Congressman Curtis of Nebraska, however, this flat plan threat represented an even more conservative alternative than conservative social insurance, calling for a policy that would represent a net cutback in federal cash payments to the aged. This flat plan movement gathered steam so quickly that Commissioner Altmeyer privately acknowledged that compromise with its supporters was unavoidable. He was prepared to offer to the Eighty-second Congress one of his double-decker study group proposals in hopes of achieving a compromise that would "satisfy the flat-pension advocates and also preserve the advantages of the existing system."[89] Political events were such, however, that Altmeyer was saved from taking this action, and by late 1953 it had become clear that President Eisenhower had accepted conservative social insurance. This marked the end of the Republican flat plan threat, but until Eisenhower made his position clear, SSB leadership suffered some very uneasy moments.

Republican Conservative Threat

The flat plan danger signals began in 1949 Senate and House hearings on social security amendments. Senator Taft of the Senate Finance Committee and Congressman Curtis of the House Ways and Means Committee had each called for a complete reexamination of the social security system, urging that a flat, universal pension system be considered as an alternative to both public assistance and social insurance.[90] The 1952 Republican convention platform likewise contained a statement urging study of such a plan. During the presidential campaign, Eisenhower made no commitments about the future of social security. His election marked the end of the long Roosevelt-Truman era in which conservative social insurance principles had developed, and Altmeyer faced the new Republican administration with "considerable trepidation," anticipating efforts to dismantle the New Deal–Fair Deal social welfare programs.[91] His uneasiness was heightened by the fact that his own departure from governmental service was imminent; his retirement was scheduled for 1953, resulting in a change of leadership at a critical time in the organization's history.

In his January, 1952, State of the Union address, President Eisenhower still gave no clear indication of his long-range plans for social security, and other events were not encouraging. The national Chamber of Commerce had launched a public campaign in favor of a universal flat pension system such as the one favored by Congressman Curtis; the new Republican-appointed federal security administrator appeared to be supportive of the Curtis–Chamber of Commerce proposals; and Curtis himself was given a special Ways and Means subcommittee to investigate social security and develop a flat plan alternative.

The United States Chamber of Commerce proposal, endorsed by its national membership in a 1952 referendum, called for a universal flat pension to be added to the existing social insurance system. Under this system, every United States citizen at age sixty-five would receive a minimum retirement benefit of $25 a month. Above this minimum, the existing system of wage-related benefits would be retained and occupational coverage universalized. The system would be financed exclusively through employer-employee payroll taxes with existing social security reserves used to pay the initial flat minimum pensions. In subsequent years, the reserve feature would be eliminated entirely, and system receipts and payments would be balanced annually through adjustment of the payroll tax. Coupled with this would be abandonment of the federal-state old-age public assistance system. For those aged dependent upon public assistance, this would constitute a retrogressive step since over four-fifths of them were already receiving monthly benefits in excess of $25 a month.[92] Opponents of this proposal also pointed out that the year-to-year balancing of benefits and taxes would provide little long-range stability for workers or retirees.

While the Chamber of Commerce proposal represented a short-run retrogressive step, SSA leadership, in an interesting exercise of long-range strategic analysis, was warned of the chance that its adoption would revive an old liberal foe: the Townsend Plan. The transformation of an immediate conservative threat into a long-range liberal threat was possible because: "The obvious inadequacy of $25 a month as a standard of life for the aged would bring about immediate pressure for raising the minimum benefit. The whole potential political strength of the movement for Federal old age pensions in a population of older people would be directed toward this single goal. The present braking effect on this pressure of the relationship between contribution and benefit entitlement would be eliminated."[93] Despite the Chamber of Commerce's support of the payroll tax, the $25 flat plan proposal might result in political pressure to abandon it at a later date. A $25 per month blanketing-in would damage the social insurance "principle of equity" under which benefits were related to contributions. "This would in turn remove the major reason for continued support of the payroll tax as a means of supporting this program by labor and other organizations committed to the ability-to-pay concept of taxation. Should the payroll tax be eliminated . . . the pressure for a Townsend Plan type federal old age pension program would be further strengthened."[94] (One interesting side effect of a Townsend-like system that would thus emerge: "It would create an aristocracy of old age pensioners in the poorer sections, especially in the rural areas."[95])

The Chamber of Commerce initiative appeared to be gathering support in the Eisenhower administration. Federal Security Administrator Oveta Culp Hobby in February, 1953, appointed a five-person group to advise her on new social security policy. Three of the five members were from the Chamber of Commerce's social security committee, there were no representatives of organized labor, and even Congressman Curtis (who by now had emerged as the congressional leader of the flat plan movement) was invited. This offered Curtis a double policy platform since he had just been given chairmanship of a special Ways and Means subcommittee to investigate social security. However, at this point, political factors began to shift in favor of conservative social insurance. The Hobby advisory group was announced at the same time that the Chamber of Commerce attracted attention by launching a national campaign in favor of its proposal. These events triggered a protest from organized labor; the ensuing pressure was sufficient to cause Hobby to expand her advisory group to twelve and to include organized labor representatives (who could be counted on to support conservative social insurance). The mobilization of organized labor in opposition to the Curtis–Chamber of Commerce movement is credited by Altmeyer as being a major factor in the Eisenhower administration's eventual decision not to support a flat system proposal. This critical factor was buttressed by the solid social security support in the Congress as expressed by such powerful figures as Senator Byrd of the Senate Finance Committee. (Byrd had spoken of the social security reserve funds as a "sacred trust" and criticized the Chamber of Commerce for wanting to violate them.[96]) The continuing Democratic support remained crucial for conservative social insurance throughout the 1950s, for after the 1954 elections the Democrats controlled Congress even though the Republicans retained the White House.

Congressman Curtis held hearings for his investigatory subcommittee in August and November of 1953, but by the time his hearings were under way it is probable that the Eisenhower administration had already assessed the political situation as not permitting the abandonment of conservative social insurance. This is suggested by the fact that Hobby's advisory group completed its work that summer, limiting itself to simple recommendations for social security occupational coverage extensions, but avoiding discussion of blanketing-in, double-deckers, or flat plans. The president, upon Hobby's recommendation, submitted the report to Congress. Curtis may have sensed a movement on the part of the Republican administration to accept conservative social insurance, since at one point he made the political blunder of publicly chastizing his own administration for not cooperating with his subcommittee. In several press releases he blasted Hobby (who had become Secretary of HEW). "It is hard for one to believe that Mrs. Hobby has been insincere in her statements about improving social security, but the fact remains that her Department is not cooperating with the House subcommittee."[97] And, again, in a direct challenge to Hobby: "All we want are the facts. We intend to get them. I will not tolerate delays, evasive answers, or anything that falls short of full cooperation."[98] By the end of 1953, however, it was clear that Eisenhower was not going to challenge social security, and Congressman Curtis admitted defeat, essentially abandoning the flat plan drive. He explained to his constituents in Nebraska, "Without hesitation, I freely admit that I do not now adhere to all I said in my minority report of 1949. . . ."[99] (This was the report in which he launched his attack on the inadequacies of conservative social insurance and advocated its replacement with a flat pension system.) President Eisenhower removed all doubt about his stance in his 1954 special message to Congress on social security, in which he proclaimed the social security system "the cornerstone of the Government's programs to promote the economic security of the individual" and pledged himself "to preserve its basic principles." [100]

Prior to the defeat of his flat plan campaign, Curtis had conducted two sets of lively hearings to investigate social security. Commissioner Altmeyer stepped down from office in the spring of 1953, and soon thereafter Curtis invited the former commissioner to submit a written statement to the subcommittee outlining the principles underlying social security. Altmeyer declined to do this, explaining: "You have consistently attacked the basic principles underlying contributory social insurance. . . . By criticizing the fact that insured persons who are well-to-do as well as persons without resources receive the benefits . . . you seem to be in favor of some sort of means test. And, of course, you have always contended that old-age and survivors insurance system is not insurance, although it is so designated in the law itself." To submit the requested statement, Altmeyer felt, "would greatly harm rather than help the cause of social security" since any investigation by Curtis was bound to be "biased." [101] Curtis then subpoenaed Altmeyer, prompting a Democratic member of the subcommittee to scold Curtis. "Bringing a man like [Altmeyer] . . . here under subpoena, Mr. Chairman, you ought to be ashamed of yourself." Altmeyer was then asked if he were bound in "chains or wristlets." [102]

Curtis wanted to demolish the insurance imagery of the system; he saw this imagery as a prime source of the system's political strength, and undercutting it by portraying it as a fraud would make the system vulnerable to replacement by, or at least compromise with, a flat plan. Turning to the insurance imagery, Curtis and his staff focused on the defensive Supreme Court strategy of the 1935–37 period, the avoidance of all insurance imagery, which was followed by the SSB's unilateral adoption of it following the positive Court opinion. Insurance terminology was missing from both the 1935 Act and the Supreme Court decision, they pointed out; in fact, the government's defense brief to the Court specifically repudiated private insurance imagery. "The Act cannot be said to constitute a plan for compulsory insurance within the accepted meaning of the term insurance." [103] A lengthy recital of Altmeyer speeches, press conferences, administrative reports, and publications was then made documenting the SSB's speedy adoption of the terminology after the Court decision. Turning to the 1939 amendments in which the system for the first time received statutory characterization as insurance, Curtis's staff quizzed Altmeyer. "When [your staff] . . . was engaged in drafting suggested amendments to the Social Security Act for consideration by the Congress, which . . . ultimately resulted in the 1939 amendments, you told your staff to use the word 'insurance' and related terms, whenever it was possible . . . is that correct?" [104] At first Altmeyer could not recall if that had happened, then, angered, "I am not going to be cross-examined . . . and my answers distorted by you or anybody else, and get that straight." [105] Eventually, however, he conceded the point. "Probably I did, because I believe it is insurance, you see." [106] What Altmeyer adamantly refused to concede, however, was that there was anything misleading about the insurance terminology. Curtis's charge was that the SSB had deliberately cultivated public misunderstanding, encouraging citizens to look upon social security as a two-party contract between an individual worker and his government—all this to foster political acceptance of the system. Curtis's point was that no such individual contracts existed; in a strict legal sense, *contract* referred to a two-party agreement which could not be altered without the agreement of both parties. Congress could at any time unilaterally choose to modify or abolish the social security benefit structure, Curtis argued; therefore social security rights were statutory, not contractual. The public imagery adopted by the SSB implied otherwise, Curtis asserted, and pointed to the pamphlets and speeches telling American workers their social security cards represented insurance policies with the United States government, that payroll taxes were insurance premiums similar to private insurance premiums, and so on.

As an example of Congress's ability to alter the benefit structure at will, Curtis pointed to several post-1935 changes which had deleted certain benefits. In 1939 the lump-sum payment provisions had been eliminated. (Under this policy, single people who died without dependents had a social security benefit added to their estates.) In 1950, the benefit increment had been eliminated. (This was a provision which increased a beneficiary's primary insurance amount by 1 percent for each year of covered employment.) Here were benefit rights which Congress had deleted without the consent of individual policyholders, Curtis argued. The SSB's private insurance imagery camouflaged the extent to which benefits were dependent upon a particular Congress's inclinations. Curtis entered into the record letters from disgruntled citizens complaining about the deletion of these benefits with the writers claiming Congress had violated their social security "policies."

Altmeyer conceded that individual contractual rights did not exist, denied that system imagery implied them, and asserted that the letter writers Curtis referred to did indeed have an incorrect perception of social security as an individual insurance contract. However, that did not mean most Americans had that misunderstanding nor could that error be attributed to system imagery. As for the benefit alterations, Congress could modify benefits at will; however, on balance Congress liberalized benefits more than it curtailed them and that trend would continue. In his greatest public departure from the language of insurance rights, benefits, and premiums, Altmeyer acknowledged that the fate of social security ultimately rested on the mood of Congress rather than the technical provisions of any "policy," that fundamentally what guaranteed social security was Congress's "moral obligation, which I think is stronger than any written contract." [107] A young worker entering the system, while having no contractual guarantee that his "policy" would still be in effect when he reached retirement age, could count on Congress's moral obligation (and the growing political clout of the aged) to assure that he would get the benefits promised him.

The Curtis attack on insurance imagery was not followed by similar moves from the Republicans; in fact, the Republican acceptance of the principles of conservative social insurance was relatively quick and thorough, and provided a remarkable degree of policy continuity in a period of political transition. For example, on the issue of blanketing-in, we find the new administration opposed because "The failure to cover more persons . . . in 1935 was an error which cannot be corrected retroactively without . . . grave dangers." [108] These dangers were listed as a breakdown of the contributory and wage-related principles and the buildup of pressure for a general revenue subsidy for social security. We even find a continuation of the Altmeyer tradition of incongruously using the charge of regressive financing against competitors of regressively financed social security. Blanketing-in "would shift the impact of supporting our present aged from progressive general revenue taxation to flat-rate payroll taxation on low-bracket earnings. Arguably, this would be a measure designed only to help the wealthy." [109] (Such shifting would occur to the extent that those blanketed-in would be able to leave public assistance rolls.)

By 1956 HEW Secretary Eliot Richardson was interested in a version of blanketing-in but was dissuaded by the Republican-appointed SSA Commissioner Schottland with the following argument. "In spite of the greater equity that might achieved for some of the present aged . . . [through blanketing-in], the potential threat to the contributory, wage-related character of OASI [Old Age and Survivors Insurance] is such that we would recommend that the Department not support [it]. . . ." [110] Again, in 1959, Secretary Richardson was interested in a blanketing-in move, by this time a severely limited one restricted to those seventy-two and over. In discussing the pros and cons of the proposal, SSA Commissioner Mitchell warned that such a move, by violating the contributory and wage-related principles, could succeed in "undermining the public confidence in OASDI [Old Age Survivors and Disability Insurance], the new benefits could jeopardize the earnings-related contributory program." [111] Richardson subsequently backed off from the proposal "because of strong opposition from various quarters, particularly the AFL-CIO which is still opposed to blanketing-in if it is tied in with the OASDI system, because they feel it would destroy the contributory character of the system." [112]

While by 1959 the AFL-CIO had emerged as a prime defender of social security, by that same year another social security ideological leader and political strategist, Wilbur J. Cohen, had begun to reconsider his opposition to blanketing-in. Cohen, at the time out of the SSA and a social work professor at the University of Michigan, wrote SSA actuarial staff proposing a modified blanketing-in move. "I believe that now that the contributory wage-related OASDI program has been reasonably well accepted by both political parties and is reasonably well insulated from basic change that there would not be as much of a threat (if any) to basic principles if a satisfactory blanketing-in proposal could be worked out."[113] Cohen proposed a temporary blanketing-in of those "over 70 or 72" to be financed out of payroll taxes, with a benefit level "at about $40" but nonpayable to anyone receiving public assistance in that amount.[114]

A restricted, temporary blanketing-in provision was enacted in 1966 such that all noninsured persons who attained age seventy-two before 1968 were eligible for special reduced benefits of $40 per month for an individual and $60 for couples with benefits reduced by an amount equal to any public assistance payment or federal, state, or local pension being received. Benefits were financed from general revenues. Nearly three-quarters of a million people qualified for benefits the first year; by 1972 their number had been reduced to four hundred fifty thousand.[115] Thus even with the strong political position social security had achieved by the mid-1960s, and after thirty years of studying the problem of the unprotected aged, the incorporation of a flat plan element into conservative social insurance was kept within tight, restrictive limits. Even this modest step was biased against the poorest of these very aged, as pointed out by Brookings Institution economists.

> Ironically, among old-age assistance recipients, the special age-72 benefit discriminates in favor of the less poor in all states where the basic assistance payment is larger than $40 a month ($60 for couples). Only those assistance recipients with sufficient outside income or wealth to have their benefits reduced below the level of the special age-72 benefit find it worthwhile to renounce public assistance and to accept social security. The denial of special age-72 benefits to public assistance, recipients—a group of the aged which, on the average, is more needy than are the remaining aged . . . is arbitrary.[116]

CHAPTER 4
Maintenance of Internal Orthodoxy

The previous chapters have shown top SSB/SSA leadership busy dealing with policy competition in the external policy arena. Throughout this period, leadership also maintained a tight rein over its own staff, insuring that deviations from the social security ideology did not develop into an internal threat to the dominance of conservative social insurance. This chapter surveys those activities by examining leaders' relationships with research staff and actuarial staff. For reasons discussed in the first chapter it had been expected that the executive leadership would emerge from this study as mediators between a proredistributional research unit and an antiredistributional actuarial unit.

However, instead of functioning as a mediator, the chairman/commissioner called the shots in the agency, keeping policy development tightly in check and viewing the other two departments as agents for carrying out technical studies on demand. With the exception of a few early incidents, little evidence was found that research staff acted as a redistributional pressure point. Early on, the research unit confined itself to a policy development stance that was well within the parameters of the social security ideology as enunciated by Chairman Altmeyer. Open policy disputes between these two units were rare. On the other hand, relations between the actuarial staff and the chairman's office were marked by wide policy differences. While research staff apparently did not protest the reactive role expected of them, the chief actuaries did and sought to expand the role of the actuary as an independent, influential agent in social security policy formation. This actuarial independence was expressed in a relatively flexible approach to the social security ideology, frequently—to the discomfort of the chairman—actuaries were willing to adapt or discard elements of the ideology. Characterizing the redistributional stance of the actuarial staff cannot be done simply; the most succinct description possible is to say that, compared to the chairman's office, the actuarial unit was in many respects more liberal in the short-run, but from a long-range perspective was more conservative. This characterization is explained on the following pages.

Actuarial Leadership: Williamson

The two chief actuaries during the period studied were W. R. Williamson (1935–47) and Robert J. Myers (1947–70). Williamson's first contact with the emerging social security system was in 1934 when his employer, the Travelers Insurance Company, loaned him as a consultant to the Committee on Economic Security. Williamson then accepted employment with the SSB in 1936 as its actuarial consultant. Myers, too, had worked for the CES before joining the SSB, and eventually succeeded Williamson as chief actuary. There were many similarities, but some important differences, between the two. Both eventually resigned in protest, citing severe policy disagreements with agency leadership and each going public with his criticism. Each felt the social security system misused both actuaries and actuarial concepts. Williamson never really accepted the concept of social insurance, preferring instead a low-level flat pension system. Myers for many years privately sympathized with Williamson's flat plan preferences, but eventually he made peace with the concept of social insurance, accepting it as a legitimate, desirable policy as long as it did not compete with private insurance. Both actuaries were fearful of social insurance's encroachment on private insurance and this was an important factor in the resignation of each.

As early as 1936 Actuary Williamson was sensitive to misuse of insurance terminology, and he did not hesitate to chide leadership for it. For example, he criticized Chairman Altmeyer over a radio speech Altmeyer had made in which he asserted that retirees under social security would receive benefits "just as they would . . . from a private insurance company." The world *somewhat* should have been substituted for *just*, Williamson pointed out, for "there are a number of differences between . . . these benefits . . . [and] private insurance companies." No, Altmeyer replied, "substituting 'somewhat' for 'just' would entirely destroy the point I was making that individuals receive their benefits without a means test, *and in this respect, at least*, they are in the same position as . . . benefits from a private insurance company."[1] Williamson repeated his objection. Altmeyer didn't budge and curtailed the argument. "I guess we will have to call it quits, you still apparently assume that the sentence . . . indicates . . . benefits are analogous to private insurance *in all respects*; whereas I am pointing out that they are analogous . . . [only in that] they are paid as a matter of right and not on the basis of need."[2] Neither man considered this to be hairsplitting. Altmeyer was determined to appropriate private insurance language as powerful system imagery and Williamson was intent on preserving the integrity of concepts from his profession. This early skirmish was a harbinger of deepening policy differences that would divide the two men over the coming decade. By late 1936, Williamson was urging SSB leadership to cease referring to premiums and actuarial principles when discussing the social security system. Although the SSB was cautious about using these terms publicly prior to the 1937 Supreme Court decision, internal usage was common. "It is suggested that the phrase 'accepted actuarial principles' be abandoned in favor of 'proper fiscal policy' and that 'premium' be abandoned in favor of 'appropriations'. . . . There are 'accepted actuarial principles' but they seem to have no specific application here. There should be a great improvement in public understanding by this modification."[3]

In the decade following the act's passage, Actuary Williamson became increasingly dissatisfied with what he considered the SSB's abuse, not just of insurance concepts, but of professional actuaries themselves. By the mid-1940s he had come to the conclusion that actuaries had been brought into the SSB as window dressing, merely to serve as elements in the insurance imagery. "There is lip-service to 'actuarial science' as a sort of mystic salvation, though actuaries have usually had rather short shift."[4] "There is the intention not to consult the actuary under most circumstances and when he is consulted his material is very commonly garbled in its use and he is not presented as a professional man in connection with Congressional hearings."[5] He resented being overruled by Altmeyer and Cohen (who were both labor economists). "Undoubtedly a great deal of the difference of opinion between actuaries and labor economists lies in the conviction that all commercial insurance is bad. . . ."[6] Nonactuaries, he felt, were both careless and devious in their use of fiscal data.

> We have no right to present as of actuarial soundness the work done by non-actuarial persons whether they be statisticians or economists.[7]
>   The statistical data used by the administrators of these programs is not made fully available to the critics of the program. When they start to discuss the structure of the plans they cannot get their hands on the essential material. They are almost bound to make quantitative errors. The proponents of the program criticize the critics and shift attention from the subjects to minor details.[8]

Williamson himself felt he had been subjected to blatant attempts by agency leadership to isolate him because of his ideological and policy differences of opinion. When SSA headquarters were moved to Baltimore, Williamson had to remain in a Washington, D.C., office, distanced from the agency's decision-making center. "The creation of a separate actuarial section in Baltimore, with limited authority, was specifically to remove that section from the unorthodox viewpoint of [myself] . . . and, second, to place control over this section more clearly with the administration. . . ."[9] Actuarial influence on policy should be expanded, not curtailed, he argued. More business sense (such as could be provided by giving actuaries more influence) was needed in the running of the SSB/SSA; the agency suffered from both a generally ineffi-

cient administration and a "general tone of sentimentality as to the needs of
. . . clients."[10]

Because of his conviction that the SSB was misusing insurance concepts,
Williamson had a much more flexible attitude toward the contributory and
wage-related principles than did the chairman. Social security was something
so distinct from private insurance that it made little sense to apply the principles of the latter to the former. Williamson did not endear himself to agency
leadership when he failed to take the contributory and wage-related principles
seriously. Statements about wage-relatedness being an expression of American values caused him to scoff, "American—my eye, it is a direct importation
from Germany."[11] He could be caustic about the social welfare benefit structure which channeled the highest benefits to those with the least need. "It is
perfect nonsense to pretend that the special favoritism for the higher paid persons . . . has anything to do with 'reducing dependency.' "[12] This produced a
situation in which social security "loses sight of social values by overstressing
individual equity."[13] Further, regarding the wage-related principle, "All the
evidence shows the objective to be a petty one—then every possible effort is
made to keep from following the basis outlined."[14] The contributory principle, too, "is honored in the breach rather than the observance"; "the emphasis upon contribution is pure lip service."[15]

Williamson felt that when the system went off a full reserve, individual
annuity basis with the 1939 amendments, the connection between an individual's taxes and benefits had become so tenuous that calling the system contributory and wage-related made little sense. Early retirees, especially, would
collect benefits far in excess of total taxes paid; this fact made Williamson
scornful of attempts to label the benefits as earned or beneficiaries as self-
supporting. The addition of dependents' benefits meant wage-relatedness had
been so diluted as to become an empty term: how could the system be wage-
related when two workers with identical earnings and tax payment histories
would receive drastically different benefits simply because one had dependents and the other didn't?

These criticisms did not mean that Williamson preferred a strict annuity
system; to the contrary, he preferred a pay-as-you-go flat plan system with
only minimal reserves, an approach he had pressed for in the Committee on
Economic Security. He preferred a system that would pay higher benefits than
those paid at the lower end of the social security benefit scale, yet not as high
as the highest social security benefits. An old-age system should more frankly
address the needs of the poorest of the aged, and pay for those benefits as they
come due, not defer the costs the way the social security system did. Social
security was deferring costs because it was making long-range promises of
benefits, yet not bringing in sufficient payroll taxes to meet those eventual
costs: the deferred bill would come due around 1980 or 1990 when the general

revenue contribution would be needed. Long-range plans also called for escalating payroll taxes between 1939 and 1980. To Williamson, this cost deferment smacked of fiscal irresponsibility. What right had the current generation to go easy on itself with fairly low payroll taxes and insufficient benefits for its poorest aged, yet commit a future generation of workers to support the current generation, when its time came, through high payroll taxes and generous benefits? Williamson considered it a question of intergenerational justice: the system "turns its back upon the social responsibility of today, and also fails to shoulder adequate provision for tomorrow." [16] Through its misleading insurance terminology with its imagery of self-support, the system blurred the extent to which a large deferred social security bill was going to come due in a later generation of workers. This hidden cost element was of great concern to Williamson; he was scornful of the Altmeyer strategy of soft pedaling the eventual need for a general revenue contribution. He worried that shifts in the population age structure would aggravate the payroll tax burden for future workers, with "a reducing population to carry an increasing benefit schedule." [17]

In addition to the intergenerational justice aspects of the cost deferment approach, Williamson was concerned that the projected increased role for social security would threaten the private insurance and banking industries. The insurance imagery of the system created an illusion of self-support, he argued, it disguised the extent to which long-range costs were deferred; this enabled liberals to push through unreasonably high benefit levels. Williamson believed social security should never constitute the sole retirement income for a citizen; everyone should be encouraged to supplement social security with private insurance and personal savings. He was deeply suspicious that Altmeyer was committed to an expanded social security system that would eliminate the need for private insurance protection. A low level, pay-as-you-go system would forestall this.

Williamson's stance in the short-run made him more liberal than Altmeyer. Williamson endorsed blanketing-in and higher minimum benefits. His discarding of the social security ideology allowed him to advocate these and other liberalities that Altmeyer could not tolerate. Williamson liked the idea of bringing women into the social security system, whether they worked in or out of the home, on an independent basis, not just as dependents of a wage-earner (a truly radical idea for his time and one that was to gain attention by the middle 1970s). In 1936 he wrote the chairman of the SSB: "I see no permanent justification for eliminating from a program of this sort, the housewife who has not had a specific wage. . . ." [18] and, again, in 1948: "Women who have children rarely have uninterrupted employment records and the continued insistence that women shall get smaller benefits because of this brevity of their earnings records or as wives or widows is unnecessary discrimination against them." [19]

Williamson had deep policy differences with organizational leadership, yet it is questionable that he had any significant impact on the production of organizational policy positions. For one thing, he had a penchant for overblown rhetoric which diminished his influence, making it possible to dismiss his assertions as exaggerations, and at times the rhetorical excesses obscured his meaning. For example, he was capable of branding conservative social insurance as a foreign import based on "a philosophy of scorn for the established systems, a structure of acceptance . . . of broad social justice which, crudely, sounds more like a Russian structure than an Anglo-Saxon structure." [20] Despite his arguments for relaxing the wage-related principle so as to meet more fully the needs of poorer retirees, he was also capable of arguing that in the upper reaches of the benefit structure, benefit levels had gone too high, producing an "easy money" situation which would result in our citizens choosing "softer and less vigorous ways." Indiscriminately high benefits of the existing system were "very much like the letting loose of DDT over great expanses of country so that the very balance of nature is changed and the long-range end product is almost impossible to predict." [21] Williamson added, cryptically, "Unquestionably we have gone too high in the level of many of our benefits for spinsters and bachelors, so that we have actually had the result of unsettling these persons in a very awkward way." [22] At times his comments reveal a professional isolated from the realities of poverty. Consider his comments on actuarial pay. "In governmental programs of social insurance . . . the poorly-paid actuary is all too apt to ally himself with the underprivileged and to suggest benefits from too personal an approach to the problem. . . . A well-paid actuary would be less biased." [23] Or consider a speech in which he argued that governmental programs for economic support should be kept within strict limits. All citizens should be expected to help themselves through purchasing private insurance as individuals or through group plans. In addition, every citizen should make use of savings accounts. "There are banks, too, convenient for the accumulation of funds for the western trip, for the Alpine jaunt. . . ." For Williamson, (the man who could advocate a social security poll tax) "paying one's own way" through life was a "God-given right." This, in turn, implied that the payment of private insurance premiums, the accumulation of private savings, and the paying of social security payroll taxes were not burdens but rights that he jealously guarded and that he sought to extend to all citizens. When he urged substantial payroll taxation for the poorest of workers he was, in his opinion, extending them a right, not imposing a burden. [24]

Evidence indicates that Williamson's perception of himself as isolated from the real organizational decision making, as functioning primarily as a symbol of insurance, was an accurate one. Little evidence was found of direct communication between Altmeyer and Williamson after the early skirmishes over insurance language. Most of the statements quoted above come from correspondence with fellow actuaries or from memoranda that were sent "to the files" with no evidence that they went any farther. Another example of this is a thick collection of Williamson's memoranda in the mid-1940s critiquing a publication written by Cohen and Falk that argued the need for social security's extension to the farm population. Williamson had critiqued the publication's rhetoric, assumptions, logic, figures, and recommendations at great length. Yet, in the end, he consigned his memoranda to the files with a cover note saying he was simply filing them for future reference, having decided it would serve no purpose to send them to Cohen. This was striking evidence of his isolation and sense of powerlessness.[25]

Williamson resigned in 1947 and publicly aired his policy differences in speeches, articles and, in 1949, in testimony before a congressional committee considering social security amendments. His comments appeared not to have caused much of a stir, considering the fact that here was the SSA's former chief actuary testifying that the social security system was unwise and fiscally unsound. Perhaps his rhetoric again diminished his impact. He criticized social security by offering his own low-level flat plan system as an alternative, but clouded the issues with convoluted rhetorical and philosophical asides. He condemned social security as having its roots in central Europe (in Bismarck's Germany, where social insurance originated), while his approach had western origins: the writings of J. Walter Dittel and Oscar Barahona, Costa Rican actuaries who had designed the Guatemalan social security system.[26]

Actuarial Leadership: Myers

Williamson's successor, Robert J. Myers, for many years quietly sympathized with Williamson's flat plan preference, describing it in 1948 as one which "I quite strongly favor in general and which I have found a considerable support for among many of the younger actuaries."[27] Eventually, however, he came to terms with conservative social insurance and became one of its defenders.[28] This position, however, was not reached without deliberation over the appropriateness of insurance terminology.

> There may be discussed the wide usage of the word "insurance" and, also, to a lesser extent "actuarial" among those here in Washington. In certain ways, this is a rather amusing matter although it has many serious implications. The word "insurance" is used to describe the program because of the great faith and trust

of the American people in the institution of insurance as developed by the various companies. . . .[29]

While his predecessor had repudiated insurance imagery as cover for liberals, Myers eventually endorsed it for the opposite reason: the imagery provided a brake against undue liberalizations with its emphasis on contributions and no "free" benefits. Like Williamson, Myers feared the encroachment of social insurance on the business of private insurance, referring to Altmeyer and Cohen as expansionists. For Myers, the insurance terminology offered a tool for keeping expansionism in check.

Like Williamson, Myers felt SSA actuaries were not being used appropriately. For him actuaries should have been the "eyes and brains" of SSA as they were for private insurance companies. SSA actuaries, not economists, should do both public assistance and social insurance fiscal analysis. Economists had been doing most of the public assistance work, and "certainly no greatly significant results could be expected from a staff of economists whose knowledge and ability with mathematics is limited, if it existed at all."[30] A measure of Myers's pride in his actuarial background is given by his 1964 refusal of an offer to be retitled deputy commissioner of SSA; Myers preferred to retain the title of chief actuary.

Like his predecesor, Myers was suspicious of hidden costs in social security. He opposed any eventual general revenues contributions and suspected that organizational leaders pressing for social security expansion were trying to soft pedal the long-range costs by a foot-in-the-door strategy of requesting a small beginning from Congress in hopes of expanding it in later years. This gradualist approach he disliked, and expressed his disagreement to Cohen, one of the organization's leading political strategists. In reviewing a Cohen proposal for benefit increases, Myers commented:

> At no point, in discussing your short-range objectives, have you mentioned the considerably higher contributions rates that would be necessary, nor have you mentioned whether you favor a government contribution (which I am opposed to because it hides the real cost from the working contributors who, as a group, in reality also have to bear the cost of the government contribution but who cannot see it as easily as the payroll deduction of their own contributions).[31]

And, again: "A number of your benefit liberalizations are suggested as being done a piece at a time. Personally, I would prefer doing everything I thought desirable at one time and squarely facing the issue rather than having deferred costs. Is the element of gradualism (or, as some would say, the 'camel's nose in that tent') approach really necessary?"[32]

Though Myers was opposed to long-term expansion for social security, he, like Williamson, was frequently more liberal in the short-run than Altmeyer. Myers proved himself more flexible in the application of the contributory and wage-related principles if it meant making the benefit structure more responsive to the needs of the poorer of the aged. With Myers, there is extensive evidence of correspondence with Altmeyer on these issues. Unlike Williamson, Actuary Myers restrained his rhetoric; he was a master technician with the details of social security financing and his policy disagreements were grounded in these technical fine details. The difference in the Myers and Altmeyer utilization of the organization ideology will now be surveyed by studying the following issues: the increment, the retirement test, and blanketing-in. Clashes with Altmeyer's Republican successor will be illustrated with the purpose of benefits debate.

Increment

The increment in social insurance benefits during the early years was both an expression of and buttress for the wage-related principle. The basic benefit formula related benefit size to average wage levels; to this basic amount, was added an additional 1 percent benefit increase for every year worked in covered employment. During the 1940s, debate arose both inside and outside the SSB over the appropriateness of this benefit increment. Those seeking the elimination of the increment argued that these funds could better be used either to grant an across-the-board increase in benefits or to increase the minimum benefit level. Thus, the issue was one of trade-offs between benefit level adequacy versus additional buttressing of the wage-related principle. In the internal debate of the late 1940s, Chairman Altmeyer was a strong supporter of the ideologically important increment; in this he was opposed by Actuary Myers. Altmeyer acknowledged that "the recognition given to individual equity through the increment is relatively small in any one year. Nevertheless, it is of great importance psychologically." [33] For Altmeyer, the addition of the increment in the 1939 amendments had served as a symbolic counterbalance to the addition of dependents' benefits in the same amendments; the latter provision had been a step away from a strict private insurance model, the former with its embodiment of the contributory principle had provided Altmeyer a sense of maintaining ideological balance. [34]

Altmeyer called for the preparation of an elaborate ideological defense of the increment that reflected his continuing concern for shaping social policy around both perceived threats from policy competitors and allegiance to ideological principles. The defense began with the premise that the increment's removal would represent a dilution of the contributory principle which would "mean removal of one of the insurance factors. It would open the door to further dilutions of the contributory principle." In response to the argument that the funds freed up by removal of the increment should be spent on raising the minimum benefit levels to bring them closer to a subsistence level, the defense paper countered that "The attempt to fix rigidly all benefits . . . at a level of subsistence does not harmonize with the American system of individual initiative and incentive to personal effort." The defense continued: "Income differentials are so prevalent in America," and these differentials have been reflected in private pension plans so consistently that "familiarity with these practices has conditioned many American workers to expect differential benefits, with differences based on varying lengths of service as well as on differential annual incomes. . . . *All* American systems . . . should reflect the prevailing economic custom of wide differentials in individual incomes. . . ." Finally, removal of the increment would make the system vulnerable to a long-time competitor: "Because removal of the increment is a long step away from the contributory principle, it may breed a new type of 'baby Townsend' plan. . . . Or, removal of the increment may pave the way for old-age relief based solely on need as a substitute for the present programs."[35]

In his opposition to Altmeyer, Myers argued for using the increment funds to raise general benefit levels. "In regard to the benefit formula, I need hardly state that I believe complete elimination of the increment would be desirable . . . if the amounts being paid today are not thought adequate, I would go along with increasing the benefit formula still further if the increment were eliminated. . . ."[36] Staff in the old-age insurance bureau sided with Myers, arguing that insistence on retaining the increment would adversely affect efforts to liberalize the basic benefit formula in Congress. "We still feel that the increment is likely to affect unfavorably the chances for liberalization of the basic formula and that in case of a showdown we should do all we can to drop the increment proposal and to protect the formula liberalization."[37]

In the brokering of the 1950 Social Security Amendments this trade-off was made: the increment was dropped and the basic benefit formula was liberalized, though Altmeyer viewed the increment's departure with a sense of dilution of basic policy principles. Three years later he was to describe the increment as something "very dear to my heart" and recommended its return to a Ways and Means subcommittee, but the recommendation was not acted upon.[38]

Retirement Test

Altmeyer and Myers differed over the retirement test (or work clause) policy with the debate illustrating, as the increment debate had, the actuary's more flexible approach to the work-related and contributory principles. The retirement test is that policy which, in its absolute form, required the aged to be without earnings in order to collect retirement benefits. The 1935 Act specified that a single dollar of earnings in a month would mean forfeiture of that month's retirement benefit. By 1939 Congress had decided earnings up to $15 a month would be allowed, but a single dollar of earnings beyond that would mean a total loss of benefits for that month. In 1950 Congress raised the allowable earnings limit to $50 a month with an absolute benefit cutoff beyond that point. Not until 1960 was a tapering-off principle introduced such that one dollar of benefits would be withheld for every two dollars of earnings between specified limits (thus rewarding work, within limits). The retirement test, in all its forms, has been a controversial element throughout the program's history with many beneficiaries arguing for the right to supplement their social security checks by continuing to work without penalty. (In part, this beneficiary demand has been stimulated by the success of the SSA's own efforts to portray social insurance benefits as an earned right. Retirees come to look forward to their benefits with a sense of property rights; resentment follows the realization that these rights are contingent ones.)

Chairman Altmeyer was a consistent supporter of an absolute retirement test, having been unhappy with the $15 per month clause introduced in 1939 and the $50 clause in 1950. Cost was one reason for his opposition; a policy that allowed employed people to collect benefits would increase the total cost of the retirement system. More important to him, however, were ideological and strategic reasons. Again, his policy stance was based on a commitment to the principles of conservative social insurance and a continuing fear of flat plan advocates. Changing the retirement test concept would, "by violating the principle of relating benefits to loss of income, . . . increase the support for universal pensions payable regardless of loss of income or established need. . . ." [39] In an attempt to mollify the critical beneficiaries, Altmeyer proposed a reward for those who respected the retirement test. He suggested that the monthly retirement benefit be increased for each year that a person deferred retiring after reaching the minimum retirement age.

Myers considered much of the criticism of the absolute retirement test justified and the all-or-none principle inequitable. His evaluation of the retirement test was not conditioned by the chairman's persistent fear of flat plan competitors. Myers opposed Altmeyer's suggestion for an incentive to respect the retirement test because it "largely benefits the higher paid and steady workers." Myers suggested as an alternate reform a proposal which would benefit "primarily the low-paid workers and the intermittent workers from whom most of the criticism seems to come." He supported a bill in Congress calling for a tapering off of retirement benefits rather than a total cutoff so that a beneficiary could come out ahead by working. (The general principle of the proposal was that benefits to be withheld should not exceed the earnings causing the withholding.) Myers acknowledged that this would fundamentally change the conception of the retirement test, but "quite properly so" for "nobody should lose money by working" even in the social security retirement system.[40] Neither Myers's nor Altmeyer's proposals were enacted in the 1950s, but a tapering off version became law in 1960. The important point for this analysis is that the retirement test debate illustrates differences in the flexibility with which the principles of conservative social insurance were approached by the chairman and the actuary, with the flexibility being conditioned by differing perceptions of environmental threat.

Blanketing-In

Another issue on which Myers disagreed was blanketing-in. Myers simply did not agree with Altmeyer's assessment that blanketing-in would be a violation of fundamental ideological tenets or would make the social security system vulnerable to flat plan opponents. Actuary Myers's support for blanketing-in continued throughout the 1950s and brought him into policy disputes with the Republican-appointed successor to Altmeyer, SSA Commissioner Schottland and his staff. By 1953, the SSA was preparing legislative strategy for a drive to increase retirement benefits but to block continued blanketing-in efforts. Conservative opponents in the Congress fought benefit increases and, as one of their weapons, used the system's own insurance imagery against it. Increasing benefit levels to those already retired on social security would constitute a "raid" on the social security trust funds, the argument went. If the SSA were serious about its insurance language, current retirees should be kept at the benefit level specified in the social security retirement "policy" they had purchased with their payroll tax "premiums." To grant them an "unearned" benefit increase would constitute a raid on the payroll taxes the current work force was paying in toward its own retirement. SSA staff went to work developing a rebuttal for this raid argument; at the same time, however, SSA leadership (with the exception of Actuary Myers) was quite willing to let the raid argument stand as a bulwark against blanketing-in. The commissioner requested development of a policy position paper that would defend a general benefit increase against raid charges but would brand blanketing-in as a trust fund raid.

Myers supported the benefit increase, but for him blanketing-in was also desirable and ideologically defensible. SSA staff member Robert Ball fashioned the defense for the benefit increase by asserting that the benefits implied in the social security retirement "policies" were not specific dollar amounts but were best expressed by the generalized concept of support.

> The protection . . . is not in the form of a benefit of a given dollar amount but is more akin to a specified amount of wage replacement adjusted in the light of

changing conditions. . . . To maintain the basic character of the benefit protection through benefit increase to those already retired cannot be considered a "raid
on the· trust fund" since it is clearly within the established purpose of the
program.[41]

Myers accepted this rationale, "It is, of course fallacious for the present
contributors to argue that they have bought an insurance contract at fixed
rates. . . ."[42] But he argued that this rationale necessarily implied approval of
blanketing-in since the same issue was at stake: "Both consist of giving benefits (definitely desirable from a social adequacy standpoint) to persons who
have made no contribution for such additional benefits."[43] The wage-related
and contributory principles had never been followed strictly at the individual
level Myers argued, and it was inappropriate to use them as weapons against
banketing-in. These principles were not endangered by those "now currently
on the OASI roll who have paid for only a minute fraction (generally less than
5%, and in many cases less than 1%) of the value of their benefits,"[44] nor
would they be endangered by blanketing-in the "neglected group" of aged.
Additionally, Myers argued, there were both public and private precedents for
blanketing-in: it had been done under private pension plans in industry and the
federal government's own railroad retirement system had blanketed-in its new
retirees for several years with no contribution required.[45]

Myers's superiors, however, still opposed blanketing-in as a trust fund
raid, despite Myers's repeated arguments that these two policy positions,
taken together, were "illogical."[46] Throughout the 1950s, as the SSA maintained its hard line against blanketing-in, and regularly marshalled its arguments in its congressional briefing books, Myers just as regularly critiqued
them. He took particular aim at the regressivity charge the SSA was prepared
to use against blanketing-in. (Since many of those blanketed-in would be
shifted off old-age assistance, there would be a shift from progressive to regressive financing structures.) This was supreme ideological inconsistency, in
Myers's opinion, and he labeled the regressive argument as "an argument that
completely ignores the existing situation. . . . The logical extension . . .
would lead to abandonment of the contributory principle."[47]

Purpose of Benefits

The "purpose of benefits" debate occurring in 1955 between Myers and Republican-appointed SSA Commissioner Schottland and Deputy Commissioner
Mitchell demonstrates: (1) the continuing importance attached to system rhetoric and image within the SSA, and (2) the actuary's unease over social security "expansionists" even under the Republican administration. In June,
1955, Myers participated in a commissioner's office legislative strategy meet-

ing to prepare a SSA report opposing a Senate bill to eliminate the retirement test. Such a move would be unwise, the report produced by the group read, since the purpose of retirement benefits had always been "partial replacement of loss of earnings" and, if benefits were received simultaneously with earnings (through elimination of the retirement test), then the basic concept would be undermined. While Myers did not quarrel with opposing elimination of the test at this time, he objected to the "partial replacement of earnings" rationale as being an "incorrect and misleading" statement. The danger in such a statement "as I see it . . . is that it has no stopping point until full replacement is reached." [48] In a flurry of memos after the strategy meetings, Myers argued for dropping the phrase and simply referring to "wage-related benefits." Myers put his concern in a memo to SSA Commissioner Schottland, and to emphasize his point, routed a copy to Schottland's superior, HEW Secretary Perkins.

Deputy SSA Commissioner Mitchell was puzzled by Myers's concern with the fine points of language.

> I find it a little difficult to follow Bob's reasoning . . . Bob finds no stopping point to the "replacement" theory. To me this is like arguing that if you give a needy man a pair of dungarees you can't stop until you have fixed him up with a complete wardrobe including a dress suit . . . it suggests that there is a plot to promote ultimately an OASI benefit equivalent to *total* earnings. I have never heard anyone espouse such a cause. [49]

Deputy Director Ball of the OASI Bureau also defended the replacement theory as one which, "when properly used, . . . is helpful. . . ." He pointed to the use of the replacement terminology in a 1950 Senate report on a social security bill, indicating its use was not a new move by the SSA. [50] In rebuttal, Myers pointed out that use of replacement terminology earlier than 1950 could not be documented, and even the 1950 Senate report phrase could not be taken as an independent expression of congressional intent since "of course, we all realize that the statements in the Congressional reports . . . were prepared by . . . [SSA] personnel." [51] Replacement terminology was not used in the language of the original act nor in the years between 1935 and 1950, Myers argued, and its adoption in 1955 signaled a profound shift in policy orientation. For him, it was evidence of growing "expansionism" in social security which would threaten private insurance enterprises. Replacement terminology remained in use over Myers's objection: "I continue to believe that the 'replacement theory' calls for larger and larger benefits until the OASI program becomes the principal (if not sole) source of retirement income for the great majority of individuals. . . ." [52]

Myers became increasingly restive through the 1950s and 1960s as social

security expanded into new areas such as disability and health insurance. Benefit increases were being enacted without full appreciation of the long-range
financing burden, he felt, and he feared the eventual need for a general revenue subsidy. He resigned in 1970, going out with a blast at social security
expansionists by warning in a *Reader's Digest* article that these expansionists
wanted to obviate the need for any private insurance or personal savings
through raising social insurance benefit levels inappropriately high.[53] In an interview with a *Chicago Tribune* columnist, he made similar charges: expansionists were working with "almost religious zeal" to swell the role of social
security; this would harm private insurance, dry up investment funds for private industry and, in the long run, encourage government "ownership of productive activities." SSA and HEW administrators, in this expansionist drive,
were undermining the conservative policies of President Nixon. "Wilbur
Cohen [HEW Secretary under Johnson] might just as well be secretary as far
as any change in attitude is concerned."[54] In another parting shot, Myers defended the concept of social insurance. "The insurance concept is no myth
and is, in fact, one of the real underlying strengths of the program." The insurance concept implied payroll taxation and was a bulwark against dangerous
general revenue financing.[55]

Myers played a different role in the organization than Williamson did.
Myers was obviously listened to, yet there is no evidence to suggest he was
influential in determining final agency policy positions. Altmeyer would listen
to and debate with him, yet ultimately Altmeyer formulated the organization's
policy position. If anything, the internal debate with Myers merely served to
sharpen Altmeyer's skills in defending his positions outside the agency. Once
Altmeyer had defended a position against Myers, such as the argument against
blanketing-in, Altmeyer could confront external critics with the knowledge
that he would be unlikely to encounter as capable an opponent. In the series of
policy disputes between the two men, there is no evidence of Altmeyer ever
changing his position in response to Myers's disagreement. The one issue that
Altmeyer lost, the increment, was lost in Congress, not in debate with Myers.

Research and Statistics Department

The Bureau of Research and Statistics was headed at first by Walter Hamilton,
who came to the agency from the economics department at Amherst College.
He was quickly succeeded by I. S. Falk. Falk had been a health research associate for the Milbank Memorial Fund, had joined the CES to handle its health
insurance studies, and subsequently joined the research department of the
SSB. After Hamilton's departure, Falk headed the department during the
period studied here. The materials surveyed on communications between Falk
and Altmeyer indicated nothing approaching the policy differences between

the chairman and the actuaries. Falk carried out research assignments on request and, apparently, did not see his role as that of a prodding, independent voice in the agency. Only in the earliest years of the organization were there scattered incidents suggesting the research staff's willingness to go beyond ideological bounds in the interests of responding more fully to economic need. These inclinations were snuffed out fairly early in the department's history. The Ewan Clague comment on the antiredistributional consequences of adopting private insurance imagery was not followed by debate on the issue once Altmeyer made his position clear. Clague subsequently transferred to the unemployment insurance department and, later, out of the SSB. Mulford's 1936 abandonment of an article of faith by defining the payroll deduction as a tax instead of a premium and investigating its regressive impact on labor was not followed by similar attempts once Altmeyer squelched his conclusions. Shearon did no further needs analysis once it became clear Altmeyer saw her work as ideologically threatening, and she transferred out of the SSB. Altmeyer's testimony before the Downey committee demonstrated his willingness to obscure need data in the interests of ideology and strategy, as do the withholding of the double-decker study group's technical studies throughout the 1940s and Williamson's charge of deliberate distortion in the Townsend plan cost estimates supplied to Congress.

The closest the SSB/SSA came to going public with research staff studies of the relationship between income distribution and social security is found in the work of Selma Mushkin in the late 1940s. Two articles derived from her work were published in the *American Economic Review*.[56] Even then, however, her studies did not analyze the impact of social security on income distribution. Income distribution was taken as a given and was simply treated as a factor in estimating social insurance's impact on aggregate consumer spending.

These studies must be understood in terms of widespread fears that the post–World War II economy would enter a recessionary phase marked by escalating unemployment. All governmental programs were under fire to assess their impact on postwar employment levels. Social security leaders felt in a vulnerable position on this issue: their program had consistently been criticized as having a depressing effect on employment. Payroll taxes, it was argued, reduced consumer spending which in turn depressed business and aggravated unemployment. The Mushkin studies constituted a rebuttal to these arguments rather than an analysis of social insurance's role in improving the distribution of income.

The articles are prefaced with presentations of the contributory and wage-related principles and recitals of their virtues. Following this, the composite impact of social insurance taxes and benefits on aggregate consumer spending is analyzed. Given the existing American income distribution, Mushkin and her colleagues had estimated that the total composite effect was favorable to increased levels of consumption. The taxes and benefits "affect the spending-saving decisions of families in each income group . . . producing either a ten cent or twenty cent increase in buying power per dollar of disbursements and of taxes, depending upon . . . [assumptions as to marginal propensity to consume]." [57] There is no analysis of the components of the aggregate increase in consumption; that is, no discussion of the composite effects on poor and rich. Nor is there any discussion of social insurance's impact on income distribution in terms of reducing or escalating the inequality in that structure.

Additional examination of Mushkin's work reveals the ideological context which apparently always conditioned the SSB research function. The consumption and employment conclusions quoted above were published in 1947 and, importantly, were based on 1941 data which reflected a 10 percent unemployment level. The level of unemployment was a key factor in determining the composite effect on consumption. Mushkin's analysis had gone on to show that at conditions approaching *full* employment, the composite tax-benefit impact would be to *decrease* consumption significantly and *aggravate* unemployment. Thus, there was apparently a fundamental, inherent contradiction between social security financing and maintenance of full employment.

This contradiction worried Mushkin considerably, especially after President Truman in 1947 ordered the administrators of the major governmental programs to prepare analyses of their programs' effects on the goal of full employment. Research Director Falk gave the assignment to Mushkin, telling her to prepare a series of nontechnical documents for members of Congress which would describe social insurance's relation to full employment. Mushkin warned her superiors that social security would not look good in such an analysis. "If our earlier analyses are fairly accurate the conclusion must be drawn that the social insurance programs . . . do not contribute to maintaining a higher level of employment, rather they create a barrier against it. . . . The purchasing power analysis furthermore strongly argues against a step-up in the old-age and survivors insurance tax rates." [58] The last was an important point; Chairman Altmeyer, every year for the previous five years, had appealed to Congress to stop postponing payroll tax increases and to immediately hike the taxes. Mushkin felt she was in a corner. "If we confine the discussion to benefits as we have done in . . . the past we are only treating half the problem and certainly would contradict the President's request. . . . If, however, we deal with both the benefits and contributions the documents would conflict with recommendations made by Mr. Altmeyer before congressional committees." [59] Mushkin saw a conflict between the research function and the political needs of the SSB. "I think we need some guidance on this problem," she said, and then went on to suggest an escape route out of this apparent dilemma. "Drop any discussion of the present program," she suggested, and begin the analysis with a projected, expanded social insurance program, "using only a comparison of the purchasing power effects of the two programs." The projected expanded program would have benefit and tax levels adjusted to neutralize their composite impact on consumption. Mushkin even saw this as a way to speed a general revenue contribution. (Such a move would improve the impact on consumption by lessening dependence on payroll taxes.) She suggested the projected reports carry "a statement on reasons for moving from a completely self-financed system to a system supported in part from general revenues."[60] In any event, the negative effects of current financing could be ignored, the positive effects of a different financing highlighted, and the financing hot potato thrown in the lap of Congress. "The financing of an expanded program can be treated as a policy for Congressional decision."[61]

Mushkin's Research Department superior, I. S. Falk, provided the guidance Mushkin had sought. She was instructed to proceed with the reports, but to forget the strategy of avoiding discussion of the current program, for that would make it appear "that we were being evasive."[62] She should by all means downplay the financing's impact on purchasing power, and when it became necessary to refer to this point at all, Mushkin should have it "coupled with treatment of the importance of (1) the contributory principle," and (2) "the insurance argument." The values of contributory, wage-related social insurance were to be portrayed as outweighing the cost in terms of reduced consumption. As an additional protective strategy, Mushkin was told to take the position that fiscal policies other than social security were the determining ones in the general economy, and the SSA should therefore not be pressed too closely on this issue.[63]

In summary, the research department is characterized here as a unit quickly learning the ideological boundaries to its work and refraining from challenging organizational leadership; research became a tool for leadership's ends rather than an independent, broadening force in the organization. This conclusion is supported by the account of the same department offered by McKinley and Frase in their two-year (1935–37) capture-and-record account of the creation of the SSB. They say "high policy does not seem to have been the special province of the Bureau of Research" and that

> if the Bureau of Research and Statistics was to perform the central planning function for the board it would be expected that its chief opportunity . . . would be in the preparation of amendments to the Social Security Act. But in actual practice . . . its role was inconsequential. . . . Altmeyer became the motive force in the . . . amendments and in the initiation of proposals involving new policy. . . . Altmeyer's personal assistant, Wilbur J. Cohen, was as important as any member of the research staff. . . . The director seems not to have figured in either the preparatory studies . . . or in the many board and staff discussions. . . .[64]

CHAPTER 5

Containing the Public Assistance Threat

The phrase *social security* as used in the 1935 Act meant public assistance as well as conservative social insurance. Over the years, the phrase has come to mean, for most people, only the social insurance system. This is symbolic of and, in part, attributable to the SSB's drive to segregate social insurance from public assistance and to identify the agency with the more desirable of the two systems. The SSB/SSA administered both public assistance and social insurance systems from 1935 to 1963. (In 1972 public assistance was returned to the SSA.) It is the assertion of this chapter that a fundamental conflict of interest existed for the SSB/SSA during the period under study: that given the SSB's overwhelming commitment to the primacy of conservative social insurance, it did not do an equitable job of developing America's public assistance system. In this one agency were lodged two crucial policy functions for both systems: the administrative interpretation of existing legislation and the development of policy initiatives for new legislation. These functions were carried out by agency leadership, which saw public assistance as a prime policy competitor with its preferred policy of social insurance. While the whole public assistance approach such as Aid to Dependent Children (ADC) and Aid to the Blind (AB) was seen as a threat to the concept of conservative social insurance, the competition was at its sharpest in the race that agency leadership saw developing between conservative social insurance and old-age assistance.

This chapter studies the development of public assistance policy from the passage of the Social Security Act through the mid-1940s. Public assistance during this period was clearly constrained in its development, leaving large numbers of needy citizens without adequate support. This chapter does not argue that SSB/SSA actions are the total explanation for these inadequacies. Clearly, other factors contributed: public opinion, congressional dynamics and presidential decisions, for example. Nevertheless, in this complex causal situation, the SSB/SSA occupied a strategic position in the total policy formation process from which it deliberately exerted leverage to constrain the development of American public assistance. This occurred even though the SSB recognized that actual and potential clients would be deprived of needed help. To a considerable extent, then, the public assistance system can be understood as a system held hostage by its own national leadership, held hostage to the development of conservative social insurance.

The SSB saw its own public assistance system as a threat to social insurance for several reasons. The 1935 Act stipulated that the first social insurance benefits would not be paid until 1942, although payroll tax collection began in 1937. Public assistance payments began within a year of the act's passage. Might not the public become impatient with the slowly developing social insurance system and embrace public assistance as a more direct way of dealing with economic insecurity? The fears were prompted by the continuing strength of the Townsend movement and other groups pressing for universal retirement pensions. SSB leaders feared that the existence of the federal-state Old-Age Assistance program (OAA) would encourage the growth of the Townsend movements or that in some states Townsendites might even rally sufficient support to convert an OAA system into a flat pension system.

Jane Hoey, head of the Bureau of Public Assistance, summed up the SSB's fears in a 1936 planning document.

> At the present time, 42 states have passed laws to conform with the Federal Act to give assistance to needy aged. The average grant in these States is over $18 per month. During the 1937 sessions of the legislatures, practically all of the States will undoubtedly pass such legislation. If there is a lapse of five years before the contributory scheme goes into effect and the average grant after five years of contribution is less than that which can be secured under the non-contributory scheme, it would seem to me to be practically impossible to put into effect the contributory plan. There is pressure now continually in the various States to reduce the means test and to give public assistance for the aged on a flat grant basis. During the next five years, undoubtedly State laws will be amended so that by 1942 the restrictions as to the means test will be greatly lessened, and persons will expect a pension on a non-contributory basis as their right. . . . we have made a great point of the fact that persons could receive the pension as a right on the contributory basis. If, however, in a five-year period, the means test is lessened and the right of the individual is established for the non-contributory scheme, then the distinction between the two systems is eliminated.[1]

The director of the SSB's information services also saw a situation of extreme threat to the social insurance concept, warning the SSB that the "concept of old-age insurance [is] at [a] critical juncture. [A] vigorous sales campaign [is] necessary or else [we] will have to accept some compromise between 'Townsendism' and 'national insurance'."[2] Looking back on this time period in his memoirs, former Chairman Altmeyer observed that state old-age public assistance programs had to be carefully guarded for they could fan "the flames of the Townsend movement which was a factor in the 1936 elections and reached its peak of intensity during the 1938 Congressional elections. The final result might very well have been to scrap the old age insurance system before it ever went into operation."[3]

In the eyes of the SSB, a race was shaping up between assistance and insurance. Leaders were threatened by the fact that not until 1950 did the number of aged receiving social insurance benefits exceed the number receiving old-age assistance. Throughout this period, social insurance benefits were so low that many recipients had to supplement them with public assistance payments, a source of embarrassment for the SSB. People receiving such supplementation would achieve a total for the two types of payments that would equal the maximum payable under public assistance alone. Thus, as one SSB internal memorandum put it, such dual recipients "would have been just as well off if they had *never* paid any . . . social security taxes . . . people with independent means did not need this insurance . . . and the ones without independent means are about as likely to accept relief . . . as ever."[4] A decade after the act's passage, the average old-age assistance payment had increased 58 percent while the average social insurance benefit had increased 10 percent; the average old-age assistance payment was 29 percent higher than the average social insurance benefit.[5] All this hardly painted a picture of the public assistance system as a residual program, supplementing the first-line social insurance program—an immensely threatening prospect for SSB leaders. As late as 1949 the SSA was warning the Bureau of the Budget and the president that "it is nip and tuck as to whether the Townsendites and other advocates of a general pension system may win out in the race between insurance and pensions. . . ."[6] And, in surveying the administration's legislative priorities for that year, the agency pointed out that while both social insurance and public assistance needed legislative improvements, "it is clear that the strengthening of the social insurance system is by all odds the most important part of the [legislative] program."[7]

The race between the two systems was more than one of numbers; it was also a qualitative contest, a struggle on the part of the SSB to keep certain valued policy features identified with conservative social insurance and to prevent their incorporation into the public assistance system. As Jane Hoey put it in her 1936 memo quoted earlier, the ultimate threat was the loss of distinction between the two systems. For the SSB this distinction rested on several dichotomies of desirable and undesirable policy features (see table 2). During the period studied here, some states attempted to incorporate desirable policy features into their public assistance programs, particularly into

TABLE 2. Policy Dichotomies

Desirable Features	Undesirable Features
Automaticity	Means test
Rights	Gratuities
Resource protection	Resource exhaustion

old-age assistance. The SSB resisted these efforts (frequently against its own legal counsel's opinion that the SSB lacked the authority to do so).

The first pair of policy elements, automaticity versus means test, refers to the fact that income support can be delivered with or without extensive individual case investigation that exposes virtually all aspects of an applicant's life to inquiry, including nonmonetary issues such as the potential need for social casework. The SSB portrayed social insurance benefits as automatic, collected by the beneficiary after specified events such as retirement without social or economic case investigations, thus protecting the beneficiary from a possibly demeaning case investigation. The SSB wanted to maintain the image of these two stark alternatives as the only policy options; the board was threatened by proposed reforms of public assistance means testing that could make means testing less intrusive. Thus, the board obstructed state attempts to adopt what today would be termed group eligibility and declaration methods of eligibility determination. Similarly, the SSB pressured states to link assistance payments with social casework.

The notion of cash support payments as rights versus gratuities was discussed in chapter 2. Although by the mid-1940s the SSB had come to acknowledge that qualified applicants had a right to their public assistance grants, the SSB was nervous about this concept for much of the first decade of the federal-state public assistance system. An important reason the SSB disliked the Colorado 1937 old-age assistance plan, which provided a guaranteed minimum annual income (assistance plus other income) of $540 for all citizens over sixty-five, was that this would have clearly established a right to cash support under public assistance. Such a clear-cut right to support was a selling point the SSB wanted to reserve for conservative social insurance. (The Colorado plan is discussed later in this chapter.)

The resource protection versus resource exhaustion issue refers to the extent to which a person is required to utilize his/her own resources before receiving support; historically, many assistance programs have refused to help an applicant until a state of destitution had been reached. The SSB scored important political points for conservative social insurance by referring to this "spiral of destitution" as an element that was inevitable in the assistance approach, but missing from social insurance benefits which flowed without regard to resources (other than earnings). Here again, however, resource exhaustion was not an inevitable element of public assistance, but something that the SSB imposed on states, many of which were eager to protect applicants from resource exhaustion.

Despite the SSB's public rhetoric that the above undesirable elements were inevitable in public assistance, the first decade after the act's passage showed this was not the case. Some states made efforts to eliminate or mitigate the undesirable elements in their public assistance programs. The SSB intentionally created a self-fulfilling prophecy regarding public assistance's negative features, for the SSB needed a weakened, restrictive assistance system to make conservative social insurance look good by contrast and to contain a powerful policy competitor.

For implementing its strategy, SSB/SSA leadership used the Bureau of Public Assistance (BPA) which was established as the SSB's operating bureau for administering the public assistance provisions of the 1935 Act. The BPA was headed by Jane Hoey, a social worker from New York with considerable experience. Under the 1935 Act, the SSB was given the authority to approve state plans for public assistance systems; this approval was a prerequisite for federal matching funds. The federal legislation was written to provide states considerable flexibility in designing public assistance programs. States were not compelled to establish any public assistance program, but if they did they could seek federal matching for assistance to the aged, the blind, and dependent children. The BPA was given the task of providing states with technical assistance in the writing and implementation of their plans. Once a plan was in place, the SSB made quarterly reviews of state operations; the continued flow of federal funds was contingent on these reviews. The SSB had an extensive staff of auditors to monitor states' expenditures; at first, federal auditors checked every single public assistance case to see if expenditures were justified in light of the 1935 Act and the state's own plan. Later, sample checks were made. Should an audit exception be taken and sustained by the SSB, a state could be compelled to reimburse the federal government's share of the grant, and the board could threaten a slowdown or hold a nonconformity hearing to investigate whether the state's program conformed with the act. A finding of nonconformity would result in a withdrawal of the SSB's approval, a cessation of federal funds, and reimbursement by the state.

The formulation of national public assistance policy was highly centralized in the SSB. The board adopted a case development approach to policy formulation.

> In this method the federal agency issues no standards but allows states to develop their plans and they interpret the federal law. Then these state plans in a sense become "cases" to be decided by the federal agency as either meeting or not meeting the federal law. These "case decisions" in time become the policy . . .

case decisions may . . . be distributed to serve states as precedents and may in time be . . . summarized in rules and regulations.[8]

The most important of the board's case decisions were those restricting the states' abilities to define eligibility for benefits and to set benefit levels. The language of the 1935 Act contained no definition of need, leaving considerable discretion to the states in identifying the beneficiaries of their programs (within the act's limitations that federal matching funds, in the case of the aged, go only to those sixty-five and older). The SSB, in an exercise of administrative interpretation, required states to adopt an individualized need formula approach such that an individual's public assistance benefit equaled the difference between his/her requirements and resources:

$$Need = Requirements - Resources.$$

Such a formula approach obviously depended on an evenhanded application of its elements. If public assistance workers did a superficial job of determining requirements while carefully investigating the smallest resource (income, property, gifts, room, or board provided by friends or relatives), the benefit level would be depressed. This chapter analyzes the impact of ideological and strategic considerations influencing the SSB's approach to first the resources element and then the requirements element of this formula. This is followed by a discussion of the impact of such considerations on the organization's handling of public assistance legislative initiatives.

Bluffing the States: Resources

We have been bluffing in these cases to date and now must decide how far the Board will go before it is faced with a matter of withdrawing grants. [SSB Legal Counsel]

These words, addressed to the board by its legal counsel in 1938, serve to characterize much of the board's behavior in implementing the resources element.[9] The bluffing had its origins in the wide scope of administrative interpretation the board claimed under the language of the 1935 Act. When it was in the strategic interest of its long-range policy goals, the board was willing to make interpretations that its own legal counsel advised were not supported by the act's language. The board made these bold interpretations to contain the threat that public assistance posed for the future of conservative social insurance. It was necessary to constrain public assistance by imposing a strict resource policy in determining benefit levels that would pressure the states into discovering and taking into account every possible resource a client might have. In itself, such an approach to resources would depress benefit levels.

Just as important as constraining benefit levels, however, was the board's feeling that a severe application of the resources element was necessary to prevent public assistance's evolution into a flat plan system.

The board had room for administrative interpretation, first of all, on the question of whether or not public assistance grants had to be limited to the needy. The language of the act was such that one could argue there was nothing in it that prevented a state from granting benefits to those not in need. As the board's legal counsel explained, "We have advised, repeatedly, that it cannot be stated without question that a State plan must provide that recipients of assistance be in need." [10] This was a highly technical issue, raised by the fact that the word *needy* did not appear in the sections of the act specifying the conditions state plans must meet to be approved. However, based upon a reading of congressional intent as expressed in the social security bill's hearings, the board decided to make an administrative interpretation that all plans would have to make payments only to the needy. (A consequence of this decision was that it allowed the board to strike down any Townsend-like old-age assistance plans that provided pensions for all aged.) The legal counsel agreed that this need interpretation was a reasonable one. "The Board is justified in interpreting the Act to require the inclusion of needs tests in State plans." [11] But the board came to fear flat plan takeovers of state public assistance systems even with this interpretation established. For instance, a state could simply define all aged with income below a certain amount as being eligible for a flat grant per month. The state would have defined a needs test, but still pushed through a flat plan. The board wanted to block this threat, too, and decided to assume the authority to decide the *nature* of the states' needs tests. If this were achieved, the board could define them in such a way as to preclude a flat system. The board's legal counsel objected to this, saying that the board could only insist upon a test for need, it could not require a particular form of needs test or impose a definition of need on the states. The very same congressional intent invoked to justify a system for the needy also made it clear that Congress intended for the individual states to establish need definitions on their own. "The legislative history of the Act shows that . . . Congress intended that any definition of need should be established by the States. The Board's duty . . . is merely to determine whether or not there is any needs test in a plan." [12]

The board, in its drive to defend conservative social insurance from flat plan threats, rejected its counsel's advice and assumed control over the nature of needs tests. It ruled out identical benefits to all aged below a certain income level by saying that need had to be determined on an *individual* basis and flat plans treated all beneficiaries alike. But even this move, in the board's opinion, did not fully contain the flat plan threat. There was another flat plan competitor that could not be neutralized by the individual basis line of defense.

These plans today would be referred to as guaranteed income plans; they called for granting whatever assistance was needed to bring a client's combined income-assistance total to a prespecified level. Individual assistance checks would vary according to income, but all clients would be brought up to the same guaranteed level. Such guaranteed income plans were seen as being as much a threat to conservative social insurance as the Townsend Plan. For one thing, their net effect "looked like" the Townsend Plan, as one SSB staff person put it.[13]

In addition, the SSB, in an exercise of elaborate scenario writing stimulated by its insecurity over the fate of social insurance, envisioned a way in which these guaranteed income systems could evolve into an outright identical grant system virtually equivalent to the Townsend Plans. States that proposed the guaranteed income systems also coupled them with resource exemptions. That is, in determining the size of the individual assistance grant they excluded from consideration certain resources such as an owner-occupied home or a certain amount of savings or earnings ($15 a month in earnings in the California proposal, for example). Beyond this $15 per month earnings exclusion, the California old-age assistance plan called for granting whatever assistance was needed to bring the income-assistance total up to $35 per month guarantee level. The board was fearful that, under pressure from the aged, California would gradually boost the income exclusion to $35 so that all eligible aged would then be receiving identical benefit checks of $35. Individual variation would be lost, in this SSB scenario, and Townsend competitors would have won an important battle, putting them in a position to threaten the future of conservative social insurance.

States with income and other resource exemptions in their proposed plans instituted them so that an applicant would not have to drop to a state of utter destitution before qualifying for public aid, thus avoiding the spiral of destitution which the board claimed was an inevitable element of public assistance. The board, however, was willing to impose the spiral of destitution by blocking resource exemptions if this was what it took to prevent the conversion of state old-age assistance systems into flat plans. In opposing resource exemptions, the board frequently overrode the objections of its legal counsel which again argued that the board was exceeding its authority under the act. The board was aware that it was bluffing the states on this issue during the 1935–39 period; it continued to bluff and quietly prepared an amendment to the act, which was accepted by Congress in 1939 with little public attention. The amendment established the board's authority to require states to consider all resources and to determine need on an individual basis. Prior to the amendment, the board was never challenged by the states in court and its bluffing was not discovered. The following pages trace the evolution of these policies and political strategies through the 1935–39 period.

One of the first administrative interpretations the board established was that of requiring the states to administer individual means tests, complete with social investigations, for each applicant. This interpretation ruled out group eligibility procedures (as in declaring all those over a certain age with income below a specified amount as eligible) and procedures such as the declaration method of eligibility determination (in which applicants would declare they met the eligibility criteria and the state would conduct only random spot checks). These actions put the board in the position of imposing on the states the intrusive social and economic investigations it branded in its public rhetoric as degrading hangovers from the Elizabethan Poor Laws. The principle of individual means testing was established in the Ohio old-age assistance case. In 1936 the board approved Ohio's plan only after the state agreed, in every case, to: (1) conduct home visits to the applicant, (2) conduct home visits to the applicant's relatives (both those legally responsible and those not responsible for the applicant), (3) verify all income and property, and (4) utilize social service exchanges and other community resources in a social casework plan for the applicant.[14] These principles were extended to the remaining states in subsequent years. These requirements served two functions: they threw up a line of defense against flat plan competitors and they established a distinctly "social work" cast to American public assistance. The imposition of detailed case investigations helped block the takeover of state OAA systems by Townsendites or other flat plan advocates who argued for economic assistance with minimal case investigations (no investigation at all in the case of the Townsend Plan and simple income and resource checks in other flat plan proposals). Flat plan competitors emphasized getting cash directly to poor people without linking it to social casework expectations.

The requirement that public assistance workers utilize social service exchanges originated with the BPA, a department headed by social worker Hoey and largely staffed by other social workers. This requirement laid the foundation for the expectation that anyone applying for public assistance must agree to open his/her private life (and that of his/her family) to the social investigation and possible casework of the assistance worker. This fusing of social services and cash dominated American public welfare for almost four decades until the 1972 separation of services amendment clearly established a public assistance client's right to refuse social services without jeopardizing the grant. The public assistance–social work link was strengthened throughout the 1940s and 1950s as the SSB successfully sought congressional funds to assist graduate schools of social work, and the social work profession, in turn, became a supporter of the SSB and its social security ideology.

The board struck down outright flat grant systems (as distinct from guaranteed income systems) in 1936 in the Minnesota aid to the blind plan. Minnesota wanted to provide a flat grant of $30 a month to all blind persons who had incomes below $365 per year. The board hesitated when its legal counsel said it was exceeding its authority, but proceeded to disapprove the plan. Minnesota was informed the plan was struck down because it failed to determine need on an individual basis. Privately, the SSB spoke of another, political, reason for disapproval: if the rest of Minnesota's assistance programs (especially the old-age assistance) "were integrated around the plan for aid to the blind, all categories would receive pensions [flat grants]. This would . . . defeat the Old Age Benefit program [conservative social insurance]." [15]

The board, however, could not bring itself to take as decisive an action against the threats posed in 1937 by Colorado and California with their guaranteed income proposals. The SSB could not use the individual basis rationale in this case, and the board was not yet sufficiently emboldened to use resource exemptions as a weapon against the states. Colorado had passed a state constitutional amendment establishing a guaranteed monthly income for its aged: assistance would be provided in the amount needed to bring the assistance-income total to a minimum of $45 per month. Certain resources were exempt from consideration: owner-occupied homes and $300 in personal property. The BPA urged the board to strike down Colorado's plan, pointing out that the plan was a move to establish a Townsend-like flat pension system in Colorado instead of a true public assistance plan. "The Board is doubtless aware that state officials are endeavoring to forestall the operation of old-age assistance under the [Colorado state constitutional] amendment." [16] The board was inclined to agree with the BPA, but approved the plan in light of the general counsel's emphasis on the variation in individual benefits and description of the resource exemptions as reasonable.

In the same year, the board was alerted that California's legislature was considering a guaranteed monthly income plan coupled with resource and income exemptions for its aged. This escalated the board's fear of a national trend toward flat plans, and it sought ways to deter California. The general counsel again warned the board it could not legally disapprove the California proposal if enacted. Jane Hoey of the BPA disagreed with the lawyers, and in a strategy session, she offered clearly, for the first time, a new tool for combating the guaranteed income threat. She suggested the board take another leap of administrative interpretation and tell California the plan would be struck down because of the resource exemptions. Hoey offered a theory for the new tactic that would root it in the already established individual basis doctrine. "The basic exemption of a certain amount of resources from consideration makes for a rigidity of grant which precludes the grant . . . from being gauged consistently in accordance with the individual's need." [17] Hoey then went on to raise the specter of California ultimately boosting the income exemption until it equaled the guarantee level, climaxing in a flat grant system. Clearly, she said, creeping Townsendism was inherent in the California proposal. Hoey's proposal was a new one for the board, and the SSB was hesitant to use it though the board, too, was opposed to California's plans. Hoey pressed her argument: "We have insisted that each State have investigations of need in each individual case. Now we should say that in considering a grant to that individual all resources shall be considered with no exclusions of regular income." Still the board could not bring itself to use the tool Hoey had fashioned. The board instructed the BPA to send word to California that its proposed system was contrary to "good social policy" and should not be enacted, but Hoey was not to commit the board to striking down the plan.[18]

By 1938, apparent liberality in state public assistance plans was developing at such a pace that the board decided to adopt the hard line on resource exemptions that Hoey had been pressing. Pennsylvania offered an excellent test case for erecting the new antiexemption policy. Pennsylvania's aid to the blind plan called for a flat plan (as distinct from a guaranteed income) of $30 per month to all blind persons with an income below $1200 per year. In addition, the plan specifically excluded all forms of noncash income resources from being considered in eligibility determination. This meant a recipient conceivably could own tremendous amounts of personal property or be receiving considerable noncash support (room and board from relatives or friends, for example) and still receive the full $30 grant. (The Colorado and California resource exclusions had been very narrowly circumscribed so as to prevent this situation.) The board struck down the Pennsylvania plan.

The flat grant feature would have been sufficient grounds to strike down the Pennsylvania plan, since there would be no individual variations in benefits. However, the board, in delivering its decision, dwelt upon the resource exemption provision, implying that this was the major reason the plan was struck down. The state had failed to consider all resources and this prevented an individual determination of need. This time, the general counsel agreed with the board; the California and Colorado plans had called for reasonable resource exemptions while Pennsylvania's extreme version was unreasonable. The board, however, was not interested in distinguishing between reasonable and unreasonable exemptions; in the landmark Pennsylvania case the SSB had adopted Hoey's absolutist position against all resource exemption.

Having gone out on this interpretive limb, the board sought to protect itself: it needed language in the act clearly giving the board authority to impose individual means testing which included consideration of all resources. Preparations for such an amendment were underway, although the board kept them quiet; it did not want to give the states any hint that there was leeway in the existing act or that the board had been bluffing to date.

The board reaffirmed its new antiexemption stance in the 1938 Missouri and Washington cases. In both states the resources in question had to do with occasional gifts of money to aged parents from their children. In both states, the legislatures had repealed their relatives' responsibilities laws. These were acts which had compelled adult children to support their needy parents if the children had the resources to do so. These relatives' responsibilities laws (descendants of the harsh English poor laws) were common in the states, but had proved virtually impossible to enforce; such laws were becoming increasingly unpopular and were slowly disappearing. When Missouri and Washington repealed their laws, state courts subsequently ruled that should adult children make gifts of money to their needy parents, such resources should not be considered when determining eligibility for old-age assistance. Such gratuitous, sporadic cash contributions could not be considered a real source of income, according to the courts. "The court relies on the unstable character of such contributions which may be stopped at any time in its reasoning in these cases," as a BPA staff member explained it.[19]

When the state public welfare agencies, following the courts' decisions, excluded such contributions from consideration in eligibility determination, the BPA protested. The agency sent letters to the state agencies that declared this practice a violation of federal policy and threatened a nonconformity hearing which could result in a cutoff of all federal old-age assistance funds.

Legal counsel pointed out to the board that, considering the recent Pennsylvania case, the board was under pressure to follow its own precedent by striking down the Missouri and Washington plans. "The Pennsylvania Blind Plan was turned down by this Board on the basis that no matter what an individual's resources were from relatives or others, he was entitled to assistance."[20] Chairman Altmeyer, however, was reluctant to take on the states, and possibly the courts. "I think we better forget these cases," he said, as "we will not be able to maintain our position because there is strong public sentiment" against relatives' responsibilities laws. In addition, there was the fact that the board's antiresource exemption policy was based on a very tenuous interpretation of the federal law, and this would come out in a direct confrontation. After all, "There is no definition of what need means in the Social Security Act," Altmeyer said. "We are in a precarious position."[21]

The BPA strongly objected to Altmeyer's suggestion to let the matter drop. If Missouri and Washington were allowed to get away with these resource exemptions, it would start a trend. "This is just the beginning of a whittling process for if this sticks they will extend to further exemptions."[22] Altmeyer wanted to know if the board should then declare nonconformity and withdraw federal funding. This option struck him as very dangerous; it would reveal the board's bluff. The general counsel bluntly phrased the question: "We have been bluffing in these cases to date and now must decide how far the Board will go before it is faced with a matter of withdrawing grants."[23]

For a moment it looked as if the board were trapped: let the cases go and begin a whittling process; fight for its hard line position and run the risk of being exposed. Altmeyer definitely did not want to have to defend the bluffing. "I don't think it is proper for this Board to stand against the world on these cases with such flimsy grounds . . . I think we are way out on a limb in that Pennsylvania matter. . . . How in heck could we have done that?"[24] To make matters worse, a staff member reminded SSB leadership of the Colorado plan: limited resource exemptions had been allowed there. Wouldn't the board have to go back and strike that plan too?

At last, a BPA staff member, Miss Dewson, suggested a way out of the apparent dilemma: simply have the federal auditors take exceptions to the individual case expenditures instead of declaring the entire state plan out of conformity and halting the entire flow of federal funds. The board seized on this proposal; this would allow it to take some delaying action against Missouri and Washington, stalling for time so the board could get its federal amendment clearly giving it the authority it wanted. With that amendment in place as expected during the following year, the board could strike down the state plans without hesitation. Upon the board's instructions, the BPA subsequently informed Missouri and Washington: "Auditors of the Board are obliged to take exception to those cases . . . in which all income and resources have not been taken into account," and the board was able to salvage its hard line, antiexemption position.[25]

With the salvaging of this hard line position, however, the board's waffling on the California proposed guaranteed income legislation came back to haunt it. The California legislature, despite the board's warning that it would be bad social policy, had enacted its guaranteed income plan, which included limited resource exemptions. As in the Missouri and Washington cases, the board wanted to strike down the plan, but hesitated for strategic reasons. California was a hotbed of Townsendism, and the board knew it would be in for a real battle if it sought to disapprove the plan outright. The board's position was too vulnerable to risk this open clash. Thus, it sought an indirect line of attack, seeking to impede implementation of the California plan without directly declaring it out of conformity, again stalling for time in hopes of achieving a restrictive resource amendment to the federal act that would allow the SSB to kill California's policy outright.

The subterfuge adopted by the board was that of challenging California's "administrative effectiveness." The board informed the BPA that "the State statutes would not themselves serve as a basis for the rejection of plans predicated upon them," but a BPA study of the adequacy of California's public assistance administrative structure "would be desirable."[26] The BPA promptly conducted such a study and concluded there were "serious deficiencies" in the state's administrative apparatus. These were summarized as "lack of sufficient information concerning local administration; . . . a failure to provide adequate leadership and supervision of county agencies; and inadequate per-

sonnel standards and practices to assure a staff sufficiently qualified to perform their duties. . . ." [27] The BPA's findings were then used as a rationale for
slowing the flow of federal grants to California. In June, 1939, the board informed California that funds for the upcoming fiscal year had been approved
only for the month of July rather than for the usual fiscal quarter. Further, the
administrative deficiencies must be corrected or a conformity hearing would
be held, which could result in a complete cutoff of federal funds. At the same
time the board urged California's governor to press the legislature to repeal
the assistance legislation. Two months later, the restrictive resource amendment to the 1935 Social Security Act had been passed by Congress, and the
board was in a much stronger position in combating California liberality, a
battle which was to continue throughout the 1940s, despite the strengthened
position of the board.

Until the last possible moment the board had sustained its bluffing, hid-
ing from the states the extent to which it had been relying on a shaky interpretation of the 1935 Act. This is illustrated in the handling of the Iowa case.
That state's Old Age Assistance plan allowed a $30 per month income exemp-
tion. Both the BPA and the board wanted to disallow the plan when it was
considered in 1938. The board, however, in the midst of its preparation for the
new amendments, was fearful of drawing public attention to the issue by doing this. Chairman Altmeyer instructed the BPA to delay in bringing the matter before the board for a final determination.

> Iowa would have to call back its legislature if we turn this down. There would be
> a terrible to-do, which might jeapardize [sic] our amendments. I think after our
> amendments are passed we will be in a position where you can write to Iowa and
> point out . . . they will be in difficulty. . . . I would forget about it for the time
> being and bring it up after our amendments. . . . I advise you to stall as long as
> possible because when you ask the Board to decide this question, the Board is not
> going to turn Iowa down . . . on nonconformity. . . ." [28]

The fear of what the states would do if they discovered the ambiguity in the
federal law was so strong that the board refused to make public its intentions
to seek the restrictive resource amendment; Altmeyer waited until a closed
executive session of the House Ways and Means Committee was held before
even broaching the subject. In Altmeyer's words: "The Board had not made a
formal recommendation that the public assistance titles be amended to make it
clear that a state plan must give consideration to any other income and resources in determining need. This was because it did not want to give the
Townsendites the impression that there was any ambiguity in the existing
law." [29]

Fishing for Policy: Requirements

> The Social Security Board should . . . now be ready to tell the States the general
> limits which would meet approval rather than for the States to have to "fish" for
> the limits on a state by state basis. [State Administrators' Council, American
> Public Welfare Council]

In constrast to the hard line, but relatively clear, position the SSB took with
the states on the resource issue, guidance given the states on the requirements
element was marked by slowness, inconsistency, and a deliberate decision to
keep the states guessing about the limits of acceptability, a stance prompting
the above complaint.[30] The 1935–39 time period was one in which the SSB
had virtually ignored the requirements element of the formula, being intent
upon enforcing a restrictive resources policy through administrative interpretation and then buttressing that interpretation with the 1939 amendment.
The BPA during this period was fully aware that both elements of the needs
formula had to be developed equally for the formula approach to have any
meaning, but did not press the SSB leadership on requirements until the 1939
amendment had been achieved.

Once this was accomplished, however, the BPA and the general counsel
fully expected the board to turn its attention to developing a liberal requirements policy to balance out the formula. Disputes flared in 1940 when it became clear that leadership was not willing to do this. The SSB rebuffed the
BPA's suggested policy guidelines for instructing the states to be as thorough
in determining client needs as they were in determining client resources. The
result of this, as the BPA repeatedly pointed out, was to undermine the whole
concept of the formula approach, producing benefit levels virtually guaranteed to be inadequate.

The SSB-BPA controversy over the requirements guidelines soon cen-
tered around the issue of family budgeting, or essential others. The categorical aid programs established in the Social Security Act provided benefits for
certain classes of needy: the blind, the aged, and dependent children. The
family budgeting issue arising out of this categorical approach can be illustrated by a typical old-age assistance case: a husband over sixty-five has a
wife under sixty-five; both are poor and meet income eligibility requirements
for public assistance, but the younger wife cannot qualify for benefits because
of her age. Should the husband's benefit be sufficient only for his survival or
should it include enough to sustain his wife if she is normally dependent on
him and essential to his well being? A similar issue arose when a blind recipient was married to a sighted spouse. In the Aid to Dependent Children program the issue was that of providing enough for the parent or other caretaker
to live on. The BPA argued for a family budgeting approach: that in the above

cases, established dependency relationships should be recognized in the benefit level determination, especially after the 1939 mandate that any resources available to the applicant from spouses and parents had to be considered when determining the primary applicant's eligibility. The BPA argued that younger spouses in OAA and needy parents of dependent children were the two major problems; the BPA felt these should be dealt with directly, and it was willing to limit the family budgeting approach to prevent an entire household from being budgeted into an OAA recipient's check.

The BPA felt that the SSB should not merely tolerate it if states on their own adopted a family budgeting approach, but the approach should be mandated using the same administrative boldness shown in the imposition of the resource guidelines in the 1935–39 period. "The major question is whether the Board has authority to interpret need as it has interpreted every other section," Jane Hoey argued.[31] Further, family budgeting was essential to maintaining family units. In the case of the aged, family budgeting could mean the difference between a recipient being able to remain in his/her home with a spouse instead of being institutionalized. The general counsel agreed: the board had the authority to encourage family budgeting; and such a move would be consistent with the Social Security Act: "It is a fundamental purpose of the Social Security Act to assure the maintenance of the recipient . . . in the home of his choice," and this was made possible by a "family orientation" and "by giving consideration to requirements."[32] The board disagreed with its lawyer, deciding it did not have room to make such sweeping administrative interpretations, arguing that congressional intent, as shown in the debate leading to the original act, clearly indicated a desire to leave the matter of defining need up to the states. In making this argument, the board displayed skill in selectively invoking congressional intent; such intent would have applied to the board's administrative interpretation in the resource issue as well. Apparently, congressional intent was to be invoked or ignored, depending on the conservative or liberal consequences. The BPA urged the board to press for a requirements amendment to the act to match the resource amendment, but throughout the 1940s the board declined to do this. The SSB declined to impose or actively encourage family budgeting and chose to keep the states guessing as to whether such an approach would be challenged by SSB auditors.

In 1940 the BPA was given the task of implementing the 1939 resource amendment by drawing up guidelines for the states. Staff also drafted an accompanying statement on requirements. However, the SSB refused to allow any mention of requirements to go out to the states. Transcripts of 1940 SSB meetings clearly reveal the BPA's frustration when confronted with the SSB's decision not to provide clear policy guidelines on requirements assessment. The SSB did not want to provoke liberality among the states by openly sanctioning family budgeting; on the other hand, the board believed that it did not have the legal authority to rule it out. This put both the BPA and the states in very awkward positions. The states were eager to protect their plans from audit exceptions, yet the board was fostering ignorance of policy limits. The BPA pressed the SSB on this issue: "We have to send an interpretation of the Federal amendment on income and resources and that is difficult to do without relating it back to requirements as well. . . . The states haven't had guidance in family budgeting and have tried to manipulate it from one side . . . hardships are resulting."[33] The BPA pointed out that many states in the previous four years, in the absence of clear federal guidelines, had on their own experimented with variations on family budgeting. In response, the board wanted to know why a policy of simply closing its eyes to the situation couldn't be adopted. After all, board member Bigge pointed out, for the past four years "we have gotten along by ignoring it."[34] The BPA protested: "The States are not satisfied because it is difficult unless they protect their procedures from audit exceptions. . . . In the meantime, the States are limiting the development of their procedures by inconsistency and incompetent procedures."[35] By the end of 1940, when the board directed the BPA to send out strict resource implementation guidelines but with no mention of requirements, the BPA asked, "When the States say you have not interpreted requirements, what shall we say?" Bigge replied, "I don't see why there is any more necessity now for answering these questions than there has been right along." Another board staff member agreed: to provide requirements guidelines would be "putting ideas in the minds of the States."[36]

The policy of keeping states in the dark continued throughout the 1940s, prompting this public complaint from the State Administrators' Council of the American Public Welfare Association in 1945: "The Social Security Board should . . . now be ready to tell the States the general limits which would meet approval rather than for the States to have to 'fish' for the limits on a state by state basis."[37] (Some thirty years later, when looking back on the board's actions in withholding guidance on requirements, former board member Bigge acknowledged that, for his part at least, such actions were undertaken with the intent of putting a damper on public assistance expenditures and that the board had been at its "most statesmanlike" in doing so since excessive social welfare expenditures were a threat to the traditional American way of life.)[38]

Late in 1940, when it was clear the board was dragging its feet on the requirements issue, the BPA did an about-face on its earlier stance toward resource policy. The BPA's new position asserted that if the board were going to be restrictive on requirements, some loosening up on resources was needed to prevent a gutting of the whole formula approach. If essential others could not forthrightly be incorporated in grants, then the board should at least allow the primary recipient to exclude from the formula those resources needed to maintain legal dependents. The BPA urged the board to utilize its administrative interpretation powers and, if needed, to request a liberalizing amendment to the act. The board's general counsel concurred that a liberalizing resource exemption policy was desirable and legal: a rationale of "actual availability" was offered by legal staff. The 1939 amendment did stipulate that all available resources must be considered in needs determination, but, counsel argued, the board could and should consider only resources "actually available" to meet the primary recipient's requirements. Resources that were "originally with him [the primary recipient] are not actually available" when the resources have been applied to those obligations "appropriately accepted [as] a personal responsibility. . . . Origin is not the important thing. The important thing is availability." The BPA and general counsel, having failed to get family budgeting accepted through the requirements element, were trying to bring it in through the resources element. The board was not impressed and rejected this move. This marked a turning point for the BPA; until this time Hoey had supported the board in its severe resource policy. From this point on, however, she was to continue chipping away at the restrictive resource element as well as fighting the requirements battles.[39]

The board, not willing to encourage family budgeting, nevertheless felt it could not forbid it outright. A policy of indirect retardation of that approach was therefore adopted: tolerating a state plan that happened to fall within the boundaries of acceptability, yet providing virtually no direct guidelines as to acceptable limits—all this with the threat of a federal funds cutoff looming in the background for a state that went too far. The board had entertained, then rejected, the idea of taking a clear-cut position on family budgeting in a 1940 meeting. Altmeyer, referring to the family budgeting experimentation that was developing among the states, said: "I think we are stultifying ourselves in actually permitting this practice. . . . We are confronted with adopting something like this [the BPA proposal for a liberal family budgeting policy] or issuing a forthright statement that we cannot permit these other individuals to be taken into consideration . . . and therefore audit exceptions will have to be taken. . . ."[40] The BPA pointed out that should the board explicitly reject the concept of family budgeting: "We have 15 liberalized . . . State plans pending in the Bureau which have to be turned down if the Board cannot approve [family budgeting]. . . . These are the larger States and cover most of the recipients. . . ."[41] Board member Bigge pointed out that it was not necessary for the board to be forthright at all, either for or against family budgeting. "We have permitted States to do things we did not want to instruct them to do . . . I think we could do the same thing here. . . . Why take any action now on this subject?"[42] This stance of minimal direct guidance was the option the board selected, prompting the BPA representative to ask: "Then will the

Board advise us on what our procedures should be, particularly in connection with these 15 . . . liberal plans."[43] The BPA should study the situation and come back to the board with a recommendation, Chairman Altmeyer instructed, but "in my opinion these pending plans will have to be disapproved on the basis of the board's decision today."[44] Bigge agreed and offered both sympathy and a criticism for the BPA. "I realize it is embarrassing because the Bureau has worked with the States. . . . I cannot understand why this Bureau hasn't brought this matter to the Board and the States could then have been told these things were not consistent with the Board's position."[45] Subsequently, the fifteen plans were not suddenly declared out of conformity, but a process of negotiation between the states and the BPA was undertaken in an attempt to bring the plans in line with the board's wishes. The difficulty in this negotiation process was getting a clear determination of what the board ultimately would allow.

The debate between the BPA and the board over family budgeting hinged on the question of essential others. Additional persons' needs could not be budgeted into the grant simply because a dependency relationship existed, the board ruled; the additional person must be essential to the recipient's well being. Throughout the 1940s series of confrontations, the board insisted on this "essential" policy, further stating that the essential nature had to be established on a case-by-case basis through caseworker investigations of husband-wife and parent-child relationships. Case record documentation of the delivery of tangible services by the essential other were required. The BPA protested this as an unrealistic imposition; surely a spouse residing in the home with a recipient could be assumed to be essential without extensive investigation? Would not emotional support be a factor as important as delivery of physical services? A BPA staff person protested to the board that its "consideration only for physical care" would be seen by the states as "impossible of definition" and "incapable of administration."[46]

The debate continued into 1941, eventuating in the first policy guideline on requirements in six years. The sole guidance sent to the states indicated that "payments should not be extended to cover the additional needs of other members of the household unless the presence of such members is essential to the well-being of the recipient in question."[47]

Both hairsplitting and SSB determination to do as little as possible to facilitate liberality among the states reached a peak of sorts in a 1942 board meeting over the issue of burial expenses. The problem involved some states that were including in old-age assistance-grants money to bury a recipient's deceased spouse when that deceased spouse had not been eligible for benefits in his or her own right. Should the SSB permit this? The BPA acknowledged that "we think most of the States are doing it, but not telling us."[48] Federal auditors had discovered a specific instance in West Virginia of a male OAA recipient being given funds to bury his wife, who had not been old enough to qualify for OAA benefits. The auditors had taken exception to this expenditure and now the SSB had to respond to the state's appeal.

One SSB staff member began the discussion by trying to sidestep the whole issue of essential others: the expense should be allowed because "this is covering a need of the survivor and not the need of another member of the household."[49] Chairman Altmeyer, however, would not allow this, for that rationale would, in his opinion, establish a dangerously liberal precedent: it would imply that "any obligations that the categorical recipient assumes for other members of the family are part of his requirement."[50] The SSB legal counsel disagreed that the implications were that drastic. "The question is when the wife dies does the man himself need to bury his wife and it is not a question of whether the wife needs burial at all. It is a question of his need. . . . I don't see that this has anything to do with this other member of the household question."[51]

However, Altmeyer insisted on linking the burial expense issue to the essential-other issue. If the burial expense were to be allowed, it must be rationalized using the SSB's established essential-others policy. He was inclined to approve the burial expense and struggled to articulate a policy position that could define a dead wife as an essential other. The trouble was that under existing SSB policy, the essential nature of a spouse had to be demonstrated through the wife's delivery of actual services to the husband—services a dead wife was hardly in a position to deliver.

The sight of Altmeyer struggling to achieve this feat of technical interpretation sparked an interesting thought for Jane Hoey of BPA: if a dead wife could somehow be rationalized as an essential other, why not a sick or incapacitated wife? Hoey had always disagreed with the board's position that the essential nature of a husband-wife relationship had to be documented with case record verification of service delivery. This policy meant a sick or incapacitated wife who could not prepare her husband's meals, do his laundry, and so on could not qualify. Mere emotional support derived from her presence did not make her an essential other in the eyes of the board. If, however, Altmeyer was apparently on the brink of construing a dead wife as essential, then logically, a sick wife could achieve that status, too. "Does this mean that if the wife is sick, she is still essential to his well being?" she asked Altmeyer.[52]

At this prospect, Altmeyer began to waver. "I don't know. I'm trying to interpret this."[53] Board member George Bigge had some thoughts on the subject: a wife could remain essential if her illness were brief. "The fact that she was sick for a day or a week, you certainly wouldn't deduct. Would you for a month? I don't know. Suppose she became chronically ill and the recipient is getting along without her services. I don't know where you draw the line."[54] Ellen Woodward, the sole female board member, argued that the board should

automatically consider a wife as essential. "I think the burial expense should
be allowed. I think the wife certainly should be considered as essential to the
well being of the husband . . . the wife should be accepted as essential without any proof, unless there is proof to the contrary. . . ."[55] However, Chairman Altmeyer saw this as posing a dramatic expansion in liberality. "All I can
say is we will say we are not raising a question with respect to this payment of
burial expenses and let the rationale go because it seems impossible to develop a rationale."[56] Bigge agreed, "Yes, it affronts me to think he should
have to give her a pauper's burial."[57] The BPA, however, pressed for a formal
statement of policy to protect similar cases from audit exceptions. Altmeyer
proposed, and the board accepted, the following revision in the essential others guidelines. The original 1941 policy stated that

> payments . . . should not be extended to cover the additional needs of other
> members of the household unless the presence of such members is essential to the
> well-being of the recipient in question.

The March 24, 1942, revision directed that

> payments . . . should not be extended to cover the additional expenses incurred
> because of the presence of other members in the household unless the presence of
> such members is essential to the well-being of the recipient in question.[58]

This constituted the sole general policy statement issued by the board to the
states; there was no direct, clear-cut statement to the effect that burial expenses for deceased ineligible spouses were legitimate budget expenses. The
SSB was afraid that such a statement would put ideas in the heads of the state
public assistance administrators. It was left to the BPA, in its consultations
with the states, to go beyond the obscurity of the revised policy statement and
inform the states directly that such burial expenses were allowed, but in thus
being frank, the BPA exposed itself to angry charges from the board of promoting excessive liberality among the states.

The debate over essential-other guidelines continued, after the burial expense case, throughout 1943. The board's acceptance of the burial expense
policy modification had been grudging; the SSB feared that the states might
take the issue and run with it. What expenses other than burial expenses might
they try to incorporate under the new clause? Control over this new policy
hinged on restricting the definition of an essential other. The board did not
want to do anything that would allow public assistance to drift away from intensive, individual case investigations for each benefit allowed (one of the
very features the board's public rhetoric claimed was an inevitable, humiliating aspect of public assistance). The board continued to push for specification
of tangible service delivery in the case records as proof of an essential rela-

tionship. At one point the BPA wanted to send out state guidelines which listed categories of persons who might be essential to a recipient; individual investigations would still be required to verify this. In the case of dependent children, states should consider whether the parent, or adult acting in the place of a parent, was essential. Older siblings of the dependent child could not be so considered, the BPA suggested, indicating its willingness to build in constraints on the states' ability to define essential others. In the case of old-age assistance, states should see if spouses were essential, but adult children still residing in the home and siblings of the primary recipient would be excluded from being an essential other. The BPA suggested that instead of trying to define essentiality in terms of a certain number of tangible services, the board should move in the direction of this categorical approach. The board refused. Board member Bigge, in particular, did not want to put ideas in the mind of the states by suggesting categories of essential others: states might interpret this as encouragement to routinely consider all spouses and parents as essential—a dangerous expansion. The Board urged the BPA to keep the situation open, and to make the states start virtually from scratch in each case to demonstrate the essential nature of an individual. During the course of the 1943 debate, the board leaned toward providing some guidance to the states by considering a guideline that defined an essential other as one who would "render specific services of a kind, which, if the applicant were living alone, would have to be provided for him."[59] The BPA strongly opposed this proposal, which would still put the states in the position of documenting a wife's essential relationship through a description of the tangible services she delivered—an unreasonable burden to place on caseworkers and an unwarranted intrusion into family life.

Finally, the BPA made a point-blank challenge to the board. The BPA could not carry out existing guidelines on essential others unless the board itself were to offer the BPA some guidance by answering these specific questions: (1) Did the board want and could it help to define a listing of essential services? (2) Did the board want "to define the duration of inability to perform essential services (because of illness or absence)"? (3) Did the board want to limit essential services to "physical services such as washing, cooking, etc., thus excluding those emotional relationships normally included in the total scope of a marital or parental relationship"?[60]

At this confrontation the board paused. Its debate over the burial expense issue had revealed to it the conceptual swamp it would enter if it tried to specify what made a wife essential. The board modified its stance slightly and agreed that a wife's or parent's services need not be specified in writing in the guidelines or in individual case records. Board member Bigge made it clear he was acquiescing to this modest boost for the concept of essential others only with great reluctance, for it amounted to agreeing that, in the case of a dependent wife: "Her need for food is his need for food. I just don't think it is possible and yet that is what is being done. . . . I am willing to go along with this although it is closing our eyes to the fact that they will be getting money for ineligible people."[61] Although wives' services need not be specified in detail, individual investigations of husband-wife relationships still had to be conducted, and conclusions about them entered in the case record. At first there was some confusion on the BPA's part about the continuing need for investigations of wives. Jane Hoey commented: "I understood that spouses and parents you [would] establish the relationship and the fact that they live in the house and then there is [*sic*] a presumption but that you would not have to have a finding on their essentiality."[62] Individual investigations had to be made, the board directed; all that was changed was that the actual services need not be documented in case records. "They may not budget to include her in the old man's budget just because she is there," as Bigge put it. This procedure was mandated over the BPA's objection. "That will mean thousands of cases in which there would have to be individual investigations when it is pretty obvious on the face of it that there is no real question."[63]

By the end of 1943, the board decided to absolve itself formally of the responsibility for defining an essential-other relationship. The board still held the states accountable for making this determination and reserved veto power over the states' definitions. A second supplement to the essential-others policy was approved for state distribution on October 14, 1943. If a state should decide, on its own, to make provision for essential others, then "whether the presence of other members of the household is essential to the well-being of the recipient is a question to be determined by the State agencies in accordance with the State law . . . provided that . . . [the] decision is made on the basis of a finding as regards the need of the eligible individual."[64] This policy revision was not introduced without some apprehension on the part of the board. Before approving it, the board had assured itself that there was still room within the policy to constrain undue state liberality. This issue had arisen when staff member Powell asked: what if a state should issue blanket instructions to all its workers that all ineligible wives residing with their aged, eligible husbands are to be considered essential? "We would not do anything about that kind of instruction as I understand this proposal. . . . We would say that is a matter for the State to determine."[65] Bigge objected strongly to this: it must not be allowed. Altmeyer wanted to know if any states were, in fact, already taking this approach. Kansas and Nevada had procedures that bordered on this already. Do we "keep hands off on that situation?" the BPA wanted to know. This pointedly raised the issue of how much control the board wanted to retain, and Altmeyer provided the policy phrasing that would allow the board to retain as much control as it wanted. At his suggestion the phrase "provided . . . that . . . [the] decision is made on the basis of a finding as regards the needs of the eligible individual" was included. This would still allow the board a basis for demanding individual case investigations of husband-wife relationships. The board accepted this, and Altmeyer raised the other major issue: should the board go to the extent of "limiting it to the physical care"? Bigge was willing to forego that restriction as long as "blanket inclusion of specific relatives" had been ruled out. The new policy was in place: Kansas and Nevada would have to revise their procedures, and in the future any other states that appeared to be drifting toward "blanket inclusion" of wives or any other relatives were to be referred to the board for a conformity determination.[66]

This policy revision had several consequences: it continued the position of doing virtually nothing to pressure those states that were ignoring family budgeting to adopt it. The revision put the burden of defining essential other on the states, while the "provided that . . ." clause still gave the board the power to impose financial penalties should the board dislike the definition. Thus, the states were kept in the position of fishing for the limits of acceptability. Finally, the revision put the BPA in a very difficult spot. The BPA was mandated by the board to provide technical assistance and consultation to states in writing plans and setting up administrative structures, even to the point of helping states devise forms for case records. All this was part of Chairman Altmeyer's boast that the board was not a policy policeman, but rather the states' "partner in a great cooperative undertaking."[67] Whenever ambiguity, obscurity, and gaps in specification were built into board policy statements, the BPA personnel were the first source state officials approached for guidance. In this case, the BPA staff were asked for advice on what would constitute a definition of essential other that would not provoke an audit exception from the board. The BPA gave this advice based on their understanding of the board's intentions; however, as discussed below, such guidance prompted the board to censure the BPA for promoting family budgeting among the states.

As early as 1941, the BPA had reported that some form of family budgeting was "nearly universal" among the states in actual practice, although only twenty-one states reflected the policy in their official state plans. The board began to suspect that this spread of public assistance liberality was being encouraged by the BPA; this suspicion produced some sharp exchanges between the board and the BPA which resulted in a motion that a formal admonition to the BPA be entered in the minutes of a 1943 board meeting. The BPA must not, the proposed admonition said, seek to encourage family budgeting among the states. Board member Bigge, a strong supporter of the admonition, asked if the BPA would abide by the warning, prompting BPA staff to ask: "If they ask for advice what do we say? They do ask for our opinion. . . . I don't think that we set out to promote but . . . with a request from a

State for advice given their setting, their law, etc. how shall we develop the manual [public assistance manual]. . . ?[68] Chairman Altmeyer was impatient with this question. "I think you are conjuring up difficulties that don't exist because if a state law refers only to the individual's need in a very strict sense . . . there is nothing that can be done. . . . so I don't think there is any difficulty." The formal admonition was entered into the record because, in Altmeyer's words, "some members of the Board feel you have been pushing the States to adopt a broader concept of need than they would have adopted themselves."[69] Despite the warning, this issue was to be a continuing source of friction throughout the 1940s, with board member Bigge especially suspicious of the BPA. Shortly after the formal admonition was adopted, Bigge quizzed the BPA.

> *Bigge:* Wouldn't you feel called upon even with this [the formal admonition] . . . to tell the States it is good social work practice to determine the need for the whole family group . . . and to get as much from this fund as possible. . . .

> *Slocum [BPA]:* We would if you wanted us to, but we didn't know you wanted us to. We never have.

> *Bigge:* We have not wanted it said but I think you have been saying it. . . . We have said they cannot do it but the Bureau nevertheless has promoted that point of view.[70]

The board continued to worry about the spread of family budgeting and in 1944 instructed the BPA to prepare a state-by-state analysis showing the extent to which states were exceeding the conservative essential-others guideline adopted after the West Virginia burial expense case. The board found the results of this survey very disturbing: in Old-Age Assistance, thirty-two of the fifty jurisdictions would need to revise their plans to come within a strict interpretation of the essential-others guideline. The same was true of thirty-four out of thirty-five jurisdictions in Aid to the Blind and forty out of forty-nine in Aid to Dependent Children. The acceptable OAA plans included three types: (1) Twelve plans that provided for no essential others, with payment level being equal to the difference between the individual's requirements and the income available to him/her, (2) Two plans in which essential-other payments included only the requirements of the spouse, and (3) Four plans in which payments including requirements of a person other than the spouse with a recording of the specific services that made that person essential (see table 3).[71] The remaining thirty-two OAA plans needed revising. Of these, nine utilized a household deficit approach: payment was equal to the difference between the requirements of all members of the household in which the recipient lived and all of the income available to them (see table 4). Eighteen OAA plans exceeded the guideline with payment procedures that included the requirements

TABLE 3.   OAA Plans Meeting SSB's 1943 Essential-Others Criteria as of April, 1944

State	Individual Budget Computation	Includes Requirements of Spouse Only	Includes Requirements of Other Essential Persons
Alaska	X		
California	X		
Colorado	X		
Delaware	X		
Illinois	X		
Indiana	X		
Iowa	X		
Massachusetts		X	
Michigan			X
Minnesota	X		
New York	X		
North Dakota			X
Ohio			X
Oregon	X		
Rhode Island		X	
Texas	X		
Utah			X
Wisconsin	X		
Total	12	2	4

of persons other than the spouse, but without case record documentation of the specific services which rendered the additional persons essential (see table 5). The remaining five offending OAA plans contained lesser deficit procedures with payment equal to the lesser of (a) the individual's requirements-income deficit or (b) the household's requirements-income deficit.

The board was upset: the thirty-two offending OAA plans had all been approved by the board over the preceding nine years upon recommendation of the BPA. Some approvals had been granted in the 1935–39 period when the board, preoccupied with nailing down a restrictive resource clause in the needs formula, had not once considered the requirements element. Other approvals had come in the 1940–1943 period in which the board had turned to requirements, but had developed its policy of indirect retardation of family budgeting. During this nine-year period the BPA had worked with the states in developing their OAA plans; during the 1935–39 period the BPA had done this work with the expectation that the board would turn to a liberal requirements policy once a restrictive resource policy had been established. However, for the last three years the BPA had to live with the realization that the board was not serious about an even-handed application of the needs formula approach, being intent, instead, on an imbalanced application that would

TABLE 4.   OAA Plans Exceeding SSB's 1943 Essential-Others Criteria
           through Use of Household Deficit Method as of April, 1944

States	
Arizona	New Mexico
District of Columbia	Pennsylvania
Idaho	Virginia
Maryland	Wyoming
Montana	

TABLE 5.   OAA Plans Exceeding SSB's 1943 Essential-Others Criteria by Including
           Requirements of Others without Specification of Essential Services,
           as of April, 1944

States	
Alabama	Nevada
Arkansas	New Hampshire
Florida	North Carolina
Georgia	Oklahoma
Kansas	South Carolina
Louisiana	Tennessee
Maine	Vermont
Mississippi	Washington
Missouri	West Virginia

serve to depress benefit levels. The fact that the board found itself facing, in 1944, thirty-two jurisdictions in which OAA plans exceeded its essential-other guidelines is attributable to several factors. First of all, the board's guideline itself was very late in coming, not being distributed to the states until 1942; states had had to develop their plans virtually in a policy vacuum regarding the requirements element of the formula. Secondly, it is possible that the BPA sought to encourage liberal essential-other practices among the states: in the first five years out of an expectation that the board would naturally adopt this approach to complement the restrictive resource element, and in the latter four years in an attempt to fight against the board's emerging restrictive stance towards requirements. In any event, the board itself felt that the BPA had been deliberately circumventing it by encouraging liberality in state essential-other procedures. As board member Bigge put it when informed of the above thirty-two OAA plans that exceeded the board's guidelines: "I don't think we have said anything in the past five years that . . . [would] permit that. In fact, we have said the opposite." [72]

In preparing the above analysis, the BPA had anticipated the board's negative reaction. In a strongly worded accompanying statement, the BPA made clear its position that the board, in its drive to constrain public assistance growth, had for nine years been slighting the real issue in American public assistance: widespread inadequacies in payment levels. Any impression of extensive welfare liberality that might be derived from the above analysis was misleading, the BPA reported, since in most states with apparently liberal OAA plans, "practices and resulting payments are more limited than the plans might indicate." Further:

> Practices observed through administrative review indicate that in determining need there is frequently overstatement of available income from relatives, either inside or outside the home, omission of certain requirements at an amount less than the actual cost or below the State standards. Records often indicate that needs exist that are not considered when the assistance plan is computed. In addition to the above limiting practices, the standards for determining requirements often are low, and in a number of States a percentage cut on payments is in effect. . . .[73]

All of these were restrictive practices that the board had chosen to tolerate, declining to exercise the same sweeping administrative interpretation prerogatives it had used to oppose state liberality on the resource issue. Among ten of the states in table 5 (with apparently liberal plans), more than half of all OAA recipients received average public assistance checks of less than $20 a month, even though such payments nominally provided for the needs of persons not covered in the board's policy (see table 6). Excessive liberality was not a real issue in these states, the BPA argued, for "it seems likely that payments of old-age assistance as high as $20 . . . would have been needed by a larger proportion of these recipients had the needs of only the persons designated in the Board's policy been considered. . . ."[74]

The board directed the thirty-two offending states to revise their plans and to weed their current welfare rolls. The states were ordered to accomplish this in the remaining eight months of 1944 or face the threat of federal audit exceptions. When the BPA suggested more time was needed to accomplish this task, Bigge countered that the eight months was a generous allowance. "I think that would be ample. I see no objection to giving plenty of time because I think the Bureau has been as much at fault as the State agencies. I think our people have encouraged them and worked with them to adopt the plans."[75] Despite the board's wishes that the states quickly alter their plans and practices, a lengthy process of negotiations between the BPA and individual states ensued, with the SSB overseeing the process.

The board's stance toward public assistance continued to be a restraining one throughout the 1940s. However, under continuing pressure from liberal

TABLE 6. Distribution of Benefit Levels among State OAA Plans Exceeding Essential-
          Others Guidelines as of November, 1943

State	Percentage of Monthly Old-Age Assistance Payments under $20
Alabama	75%
Arkansas	76
Florida	75
Georgia	94
Louisiana	53
Mississippi	98
North Carolina	93
South Carolina	93
Tennessee	78
West Virginia	78

states and the BPA, some modifications in both the requirements and resources elements had been achieved by the late 1940s. For example, in World
War II the SSB debated whether elderly welfare recipients in Oklahoma
should have the estimated value of the produce from their victory gardens de-
ducted from their checks. After thorough consideration of the matter, even
conservative board member Bigge was willing to exempt this particular resource, explaining that as far as "inconsequential, casual, victory gardening
by those old people," the SSB should "be realistic," and "I think I would be
willing to write off any income from a victory garden."

> *Long [BPA]:* Suppose they do have a garden that produces enough food for a
> family for a year. . . .
>
> *Bigge:* I think we are concerning ourselves about some very inconsequential
> things when we object to a victory garden.
>
> *Hoey:* We are not objecting to the victory garden.
>
> *Bigge:* All right, then, let's say we don't object.[76]

Gradually, in response to state and BPA pressures, the board acquiesced even
further by allowing states that so desired to exempt income that a recipient
used to support a legal dependent; in doing this the board reversed itself, coming to accept the previously rejected legal counsel's available income rationale
with its boost for family budgeting. The board, however, still left it on a voluntary basis; there was no bold administrative interpretation to force this approach on the states. These movements on the part of the board were the
results of continuing liberal environmental pressure from the states on the
board, as well as continuing pressure from the BPA.

Public Assistance Legislative Initiatives

While the data available on the SSB's role in public assistance legislative initiatives is not as extensive as the preceding material on administrative interpretations, there is material which can be used to identify some key decision points and the agency's rationales, rationales in which the containment of public assistance's growth played a large part.

From its earliest days the SSB was sensitive to legislative proposals to liberalize its public assistance programs, particularly when such suggestions emanated from within the agency itself. Wilbur J. Cohen (at the time special assistant to board Chairman Altmeyer) made this clear to staff member John Corson in 1937. Corson was drafting a section of the SSB's annual report to Congress and proposed the statement: "In some States, levels of payment are so low as to raise a question whether or not the Board should continue to grant implied Federal approval of such meager amounts." The board, Cohen said, had decided it could do nothing in the way of administratively interpreting existing law to raise these "meager amounts" and, furthermore, Corson ought not to imply that "the Board should like to see the Act changed in some respect so that the Board would have some power over the amounts. . . ." Cohen indicated that the board was not interested in pressing for any such policy changes. "From my own personal information, I am under the impression that the current attitude . . . of the Board itself is that we must go slow in making any suggestions for the revision of the public assistance program and leave the responsibility pretty much to the States from both the fiscal and administrative aspects in working out their own problems." Corson's sentence with its "dangerous possibilities" should "be carefully reconsidered, then, if necessary, eliminated." Discussion ensued and a toned down sentence substituted which read simply, "The Board is deeply concerned that the level of payment prevailing in some areas of the country is too low to achieve the purposes of . . . the Federal Act." [77]

A conservative response to a liberalizing impulse is found in a 1939 exchange of letters between Chairman Altmeyer and D. W. Bell, director of the Bureau of the Budget. Bell was withholding bureau approval of Senate Bill 959, a proposal to increase the federal match in the Aid to Dependent Children program from one-third to one-half (to bring it in line with the other public assistance programs). Bell would not approve the bill because it failed to contain a provision specifically requested by President Roosevelt: a guarantee that "additional Federal expenditures would actually result in either an increase in monthly allowances to present beneficiaries or an increase in the number of beneficiaries." In other words, Roosevelt wanted a mechanism to prevent the states from simply substituting federal for state dollars with no real expansion for beneficiaries. Altmeyer opposed this idea, urging the president to abstain from any action that would virtually mandate public assistance liberalization. The SSB, Altmeyer said in a letter to Bell, had already considered such a provision "as a condition for more liberal grants not only in the case of aid to dependent children but in the case of the old-age assistance and blind assistance. However, the disadvantages outweigh the advantages." No such liberalizing pressure was needed, Altmeyer urged, for he was confident that the states could be trusted to voluntarily pass increased funds on to clients since ADC "is a field that has been relatively neglected in the past" and states could be counted on to "spend at least as much and probably more" for ADC. As for old-age assistance, "it is probable that some states may be able to reduce their previous levels of expenditures," and this must be allowed. In this letter Altmeyer did not indicate what evidence led him to think the need for OAA expenditures would be declining in the near future when, in fact, his own research staff at the time was pointing out to him the widespread inadequacies in conservative social insurance and public assistance. A more likely reason for Altmeyer's position was its restraining effect on a social insurance competitor. The Bureau of the Budget took Altmeyer's statements at face value and withdrew its objections.[78]

Perhaps the most striking and candid expression of the SSB/SSA's opposition to legislative liberalization took place in 1950. Wilbur J. Cohen (then technical advisor to Commissioner Altmeyer) expressed the agency's opposition to a bill prepared by Senator Claude Pepper that would allow old-age assistance recipients to work to a certain extent without suffering a reduction in their assistance checks (the resource exemption issue). The bill called for the exemption of income which, when combined with the amount of public assistance received, would not exceed $100 a month. Cohen responded:

> The approval of this amendment would have an undesirable effect upon the contributory retirement system by establishing a policy that $100 is the amount eligible persons should receive, an amount in excess of that which persons could expect to receive through the retirement system. This, it would seem, places the retirement system in an unfavorable light and holds the threat that the assistance program will continue as the primary income maintenance device for the aged. We have consistently maintained that the contributory social insurance program should have this responsibility and that public assistance should assume the role of supplementary and residual program.[79]

The Republican administration of the 1950s adopted this line of thinking readily; for example, in 1956 a bill to allow states to disregard no more than $50 a month of earned income in determining old-age assistance was defeated, in large part due to the opposition of the SSA and HEW who, according to a HEW policy paper: "stated that this provision was inconsistent with the supplementary nature of the Old-Age Assistance program . . . such an amendment would confuse the purpose of public assistance with Old Age and Survivors Insurance . . . and would tend to give Old-Age Assistance some of the qualities of a pension. They further stated that it would open up the entire question of exempt income in the assistance programs." [80]

Though the SSA maintained its anti–income exemption stance on the legislative front in regards to the aged, it acquiesced to widespread public support for an income exemption amendment in the case of Aid to the Blind. (However, the exact details of the SSA's private maneuverings for or against this legislation will have to await researchers' access to data on the congressional committees which considered the legislation. Executive sessions of these committees in which policy decisions are brokered are closed to the public and their records are not open to scholars; a researcher interested in exploring possible SSA opposition to this public assistance liberalization in these closed sessions would do well to examine the personal papers of the committee members.) In 1950 federal law was changed to allow (and by 1954 to require) states to exempt up to $50 a month in earnings for Aid to the Blind recipients.

Dependent children also received a boost in the 1950 amendments to the Social Security Act with a caretaker amendment. (The amendment was publicly endorsed by the SSA; again, it would be interesting to see if public endorsement was translated into strong SSA support in the committee's executive sessions.) This permitted states to receive federal matching funds for payments to an essential other: the needy parent (or parent substitute) of a dependent child. A scholar of American public assistance legislation, Gilbert Steiner of the Brookings Institution, has argued that this ADC caretaker amendment was omitted from the original act through oversight, and that it was not enacted in the succeeding fifteen years through oversight on the part of SSB and social work lobbyists. When the caretaker or essential other amendment finally was enacted in 1950, it sailed through Congress with very little opposition, prompting Steiner to ask, "The tantalizing question is whether it could not have been included 15 years earlier if someone had pushed it—or even nudged it along." Material presented in this chapter strongly suggests that the caretaker amendment was not nudged or pushed by the SSB in the preceding years, in a deliberate move to restrain the development of public assistance. [81]

The aged received neither an income exemption amendment nor an essential-other amendment in 1950 nor were such amendments requested by the SSB. This differential treatment of the aged is explainable by the fact that the old-age assistance-insurance race had essentially narrowed to one between assistance for the aged and insurance for the aged; the SSA could acquiesce to liberalizing pressures on behalf of the blind and children, but not on behalf of the aged.

CHAPTER 6

Caught in the Pincers Movement

As is apparent by this point, this study's conclusion is that a goal achievement, organization-as-tool view is the appropriate interpretation of administrative leadership's role in producing social security's antipoor bias. Both redistributional policy opponents and many of the needy aged themselves were caught in a social insurance–public assistance pincers movement directed by leadership. This chapter elucidates the logic of this conclusion and compares the conclusion with an important, but quite different, one reached by another student of social security. An epilogue reflects on the relationship of this conclusion to current social security issues.

Goal Stability in a Changing Environment

A brief review of organizational redistributional goals and their relation to the perceived political environment will be helpful. The reader will recall that *environment* as used in this work means everything beyond the immediate bounds of the organization; thus, *environment* encompasses the Federal Security Administration, the president, the rest of the federal government, and state governments, as well as nongovernmental elements such as the Townsend movement and organized labor. *Organization* as used here refers to the Committee on Economic Security, the Social Security Board, and the Social Security Administration. Because of strong continuity in personnel and goals, the SSB is treated as an extension of the CES. Three periods can be distinguished in the 1935–54 period studied here.

Early Period

The 1935–41 period was one in which, on balance, redistributional threats were seen as the predominating environmental characteristic. Certainly there were conservative forces in this period, but it was in this time frame that:

1. The Townsend movement peaked in membership and clout.

2. The SSB discovered and fought a surge of liberality in state public assistance systems.

3. Liberal threats emerged within the executive branch of the government (the Eccles group and the SSB's own superior, McNutt).

4. In Congress, Senator Downey emerged as a leader of liberal flat plan insurgents, conducting hearings that focused national attention on social security's inadequacies.

5. Organized labor maintained a stream of criticism against conservative social insurance.

6. Even Roosevelt emerged as a liberal threat when he endorsed a social insurance–flat plan merger.

The last environmental threat, the presidential one, was complex. Tracing Roosevelt's position on social insurance in this period shows initial vacillation followed by a right-to-left movement. Roosevelt, at first, was in alignment with the very modestly redistributive stance of the Committee on Economic Security, but later he moved out of alignment and became a conservative force on the CES after Morgenthau's lobbying. This conservatizing impact on the organization's goals was a short-run anomaly in a period of predominantly liberal pressures. This anomaly was reflective of a vacillating president's power to impose goals on the organization. In doing this, Roosevelt misjudged the intensity of the liberal forces in the environment and reversed himself. The powerfully redistributive nature of the environmental forces was dramatized by this reversal and by his further movement to a liberal redistributional point where the SSB was reluctant to follow. It was Roosevelt's acceptance of compromise with flat plan advocates in 1940, followed by Downey's hearings in 1941, that marked the peak of the liberal environmental threat. The outbreak of World War II kept Roosevelt from acting on his newfound social insurance liberality and also defused the rest of the liberal threat.

Middle Period

The second period, which covers World War II, was one of transition, in which the environment was essentially neutralized in terms of conservative and liberal pressures on the legislative front; the war effort eclipsed domestic social initiatives. All the liberal threats did not vanish with the outbreak of war, however; on the administrative (as distinct from legislative) front, liberal forays in the state public assistance systems continued to threaten leadership's social insurance goals. These were beaten back and were essentially under control by 1943, although a low-grade liberal insurgency continued throughout the 1940s in public assistance.

Late Period

The third period, post–World War II to 1954, was marked by the emergence of a conservative Republican threat to social security. Leadership perceived this as a very dangerous phenomenon, which picked up steam in 1949 with Congressman Curtis attracting national attention as its leader. This perceived threat escalated with Eisenhower's election and his initial silence on the future of social security. Crisis appeared eminent in 1953 with Curtis being given an investigatory committee and Hobby apparently joining the Chamber of Commerce camp. The zenith of the antiredistributional threat was represented by the Chamber of Commerce proposal for a low-level flat pension, regressively financed, and coupled with the abandonment of public assistance. A measure of the perceived power of this environmental threat is found in Altmeyer's private admission that compromise with the opponents was inevitable and in his preparation of such a contingency plan. (An interesting question: would the compromise with conservative foes have produced a net liberalizing outcome? This would have been the case if Altmeyer had engineered a blanketing-in compromise along the lines of the double-decker group's proposals prepared internally by his agency.) By early 1954 the conservative threat had subsided. In the face of organized labor's opposition and that of powerful Democrats in Congress, the Republican challenge was dropped; social security ideology was embraced by the Eisenhower administration, producing a remarkable degree of congruency between a conservative political environment and conservative social insurance.

Thus, despite some early goal changes, the overriding characteristic of leadership's goals during this twenty-year period of drastically changing environmental conditions was one of comparative stability: the early shifts were small and after 1939, leadership's minimally redistributive goals survived the peak of the liberal threat, as well as the extreme of the conservative threat.

Intention and Consequences

In moving to a consideration of consequences and intention with intention being embodied in ideology and strategy, we will be in a position to scrutinize the relative merits of a drift or tool interpretation of redistributional goal formation.

The organizational goals during this twenty-year period have been characterized as minimally redistributive. What is the relationship between the nature of these goals and organizational ideology? Consider a goal drift scenario: the social security ideology, and in particular the private insurance imagery at its heart, served a protective function for the modest redistributive content of the original goals, and organizational leaders intended for it to perform this protective function. The ideology provided defensive cover for liberals intent on establishing a redistributive beachhead in a conservative environment. Continuing the scenario, we would expect that unanticipated goal displacement would be revealed when these same leaders later sought to expand the redistributional content of their goals and policies, but were limited in doing so by the conservative insurance imagery. The very success of the insurance imagery strategy in protecting initial limited redistributional goals now serves to block redistributional expansion. This scenario contradicts the facts of the twenty-year period under study. An alternative interpretation is developed below.

Ideology and the Liberal Threat

The 1935 Act and 1939 amendments were not established as liberal beachheads in a conservative environment; on the contrary, they were conservative defense lines in a threateningly liberal environment. In this early period, the social security ideology served primarily to ward off liberal pressures, not conservative ones. This characterization is drawn from a study of leaders' own perceptions and strategic analyses as found in agency files and leaders' memoirs. Leaders' assessments of their early environment consistently reveal, on balance, a predominating fear of liberal pressures. Intention and organizational activism in dealing with liberal threats are highlighted in the organization's unilateral adoption of private insurance imagery in 1937. This imagery was later ratified by Congress, it is true, but the point to be made here is that to the extent that the organization could influence the total policy formation process, it threw its weight behind a conservatizing move: the adoption of insurance imagery. This imagery was adopted by leaders with an understanding of its antiredistributional consequences as spelled out in Clague's warning to Altmeyer.

The insurance imagery became part of a two-part definitional campaign which had the explicit purpose of restraining redistributional competitors, both flat plans and public assistance. The second aspect of the definitional campaign, the derogation of public assistance, further highlights both the primacy of the redistributional threat for the leaders and the intensity of their desire to contain redistributional pressures. A measure of this intensity is illustrated by two factors: (1) leadership's overriding of its own legal staff's advice in making administrative interpretations to retard public assistance and in so doing taking actions that exceeded their legal authority under the 1935 Act; (2) leadership's anger at subordinates (the BPA) who appeared to be tolerating or encouraging liberality in public assistance.

The social security ideology shaping policy throughout the whole twenty-year period was fundamentally a middle-class vision. Implicit in its statements about earning one's benefits, rewarding thrift, supporting the work incentive, and all the rest of the virtues of the contributory and wage-related principles was a vision of a smoothly functioning capitalistic society with few imperfections in its labor market. In this ideology are strong echoes of the Wisconsin model's dream of preventing need and harnessing capitalistic self-interest to serve collective social welfare ends. Old-age dependency would be prevented by requiring young workers to participate in social security. Making retirement benefits wage related would wed a social welfare end to self-interest-seeking means. Thus, just as in the Wisconsin theory of unemployment compensation, the social security ideology diverted attention from caring for the need to preventing the need.

Undergirding the ideology was the belief that the Great Depression was an historical anomaly, that fundamentally the American economic system was sound and, further, that the system, when back on its feet, would provide a job with livable wages to everyone able and willing to work. Additionally, there was the assumption that virtually everyone in society (with the exception of the blind) would be either a work force participant or have a dependency relationship to a participant (as wife, widow, or child). Thus, keying the social security retirement system to work force participation through the contributory and wage-related principles made eminent sense to SSB leadership. Their belief in this vision is demonstrated by the withering away theory of public assistance which organizational leaders offered repeatedly to Congress and the public. As social insurance matured (coverage was expanded), it was argued, the need for old-age public assistance would dwindle to virtually zero. Thus, old-age assistance was a temporary safety net for a maturing social insurance system, a net to be discarded once the economy was back on its feet and the social insurance system firmly established.

There was no room in this vision for fundamental defects in the American economy, such as structural unemployment and underemployment or the effects of discrimination which could prevent significant numbers of workers from "earning" decent social security benefits. The naivete of this vision is further shown by the inclusion of Aid to Dependent Children in the withering away theory. Not only Old-Age Assistance, but Aid to Dependent Children would dwindle as social insurance matured. This statement was based on a perception of dependent children as orphans of wage earners, who would receive social security dependents' benefits. Nonorphans who needed help due to parental desertion, divorce, or birth outside of marriage were not included in this vision of society and policy.

Flat planners and other redistributional opponents were threats precisely because they challenged this optimistic vision of the American scene, and, ironically, those aged whose needs were not being met by social insurance and old age assistance embodied threat as well. Proposals for large-scale, permanent, significantly redistributive support systems were attacked by organizational leaders because such proposals stemmed from a misunderstanding of the fundamental correctness and health of the American system.

Conservative social insurance ideology served to blunt the redistributional movements of the Depression by appearing to respond to need, but actually doing so in a way that offered little fundamental change in income distribution. The minimum benefit provision and the weighted benefit formula in social insurance allowed leaders to speak of the system as favoring the poor, while the tight limits placed on these elements undercut their antipoverty effectiveness. Senator Downey's angry outburst over the benefit formula was prompted by the illusory quality of this "weighting in favor of the poor." Similarly, the role accorded public assistance in the formal statements of ideology allowed the organization to portray itself as being responsive to acute need—thus undercutting the arguments of the redistributional proponents. Privately, however, in their administration of the program, leaders succeeded in severely retarding assistance.

The intended consequence of organizational ideology in this period was the blunting of the redistributional thrust created by the economic needs of the Depression-era aged. That the organization did not completely succeed in blocking this thrust is shown by the modestly redistributive goal movements found in the 1935–41 period. This period certainly does not reveal leaders seeking to expand the redistributional nature of their policies, but being restrained by their previously adopted insurance imagery. For these reasons, a goal achievement tool view is supported: minimally redistributive policies were the intended consequence of leaders' actions. The organization and its protective ideology were tools for this end.

Ideology and the Conservative Threat

What about the role of organizational ideology in warding off the conservative threat in the 1950s? Can the preservation of goals in this period be attributed to the ideology? In large part it can, although at first glance the opposite might appear to be true. Upon initial examination the social security ideology, with its private insurance imagery, appears as a liability before the extreme conservative attack. Congressman Curtis made the insurance imagery his principal point of attack, and in so doing he established a valid point: the SSA *had* overstated the private insurance aspects of social security in the previous years. The long string of publications and public statements about workers having insurance policies with the federal government *were* misleading overstatements intended to build upon the average citizen's concept of contractual, private insurance. Curtis succeeded in establishing this, even to the point of forcing the principal organizational ideologue, Altmeyer, to come the closest he ever did to abandoning private insurance imagery by describing social security as fundamentally a moral obligation of Congress. (The SSA apparently learned a lesson from the Curtis onslaught and in subsequent years moderated its insurance rhetoric: insurance imagery was still used, but references to workers having insurance policies with the federal government were dropped.) The intent of the Curtis attack was to demolish the private insurance imagery, undercut confidence in the stability of the system, and thus erode its political support. Altmeyer was well aware of this intent, and that is why the Curtis hearings read like a cross-examination, with Altmeyer battling every step of the way. At one point Altmeyer directly accused Curtis of doing more than anyone else to undermine public confidence in social security.

Curtis established the mythical nature of much of the insurance imagery but social security's political support certainly did not erode. The mobilization of organized labor was a major factor in averting this political defeat. Labor's role as savior of conservative social insurance was a dramatic reversal of its pre–World War II role. In 1940 organized labor called for a universal, liberal flat pension with progressive financing (asserting that social security should be a measure for the redistribution of national income) and was one of the most powerful liberal threats to conservative social insurance. It was to organized labor that Roosevelt first made the announcement of his intent to accept a blanketing-in compromise. By the early 1950s, however, organized labor had become a champion of conservative social insurance and payroll financing and a strong opponent of blanketing-in. Organized labor's changing social security stance was but one aspect of the changing character of the labor movement. This movement lost much of its radical and liberal character in post-Depression years. As labor unions became established, they became more conservative, turning away from broad issues of social justice to a concentration on issues immediately affecting union membership. The social security ideology, with its emphasis on wage-related, earned benefits, fitted in nicely with this narrowing of interest. Organized labor stopped seeing social security in terms of social justice for all the aged and began seeing it almost as another membership benefit negotiated with management. By the 1950s labor had come to look upon the social security reserves as their own reserves. Blanketing-in was opposed because it was viewed as a raid by nonunion members on labor's reserves.

Conservative social insurance, with its ideology of earned and wage-related benefits, thus succeeded in winning and consolidating the support of a changing labor movement. As unions grew more successful at increasing the wage levels of their members, they also saw the ideological virtues of tying social security benefits to those higher wage levels. In describing labor's rescue of social security as a consequence of the ideology, it is not necessary to argue that labor was in any way misled or manipulated by the SSA or its ideology. It is simply that the ideology became increasingly appealing to a conservatizing, introspective labor movement, eventuating in exactly the type of middle-class, vested-interest political support envisioned by organizational leaders.

Ideology and Strategy: Consequences for the Aged

Throughout the period studied, the formal goal of the organization was that of providing economic support for all the aged. For public consumption, the organization elaborated a "safety net" goal statement: conservative social insurance was to be the first-line support, and for those aged not falling within its protection, there was the old-age public assistance system to act as a safety net. Operative reality was that both the front-line system and the safety net were full of holes. Large numbers of needy aged were excluded from both social insurance and public assistance. Even those who did receive social insurance and assistance payments frequently received inadequate levels of support and, in the case of assistance, did so under intrusive investigatory conditions.

How should we interpret this gap between formal goal statement and operative reality? In large part the operative inadequacies were the *consequences of strategies* adopted by organizational leaders in pursuit of ideological goals. A drift view would portray these consequences as unforeseen and unintended; a tool view would see them as foreseen and intended: the difference is goal displacement versus goal achievement. The conclusion reached here is that a tool view, goal achievement interpretation is the correct one. In order to show the basis for this conclusion, it is necessary to make clear the relationship between ideology and strategy, describe the strategy under discussion as well as its consequences, and then assess these consequences in terms of leaders' intention.

Ideology is here distinguished from *strategy* in the following manner: *ideology* is a body of interrelated, normative and descriptive statements; *strategy* is defined as those plans and actions taken to advance, implement, or defend an ideological position. One should not draw too sharp a distinction between ideology and strategy, for it is frequently true that the body of ideology, in addition to goal material, contains within it prescriptions for how best to pursue the goals. (For example, the social security ideology offers the wage-related and contributory principles as both goals in themselves and as strategies for achieving other goals.) Strategy is informed, guided, and bounded by ideology; strategy is in the service of ideology. Nevertheless, no ideological system can provide specific, detailed guidance for every contingency that may arise in the world of action. Carriers of the ideology at times must make independent decisions, choosing from an array of action possibilities that option which they think will best advance the ideological position.

To illustrate: the social security ideology says that conservative social insurance possesses certain highly valuable features and public assistance possesses certain flawed features. Organizational leaders were making *strategic* decisions, however, when they decided to bluff the states out of liberal resource exemptions, deliberately foster policy ignorance and confusion among states on the requirements issue, or suppress Shearon's work and present distorted needs data to Senator Downey's committee, to list a few examples. The social security ideology does not value bluffing and dissembling; these were strategic choices made by leaders on behalf of ideological goals.

The purpose in drawing these distinctions is to spotlight the element of choice on the part of organizational leaders. Choice is important, for it both focuses us on intention and directs our attention to consequences and the anticipated or unanticipated nature of those consequences. These are concepts at the heart of the drift versus tool question.

Just as organizational leaders chose to adopt the strategies of bluffing or research suppression, so they chose an overall strategy for defending their policy goals from ideological threats such as the flat plan competitors. An overview of the strategic actions taken in the fields of social insurance and public assistance against these opponents can be provided with a pincers movement metaphor. *Pincers movement* is a military term referring to the simultaneous converging movements of two flanks to cut off an enemy from sources of support. This offers a unifying image for the strategic choices made by organizational leaders in fighting flat plan competitors. The two flanks of the movement were social insurance and public assistance. The movement, or development, of both flanks was simultaneously directed by leaders so as to complement one another in defeating competitors.

The social insurance flank was closely directed by leaders so that no support would be provided for flat plan competitors. Leaders feared that flat plan opponents would take encouragement from the incorporation in social insurance of any features that resembled flat plans; thus, blanketing-in was opposed. Of course, there were purely ideological grounds for opposing blanketing-in, but this discussion highlights the strategic considerations behind their opposition. Purely ideological opposition would resist blanketing-in because it was inherently wrong; strategic considerations for resistance sprang from the aid and comfort such a policy would provide a flat plan enemy. Actuary Myers offered organizational leaders an ideological reconciliation with blanketing-in by pointing out that blanketing-in and the raising of benefit levels to those already retired were doctrinally equivalent. Leaders, however, were not receptive to arguments of ideological acceptability; they were preoccupied with the *strategic* consequences of blanketing-in, which would provoke the flat plan opponents. This incident provides a prime illustration of the relationship between strategy and ideology: here, strategic considerations promoted doctrinal rigidity among the leaders. Once the strategic threat had subsided in the late 1950s, a prime ideologue such as Cohen could be receptive to arguments for the ideological acceptability of a watered down version of blanketing-in. Similar strategic considerations both reinforced and rigidified ideological opposition to other redistributional moves in social insurance: the raising of the minimum benefit level would "flatten" the benefit structure or liberalization of the work clause would similarly provoke flat planners.

The movement of the public assistance flank, too, was closely directed so as to deprive flat planners of support. As in the case of social insurance, leaders feared that the incorporation of any features similar to those of flat plans would encourage the activities of those opponents. Leaders controlled the movement of this flank and ruled out these features by imposing on the states a negative stereotype of assistance that limited coverage, depressed benefit levels, and mandated intrusive social investigations. Chapter 5 of this book clearly documents the strategic context of these efforts: statements of intent make it clear that assistance had to be contained to protect conservative social insurance.

In addition to the flat plan enemy, many of the nation's aged were caught in the pincers movement and cut off from support. The poorest of the aged suffered the most as a result of leaders' strategic choices. This is brought into sharpest focus in the case of those who could not qualify for social insurance benefits and needed blanketing-in but, then, had only a weakened, inadequate old-age assistance safety net to fall back upon. Were these negative consequences for the aged a case of unanticipated goal drift? The unforeseen consequence of strategy? Material presented earlier in this work shows that from the first days of the SSB's life, leadership foresaw the consequences of their choices. Beginning with the needs assessment work of Shearon in 1936 and continuing with I. S. Falk's warning to Altmeyer in 1939, agency leadership was made aware that needy aged were being deprived of support as a result of the pincers movement. The series of double-decker studies of the 1940s and 1950s repeatedly informed leadership of the price being paid by the aged; BPA added its voice in 1940 and thereafter, pointedly and repeatedly it brought to leadership's attention the negative impact on the aged of a crippled public assistance system. Clearly, the pincers movement, with its thrust against the flat plan enemy and its concomitant thrust against the most needy of the aged, was a strategy adopted in awareness of its consequences for those aged. This was no case of unanticipated goal displacement, no unforeseen drifting away from the formal safety net goal. The safety net goal was never seriously entertained by leadership in the first place. The story of public assistance in the 1935–44 period is that of SSB/SSA leadership successfully fighting against the states (and the BPA after 1940) to insure that public assistance could *not* succeed as a safety net.

The Nature of the Tool

Having put forth a goal achievement, tool view interpretation based upon a consideration of goals, environment, strategy, consequences, and intention, there remains an element left for discussion: the nature of the tool that leaders used to pursue their goals. In the SSB/SSA, leaders had a powerful resource for promoting their ideology.

Mastering the Tool

Mastery of this tool was established fairly quickly by Chairman Altmeyer. The research department showed early signs of ideological nonconformity, but was soon brought into line. The actuarial unit, headed by the ideologically nonconforming Williamson, was controlled by isolating him and dealing directly with subordinate actuaries for the needed technical work. Myers, as head of the actuarial unit, moved more directly into the decision-making arena after his conversion to social insurance, but never emerged as a strong, countervailing force to the influence of the chairman. Policy debates between the two sharpened the chairman's position, but did not result in a broadening or modifying of the chairman's views and goals.

The BPA under Jane Hoey was the closest to a truly rebellious unit in the SSB; under her guidance the BPA did achieve some limited success in diverting the chairman in his course. Until 1940, Hoey kept her department responsive to the leader's wishes in the field of public assistance, at times even exceeding the chairman in her zeal to constrain the states on the resource exemption issue. There was a dramatic shift, however, when in 1940 it became apparent to Hoey that organizational leadership was intent on an unbalanced application of the needs formula, which made a charade of that approach. Repeatedly Hoey challenged the leadership and, in the board's opinion, she and her department even subverted the wishes of the board by encouraging liberality among the states on requirements.

After 1940, Hoey, the BPA, and the states achieved some modest, liberalizing victories. The pattern in these cases was that of the board, upon discovering widespread liberality on a particular issue, ordering immediate policy reversals by the states under threats of a federal funding cutoff. This was followed by the board retreating to the extent of allowing state-by-state negotiations with the BPA. The board was reluctant to take the drastic action it initially wanted because such action would have caused a political furor. The board's deliberate ignoring of requirements had allowed states to stake out liberal policy positions and to confront the board with an accomplished fact. This was the pattern in 1940 when the board ordered that plans of states with liberal requirements policies immediately be disapproved. Hoey pointed out that would put the board in the position of striking down plans that encompassed the majority of the old age, the blind, and the dependent children clients in the United States—a situation that would be loaded with political dynamite. Upon hearing this, the board retreated to a position of ordering the BPA to negotiate more restrictive policies on a state-by-state basis. The same pattern prevailed in 1944. The relatively minor liberalizing actions by the board after 1940, though not enough to undo the crippling effect of their earlier decisions, did represent modest liberalizations extracted from a reluctant board by an assertively liberal environment which had an internal advocate.

Of the units studied (the BPA, research, and the actuarial department), the BPA was the only one to achieve any significant policy battles with organizational leadership. This is due to the fact that the BPA was the only unit that spanned the boundaries of the organization, that was able to tap directly into environmental forces (the states) and use these forces as leverage in policy disputes. The other units had no similar boundary-spanning characteristics; they were entirely contained within the organization, making them more easily controlled.

Hoey's recalcitrance after 1940 did not mean she and her department rejected the social security ideology; on the contrary, Hoey was even more faithful to the ideology than Chairman Altmeyer. For, Hoey, in her insistence on a balanced application of the needs formula, was simply insisting on bringing to reality the safety net function of old-age assistance. She never challenged the supremacy or inherent superiority of conservative social insurance; she believed in a residual, withering away role for old-age assistance. The crucial difference was that for Hoey, assistance would wither away only as need truly declined; in the meantime, need really had to be met. She refused to participate in the strategic decision by Altmeyer and the board to deliberately subvert the safety net function, which was also a subversion of one of the ideology's doctrines. Though she and the states continued to battle with the board throughout the 1940s, Hoey had waited too long to switch positions. The board's final authority in these matters—especially the board's control over public assistance legislative initiatives—was too great to prevent the fundamental retarding of public assistance from taking place.

Organizational Resources

Leaders had impressive organizational resources on hand to pursue their goals. In the field of social insurance, a major strategic resource was the benefit data and tax data of the system and the expertise to interpret them. The organization had a monopoly on knowledge of the fiscal fine details, which could become enormously complicated. Actuary Williamson made an important point when he described the strategic advantage flowing from this data monopoly. This was especially important in the time period studied, when individual members of Congress as well as committees did not have the extensive support staffs of today. Congress was extremely dependent on the organization for cost estimates of various proposals: it was difficult to find competent, independent analysis. This put critics of social security in the position of being dependent on the SSB/SSA for the data needed to back up their criticisms and flesh out their counter proposals. Leadership's willingness to take advantage of this knowledge monopoly is shown in the Shearon needs analysis incident and in the withholding of technical studies from Senator Downey. Senator Millikin had an acute appreciation of the organization's monopoly on technical knowledge and complained in a 1950 committee hearing, "The cold fact of the matter is that the basic information is alone in possession of the Social Security Agency. There is no private actuary . . . that can give you the complete picture. . . . I know what I am talking about because I tried to get that."[1]

In terms of sheer organizational clout it would be difficult to surpass the resources available to the SSB for controlling state public assistance systems. The organization had the power to approve state plans, which encompassed the power to pass judgment on the administrative adequacy of the systems, and the power to interrupt the flow of federal funds and demand reimbursement for assistance expenditures already made. In addition to direct control over the purse strings, the SSB had another strategic resource to use in imposing its will on the states: knowledge of policy.

The states were dependent on the board's interpretations of federal law; these interpretations were passed to the states by the way of BPA field representatives in a series of loosely organized, obscurely written state policy letters. Knowledge of acceptable policy was a variable to be manipulated by organizational leaders in the interests of their goals. The deliberate decision to foster ignorance of acceptable requirements policy in an effort to constrain state liberality has been demonstrated earlier. Mark Hale, a scholar of American public assistance policy, has studied this particular aspect of the board's operation in detail. Hale describes the guidelines to the states as "slow, at points cumbersome . . . divorced from operating offices of state agencies, at times obscure and often subjective. . . ."[2] Hale alludes to the potentially crippling effects of this policy obscurity, but to him obscurity was simply a result of bureaucratic red tape. Obscurity, he tells us, was simply one of several bureaucratic errors "which may have occasionally characterized the board's administration." Further, "Such mistakes are to some extent inevitable in any undertaking as extensive as that managed by the Board for the first eleven years of . . . public assistance."[3] Specifically referring to one such "error," the obscurity of state guidance on essential others policy, Hale offers this explanation. "Either because they were vague and involved or too hastily conceived (or perhaps they were developed largely in Washington with little appreciation of 'grass roots' issues) they occasionally raised more questions than they settled."[4] As previously argued, obscurity of essential-others guidelines was not a function of isolation from grass roots. The organization was acutely aware that grass roots proclivities were liberalizing ones: obscurity was deliberately fostered to curb this liberality. Nor can the guidelines be characterized as hastily conceived or as simple errors in judgment. They were debated in elaborate detail and represented considered, deliberate decisions by the board to foster policy ignorance.[5]

Another resource of the organization was its strategic position within the federal government. In battling policy competitors this gave the organization advantages analogous to those of an incumbent politician campaigning against political challengers. The remarkably long tenure of leadership flowing from the Democratic hold on the White House permitted consolidation and expansion of this positional power. This positional power was weakened by the interposition of the FSA between the SSB and the president, but SSB leadership proved adept at circumventing this barrier.

The organization's position, with its high visibility and extensive public relations resources, enhanced its ability to mount the definitional campaign to structure policy debate on terms most favorable to the organization. The promotion of private insurance imagery and the derogation of public assistance and flat plans were the principal components of this campaign.

In conclusion, the organization (CES/SSB/SSA) was a tool of considerable utility and effectiveness for proponents of the social security ideology. Its power certainly was not unbounded: it could be, and was, arbitrarily overruled by a president, and it was saved from defeat or significant compromise by the intervention of extraneous forces, as when the outbreak of World War II saved it from compromise with the flat planners. Overall, however, the picture for this period is one of organization leaders remarkably successful in maintaining the minimally redistributive character of their goals and policies. Instrumental to this success were the attributes of the tool at their service: a monopoly on technical knowledge, positional power, the power of financial veto over state programs, and the ability to manipulate the variable of policy obscurity or clarity.

Comparing the Conclusion

This interpretation of the institutionalization of social security's antipoor bias is at odds with traditional explanations—in particular its image of administrative leadership. A fuller appreciation of this conclusion can be had by comparing it to the very different conclusion reached by a major social security scholar, the Brookings Institution's Martha Derthick. We agree on the strategic importance of the SSB/SSA in the total policy-making system, that leadership's imprint is found throughout social security. But we differ in our understanding of leadership's role in producing social security's redistributional limitations. Derthick sees leadership as fundamentally in sympathy with lower income classes; liberalism was "the prevailing value," and leaders wanted their social insurance "to protect the poor in particular against misfortune."[6] She sees two limitations to their propoor efforts, one self-derived (leaders were not radicals) and one externally imposed (leaders were kept by the political environment from implementing in full their propoor goals). She tells us, "Had the executive founders been free to make the program conform to personal preferences, they would in all likelihood have made it more progressive than in fact it has been (though not, so I would judge, radically egalitarian)."[7] But to tell us that leadership was not radically egalitarian is such an understatement that it tells us very little about the self-imposed limitations to their redistributional policies. Altmeyer's arbitrary pronouncement that even a subpoverty-level wage earner's benefits should not exceed 80 percent of former average wages, for example, shows us much more than the absence of radical egalitarianism; that decision and others discussed earlier reveal a profoundly conservative stance toward income inequality. Repeatedly, leadership was faced with episodes of historical "looseness" or degrees of redistributional freedom in the environment, when political circumstances would have allowed them to do their highly significant part toward making social insurance more responsive to the needs of the poorest. Repeatedly, leadership chose not to take advantage of circumstances in this way, and frequently, in fact, actively and successfully opposed proredistributional pressures. In short, Derthick underestimates leaders' self-imposed redistributional limits and overestimates the environmentally imposed ones. This is clearly illustrated in her handling of the blanketing-in issue.

Although blanketing-in is not covered in great detail in her work, she does briefly recount Roosevelt's temporary embracing of it in 1940 and the SSB's corresponding distress, as well as describing—this time in more detail—the resurgence of blanketing-in pressures in the early 1950s. Leadership's opposition to allowing the unprotected aged to enter the social security shelter appears to give Derthick a bit of difficulty in preserving her previous characterization of leadership as bent on protecting the poor in particular, for she tells us, "Their resistance to universal flat plan pensions was so rigid and the reasons for it so little articulated in public that the logical content is hard to summarize. They were reluctant to even consider such proposals. . . ."[8] Derthick describes part of that ideological and strategic logic of resistance. She tells of the perceived threat to the contributory principle (the fear that blanketing-in would undermine uncovered workers' incentive to be covered), as well as the flat plan threat (that blanketing-in might spur on the Townsendites). However, there is another aspect of the logic of resistance that Derthick misses: the deliberate writing off of large numbers of the neediest aged. The unspoken factor in that calculus of decision making was the devaluing of the aged caught in the social insurance–public assistance pincers movement. Leadership's reasoning led them to conclude that caring for those aged would have exacted too high a price in terms of strategy and, ultimately, ideological values. This aspect of the logic of resistance, its grounding in leaders' awareness of the human cost, is missing from Derthick's discussion, probably because she did not examine the reports to Altmeyer, beginning from the early days of the program, that demonstrated the effects on the aged of the pincers movement's operation. Far from being "reluctant to even consider such [blanketing-in] proposals," leadership studied them repeatedly and in exquisite detail; they simply rejected them.

Larson's position that the unprotected aged were a problem that would solve itself through mortality rates was nothing more than an inelegant phrasing of agency leadership's own stance, a position thrown into sharp relief by Altmeyer's 1950 consternation over those unprotected aged's "great persistence in longevity." The starkness of this aspect of the logic of resistance is surely one of the reasons leadership was so reluctant to articulate it in public. Public discussion would have been risky: if pressed, leadership could hardly have afforded to say bluntly that this portion of the aged had been weighed in the scales of ideology and found to be excludable. Altmeyer did nearly admit this in his memoirs by saying, "We in the Social Security Administration were quite aware of the social need for protection of those already aged . . . however. . . ."[9] The needy, excluded aged were threatening—hence Shearon's needs analysis had to be contained, questions about including them had to be deflected with metaphors of the social insurance sapling needing time to mature before bearing its fruit, and inquiries about holes in the old-age assistance safety net had to be forestalled with rhetoric about the inevitably and inherently flawed nature of the public assistance approach.

Derthick's failure to reach the conclusions above is attributable to two factors. First, she misses the combined effect of the pincers movement through her exclusive focus on the social insurance component of social security. Thus, she sees leadership's opposition to blanketing-in in a softer light than I do, for the old-age-assistance safety net can still be seen as a refuge for the excluded. However, the simultaneous perception of the social insurance exclusion and the deliberate retarding of public assistance throws a harsher light on the matter. Secondly, in her characterization of early leadership she lets those leaders, to a large degree, paint their own portraits through her heavy reliance on official memoirs and oral history interviews conducted in the

1960s. Thus, to a large extent, she presents their official characters as they remember themselves or would like to be remembered. Use of daily agency records in this study injects a more candid, on-the-spot element.

Derthick's data sources lead to other conclusions with which I disagree. For example, she tells us that leadership felt few, if any, qualms about social insurance's antipoor bias. The fact that the system could pay the poor very little and yet pay large benefits to well-to-do people, some of whom had made negligible contributions, "seems not to have required the founders to develop defenses or justifications either to themselves or to others." [10] To document this point she refers to a 1967 oral history interview with Altmeyer.

> With apparent pride and serenity, Altmeyer once remarked that "nobody thinks they're being demeaned by getting that check, and I think they probably look forward to it. If they're rich, they probably turn it over to their wife so she can go and do something with it that she wouldn't have done otherwise. And everybody's happy, happy as a lark." [11]

I agree that Altmeyer accepted and worked for a system biased in favor of the more fortunate in society, but I disagree that he felt no need to rationalize this. The serenity that Derthick sees is the serenity of a retired commissioner who has seen his ideological battles end largely in victory. However, the Chairman Altmeyer of the 1930s and 1940s was anxious about the future of his system and felt a recurrent political need to defend, rationalize, and justify the system's antipoor bias: thus the elaborate defenses of the tax's regressivity, the doctrinal elaborations in which the benefit squeeze against the poor was couched, and the extreme sensitivity to needs data.

Another point at which Derthick's analysis differs from the present one is the handling of the Marjorie Shearon needs analysis incident. In her discussion of early expert critics of social security, Derthick accords the "curious and very conspicuous case" of Marjorie Shearon less than a paragraph. Referring to the criticism Shearon leveled against SSB policies and leaders, Derthick sees this "extreme disaffection" as stemming from Shearon's anger over not being given sufficient credit for her work in preparing the economic brief for the defense of the Social Security Act before the Supreme Court and to Shearon's belief that SSB leadership "maliciously suppressed its publication." Further, "There was nothing . . . to suggest," says Derthick, that Shearon's criticisms were not "purely personal . . . rooted . . . apparently, in emotional distress. Nothing suggests that [the criticism] . . . originated in tensions between the demands of the organization and the performance of a particular professional role." [12]

Evidence presented earlier in this work regarding the SSB's response to Shearon's needs analyses in 1941 demonstrates that there is much to suggest that Shearon's actions at that time were rooted precisely in organizational-professional conflict and that her disagreement was much more than author's pique. Her 1941 behavior in leaving the SSB and in contradicting Chairman Altmeyer's testimony in the Senate was rooted in what she saw as political infringement of her role as a professional researcher. But we can let Shearon speak for herself, as she did in a 1941 communication to Altmeyer explaining why she was about to contradict him in her forthcoming Senate testimony.

> On July 28 I shall testify at length. I have been asked to give the results of many years of study in this field. . . . My testimony will be at variance with the written testimony you presented to the Committee. Mr. Falk gave you figures on the economic status of the aged which he knew were subject to attack. . . . I greatly regret the chain of events that puts me outside the Board and makes it necessary for me to show wherein your testimony was vulnerable.[13]

Referring to a rumor that she had "stirred up" Senator Downey by leaking her report, she said "Anyone who states that I initiated the present activities of Senator Downey . . . or that I have any connection with the Townsend organization lies."[14] And, speaking of her role as a professional researcher: "I am a research worker, seeking facts and I ask only that I may present them truthfully without fear that my motives will be impugned. As a professional worker . . . I ask that reasonable steps be taken to protect my professional reputation and to permit me to comply with the requests of the Special Senate Committee."[15]

Twenty-six years later Shearon's criticisms had taken a turn which could possibly justify characterization as "curious and very conspicuous," for in 1967 she published a book in which the health insurance initiatives of Cohen, Falk, and others were attacked as socialistic efforts.[16] It is important, however, that we not let the intemperate, unsupported outburst of 1967 obscure the legitimate complaints of Marjorie Shearon two and a half decades earlier. A full examination of Shearon's early criticisms is important not only to do her justice, but also because the 1941 incident is revealing of leadership's sense of vulnerability over the system's redistributional inadequacies and the seriousness with which they sought to minimize and obscure such limitations.

Minute examination of leadership as displayed in this work is important to the extent that leadership's perceptions, goals, and actions have helped to shape policy. An accurate description is important not only for the intrinsic value found in a richer, more detailed understanding of a piece of our history—the history of the treatment of the neediest aged—but also because such material can contribute to assessment of the relative merits of drift and tool models of organizational goal formation. The material's relevance to contemporary policy issues is discussed in the epilogue.

Epilogue

Despite the passage of several decades since the last year studied here, this work can help inform contemporary policy debate. An important part of contemporary debate is the various perceptions of social security's origins: its first goals and the intentions of leaders such as Roosevelt, Witte, and Altmeyer. The financial crisis of the 1970s and 1980s has caused many people to reevaluate the system by considering its original purposes. These contemporary perceptions of original intent can be used in several ways. Frequently they can be held up as reference points or standards against which subsequent developments are judged. Peter J. Ferrara does this in *Social Security: The Inherent Contradiction*, in which he proposes to replace social security with private insurance mechanisms. This proposal is grounded in an understanding of social security as originally good insurance: its diminution through the incorporation of welfare elements began with the 1939 amendments.[1] Ferrara's critique and recommendations grow out of a view of social security as corrupted by social welfare elements.

A very different perception and use of origins is found in Bruno Stein's *Social Security and Pensions in Transition*, which concludes with a view of needed changes that are discussed against a backdrop entitled "The Goals of the System Revisited: Back to the American Founders of Social Security."[2] Stein does not argue for a fundamentalist return to original goals; indeed, he argues that leaders' original choices were conditioned by Depression-era realities and that we should reevaluate those choices in light of contemporary factors. Nevertheless, his analysis and recommendations are colored by an understanding of origins that differs from the one presented here. In Stein's view, "A principal goal of the founders was to provide for the basic needs of the aged," and "Generally speaking, the goal was achieved."[3] It is possible that a different understanding of origins would have produced a different analysis and recommendations.

As we struggle with contemporary policy choices, the present study urges us to be skeptical of appeals to abstract "principles of social insurance," as if social insurance constituted an objective, external reference point or guide to action. As the pre-1935 competition between the Ohio and Wisconsin schools of thought and the 1935–54 definitional campaign by SSB/SSA leadership show, *social insurance* is a fluid concept, a social and political construction. It means largely what we want it to mean; those with strategic placement and command of powerful organizational resources have been able to exert great influence over our perception of the concept. A detailed understanding of those influence processes and the goals they served can liberate our thinking. Closely related to this point, of course, is the seriousness with which we take the system's insurance imagery.

That insurance imagery is still a political force is recognized by the Democratic National Committee; in 1982 the committee opposed the Reagan administration's proposed changes in the system with a mass mailing arguing, "Social Security is paid-in insurance—not charity."[4] However, insurance imagery is not as powerful as it once was: its power has been eroded by both the system's funding crisis and by sophisticated analyses such as John Brittain's study of the payroll tax.[5] Wilbur Cohen, writing in 1981, shows a concern that this erosion exposes the system to redistributional critiques. "One myth which has circulated is that Social Security is not insurance. This . . . has contributed to many people believing that the Social Security *system* (contributions and benefits) is regressive—which is not true."[6] It is necessary, of course, that we recognize whatever political clout still attaches to the insurance imagery, but it is a very different matter as to whether we as policy analysts, policy advocates, or citizens choose to accord that imagery, per se, any intellectual validity or choose to encourage its further political use, especially in light of its previous antipoor uses.

Similarly, we should maintain a vigorous skepticism regarding statements of the inherent nature of income and means-testing policies. The lesson of the 1930s and 1940s is not that such programs are inevitably inadequate and demeaning, but rather that determined leadership can make public assistance inadequate, given the power to back up that determination. "Those who criticize the social security approach and advocate new income-tested programs are asserting, in effect, that we will prevent stigma by an act of will," Alvin Schorr tells us as he argues the inherent inferiority position.[7] I agree with his statement, but not his conclusion. An act of will—and power—by early leaders played a large part in crippling the emergent public assistance system. Their strategic moves blocked the evolution of public assistance into a rights-oriented guaranteed income system in many states. An act of will, coupled with power, can speed the dismantling of negative features, as demonstrated by the very real progress of the 1960s when court decisions struck down some of the more glaring stigmatizing features of public assistance.[8]

While we cannot automatically assume that early leaders' direct efforts to retard public assistance are being repeated by today's SSA leadership, we should be sensitive to the dangers of a half-hearted commitment to public assistance by current leadership. The SSA once again has administrative responsibility for much of public assistance. For a time, starting in the 1960s, welfare was given an administrative base within HEW, apart from SSA. These programs were returned to the SSA with the 1972 legislation that completely federalized Old-Age Assistance, Aid to the Blind, and Aid to the Disabled; the programs are now collectively known as Supplemental Security Income (SSI). The danger in returning public assistance to an organization with an institutional bias against it is illustrated by the SSA's inadequate showing in getting SSI payments to those who need them, an issue known as the SSI nonparticipation problem.

The first thorough published analysis of nonparticipation produced by SSA staff shows that by 1974 only 30 percent of the eligible needy aged were actually receiving SSI and that by 1981 a drastically low participation rate was still evident.[9] Two primary factors were found to account for nonparticipation: lack of knowledge about SSI on the part of the aged and "the dread of stigma associated with dependence on welfare."[10] The SSA staff report speculates about solutions: liberalizing certain income and assets requirements to preclude near destitution as a precondition for eligibility (echoing the spiral of destitution argument of early years) is discussed, as are outreach efforts to inform the aged of SSI. Outreach efforts are especially important, for we know that many needy aged are socially very isolated: they simply do not know of SSI's existence or have misinformation about eligibility requirements.

The SSA study discusses the two efforts by the SSA to inform the aged of their right to SSI; both efforts are candidly admitted to have been failures. The first, in 1974, actually aggravated the problem by dispensing much inaccurate information about eligibility. The second outreach effort is notable for its extremely limited scope. In sum, the impact of the two informational efforts "has been limited."[11] However, in a striking and revealing conclusion, the staff report does not urge a major new outreach effort by the SSA; rather the SSA, in effect, is absolved from any direct responsibility for such efforts, as they would increase SSA administrative costs. "It is virtually impossible . . . at current resource levels for SSA to do the personal canvassing and fieldwork to disseminate correct program information and overcome the stigma . . . [of] . . . participation in SSI."[12] A sense of historical injustice might cause one to argue that the SSA—the organization which vigorously helped to stamp the new public assistance system with a stigmatizing cast and which deliberately propagated informational obscurity—should be given the resources and the unequivocal mandate to overcome both stigma and lack of information today. A more reasoned argument, perhaps, would be that SSI should be removed from the SSA's sphere and given genuinely committed administrative leadership.

The importance of having an authentic SSI safety net behind social insurance is underscored by the danger of a contemporary version of the pincers movement, in which the poor are squeezed out of social insurance by the system's financial crisis. This is illustrated by the 1981 decision to eliminate the minimum benefit provision in social insurance for future beneficiaries. Elimination was one of several Reagan administration proposals advocating responding to social security's funding crunch by cutting benefits. In the course of congressional debate, the elimination was defended with two arguments. First, a portion of those receiving the minimum benefit were "double dippers" receiving a "windfall" benefit. That is, some people had spent most of their working years in an occupation uncovered by social security, such as federal civil service, in which they qualified for a reasonable retirement pension. Some of these people, before retirement, also worked in covered employment for a very short time (minimum of six quarters) in order to qualify for social security's minimum benefit, resulting in two retirement pensions. Here, it was argued, was a place to save money. Why allow these people who don't really need the minimum benefit (which was instituted to help poor workers) to collect it, especially when they could do so with very minimal contributions? These workers represent only a part of the beneficiary population that received the minimum benefit. The second argument dealt with the many extremely poor workers—just how many is not known with any real accuracy. As the *Congressional Quarterly* reports it: "Although not strictly a program for the poor, the minimum benefit has gone disproportionately to elderly women, who are more likely to be poor than other Social Security recipients. There is no way to tell how many of the people losing the benefit are poor, [the Congressional Budget Office] said." [13] Those advocating the elimination of the minimum benefit had an efficiency line of argument to deal with this second group. The truly needy could turn to welfare, to SSI, which is a much more efficient way to channel funds to the poor. As Alicia Munnell put it in her 1977 Brookings study, "The minimum benefit should be phased out because it is not an efficient welfare device, is not consistent with a wage-related benefit structure, and with the advent of SSI, is no longer needed to achieve social adequacy." [14] With the minimum benefit now eliminated for future beneficiaries, the SSI nonparticipation issue is aggravated, and a resolution is demanded in order to make a real safety net of SSI.

Beyond spotlighting the need for a genuine SSI safety net, the 1981 minimum benefit decision also highlights the vulnerability of the traditional social security ideology to the contemporary funding crunch. The elimination of the minimum benefit was resisted by traditional social security supporters, but opposition sprang from a desire to preserve the system from *any* change as much as from any desire to protect the poor. Breach of contract was the fundamental rationale of resistance, and it signaled no new interest in ameliorating social security's traditional antipoor bias.

The traditional rationale for social security's antipoor bias, as we have seen, can be described as social welfare's own version of a trickle down theory: the best way to get any money to the poor is to simultaneously give an equal, and preferably larger, amount of money to the nonpoor. Thus, the result will be the blending together of the poor and the nonpoor in the minimum benefit population. However, in a time of financial crisis, this particular blending has proven vulnerable to both need and efficiency arguments: why waste money on those not in need? Logically, we can extend that question beyond the minimum benefit to the middle and upper reaches of the benefit structure. Can we afford to be "happy, happy as a lark" about a system with severe funding problems that pays large benefits to the well-to-do? Doesn't a time of scarce resources demand that public funds go first to those who have most need of them? Wouldn't another way to control expenditures be to decrease payments to the wealthy through the use of income-testing devices throughout the benefit range?

An influential analyst such as Alicia Munnell apparently would reject such proposals, since for her the true identity of social security is that of a purist wage-replacement system. She uses an invocation of the wage-related principle to ward off such questions. "The present system can best be understood in a lifetime compulsory saving framework."[15] A traditional social security leader such as Wilbur Cohen rejects such questions: income testing is inherently degrading and, besides, such income testing of social security beneficiaries would "discourage thrift and saving."[16]

There is another group of individuals who have traditionally not supported income testing or other major departures from the social security ideology, those with a genuine commitment to caring for the needy. The members of this group have been made uneasy at times over the rhetoric that paints wage-related benefits as rewards for merit and virtue and, at times, have experienced discomfort with the antipoor bias, but these individuals have taken their strategy lead from social security ideologues. For this group, the trickle down approach has been accepted on pragmatic grounds as the only feasible way to help the poor and to maintain a sense of decency in the process. It is to this group that this study's policy implications are most pertinent, for the contemporary funding crisis calls for a fundamental reevaluation of the traditional social security ideology and strategy to preclude a worsening of the antipoor bias and a new version of a pincers movement. It is also possible that the funding crisis, with its pressures for cost savings, can be used as leverage by those interested in increasing the redistributional component of social insurance, if those cost concerns can be directed toward benefits flowing to the well-to-do. A failure to reexamine all facets of the traditional ideology will result in a continuance of social security's historic role in insuring inequality.

Appendix

This book is based on a longitudinal case study which relied heavily on primary source materials. The collections of the National Archives and the National Records Center were the most important. The following collections were consulted

Records of the Committee on Economic Security, National Archives
Records of the Chairman of the Social Security Board (1935–40), National Archives
Records of the Executive Director of the Social Security Board (1935–40), National Archives
Central Files of the Social Security Board (1935–47), National Archives
Records of the Executive Director of the Social Security Board (1941–48), National Archives
Records of the Commissioner of the Social Security Administration (1949–50), National Records Center
Records of the Bureau/Division of Research and Statistics (1946–50), National Records Center
Actuarial Records of the Social Security Administration, National Records Center

The above collections have been exhaustively inventoried by SSA Historian Abe Bortz. A very condensed version of this inventory has been published: Abe Bortz, *Social Security Sources in Federal Records 1934–1950* (Washington, D.C.: Government Printing Office, 1969). A more useful research aid, however, is the original Bortz inventory, kept at the National Archives, with its file-folder-by-file-folder description of the contents of thousands of cubic feet of records. The above materials stop at 1950; post-1950, uninventoried collections found at the National Records Center were also used in this research. They include:

Research and Statistics Files of the Social Security Board/Administration, 1936–59

Actuarial Subject File of the Social Security Administration, 1951–59
Actuarial Subject File and Office of the Commissioner Files, Social Security
    Board/Administration, 1936–59

A valuable source of material on top-level agency decision making was
found in the Official Minutes of the Social Security Board for 1935–46, the
Commissioner for Social Security Minutes for 1946–48 and the Commissioner's Action Minutes for 1948–63. These are found at the National Archives and provide brief, formal statements of issues and decisions. More valuable are the Informal Minutes kept for the 1935–63 period. In the early
years, these minutes provide virtually verbatim transcripts of the arguments
and discussions which preceded formal decisions. The Informal Minutes are
kept in the Social Security Administration offices in Woodlawn, Maryland.

Another collection that has been only superficially inventoried is the
General Decimal Files of the Federal Security Administrator, 1944–50, at the
National Archives. Useful material was found in these files by using the FSA
filing manual.

In citing the documents, I have given the sources exactly as the documents are labeled, even though there are many inconsistencies in style. This
should enable future researchers to identify the specific documents.

At the Wisconsin State Historical Society, Madison, Wisconsin, the collections of Arthur J. Altmeyer and Edwin E. Witte were useful.

Interviews supplied by the following people were important.

Wilbur J. Cohen, former staff member of the Committee on Economic Se-
    curity, former special assistant to both the chairman of the Social Se-
    curity Board and the social security administrator, and former secretary
    of Health, Education and Welfare
Abe Bortz, Social Security Administration historian
Ida Merriam, former head of the Department of Research and Statistics, So-
    cial Security Administration
Robert Myers, former chief actuary of the Social Security Administration
George Bigge, former member of the Social Security Board
Ewan Clague, former associate director and director of the Social Security
    Board's Bureau of Research and Statistics, former director of the Bureau
    of Employment Security, and former commissioner for labor statistics in
    the Department of Labor

Notes

Introduction

1. This research would have been almost impossible without the work of SSA Historiun Abe Bortz in inventorying the holdings: Abe Bortz, *Social Security Sources in Federal Records, 1934–1950* Social Security Administration, Research Report, no. 30 (Washington, D.C.: Government Printing Office, 1969).

2. Eveline Burns, *Social Security and Public Policy* (New York: McGraw-Hill, 1956); Alvin Schorr, "Income Maintenance and the Social Security Ideology," in *The Social Welfare Forum*, ed. Arthur Katz (New York: Columbia University Press, 1970); Arthur J. Altmeyer, *The Formative Years of Social Security* (Madison: University of Wisconsin Press, 1968); Edwin E. Witte, *The Development of the Social Security Act* (Madison: University of Wisconsin Press, 1962).

3. Frances Fox Piven and Richard A. Cloward, *Regulating the Poor: The Functions of Public Welfare* (New York: Random House, 1971); Sheldon L. Messinger, "Organizational Transformation: A Case Study of a Declining Social Movement," *American Sociological Review* 29 (1955):3–10.

4. Arthur J. Altmeyer, *Formative Years*.

Chapter 1

1. President's Commission on Income Maintenance Programs, *Poverty Amid Plenty: The American Paradox* (Washington, D.C.: Government Printing Office, 1969), pp. 165–66. *Redistribution* can refer to movement between various groups, such as from young to old. The present work uses the concept in the same manner as the commission, referring to the net movement of income between income classes as a result of social security's operations, that is, the extent to which social security achieves a net movement of income from rich to poor or vice versa.

2. U.S., Congress, Senate, Committee on Finance, *Staff Data and Materials Relating to Social Security Financing*, 95th Cong., 1st sess., 1977, pp. 47, 87; and Alicia H. Munnell, *The Future of Social Security* (Washington, D.C.: Brookings Institution, 1971), p. 1.

3. John A. Brittain, *The Payroll Tax for Social Security* (Washington, D.C.: Brookings Institution, 1972), p. 103.

4. Ibid., p. 91.

5. Alicia H. Munnell, *Future of Social Security.*

6. Brittain, *Payroll Tax,* pp. 178–79.

7. Munnell, *Future of Social Security,* p. 92.

8. U.S., Congress, Subcommittee on Fiscal Policy of the Joint Economic Committee, *Income Security for Americans: Recommendations of the Public Welfare Study* (Washington, D.C.: Government Printing Office, 1974).

9. Martha N. Ozawa, "Income Redistribution and Social Security," *Social Service Review* 50 (June, 1976):216–17.

10. Ibid., p. 217.

11. Ibid., pp. 217–18.

12. Ibid., p. 219.

13. Gilbert Y. Steiner, *Social Insecurity: The Politics of Welfare* (Chicago: Rand, McNally and Co., 1966).

14. Brittain, *Payroll Tax,* pp. 8–11.

15. Wilbur J. Cohen and Milton Friedman, *Social Security: Universal or Selective?* (Washington, D.C.: American Enterprise Institute for Public Policy Research, 1972), p. 90.

16. Ibid., pp. 54–55.

17. Philip Selznick, *TVA and the Grass Roots* (Berkeley: University of California Press, 1949).

18. Ibid., p. 13.

19. Selznick, *TVA and the Grass Roots*; Anselm Strauss et al., *Psychiatric Ideologies and Institutions* (New York: Free Press, 1964); Richard Bendix, *Work and Authority in Industry* (New York: John Wiley and Sons, 1956).

20. Strauss et al., *Psychiatric Ideologies and Institutions,* p. 8.

21. Eveline Burns, *Social Security and Public Policy* (New York: McGraw-Hill, 1956); Alvin Schorr, "Income Maintenance and the Social Security Ideology," in *The Social Welfare Forum,* ed. Arthur Katz (New York: Columbia University Press, 1970); Arthur J. Altmeyer, *The Formative Years of Social Security* (Madison: University of Wisconsin Press, 1968); Edwin E. Witte, *The Development of the Social Security Act* (Madison: University of Wisconsin Press, 1962).

22. Arthur J. Altmeyer, "Social Insurance for Permanently Disabled Workers," *Social Security Bulletin* 5 (March, 1941):3–10.

23. Arthur Larson, "The American Social Insurance System: Structure, Coverage, and Current Problems," in *Economic Security for Americans,* ed. Harry Willmer Jones (New York: Columbia University Graduate School of Business, 1953), p. 53.

24. Burns, *Social Security and Public Policy,* p. 157.

25. Ibid., p. 161.

26. Ibid., p. 40.

27. Ibid., p. 38.

28. Theodore R. Marmor quoting Graham T. Allison in Marmor, *The Politics of Medicare* (Chicago: Aldine Publishing Co., 1970), p. 104.

29. Charles Perrow, *Complex Organizations: A Critical Essay* (Glenview, Ill.: Scott, Foresman and Co., 1972), p. 181.

Chapter 2

1. Arthur M. Schlesinger, Jr., *The Age of Roosevelt*, vol. 3, *The Politics of Upheaval* (Boston: Houghton Mifflin Co., 1960), p. 325.

2. Frances Fox Piven and Richard A. Cloward, *Regulating the Poor: The Functions of Public Welfare* (New York: Random House, 1971), pp. 100–104.

3. Roy Lubove, *The Struggle for Social Security, 1900–1935* Cambridge, Mass.: Harvard University Press, 1968).

4. Ibid., p. 174.

5. Ibid., p. 170.

6. Ibid., p. 172.

7. Ibid., p. 174.

8. Ibid., p. 178.

9. Edwin E. Witte, "Social Security: A Wild Dream or a Practical Plan?" in *Social Security Perspectives. Essays by Edwin E. Witte*, ed. Robert J. Lampman (Madison: University of Wisconsin Press, 1962), p. 11.

10. Lubove, *Struggle for Social Security*, p. 176.

11. William E. Leuchtenberg, *Franklin D. Roosevelt and the New Deal* (New York: Harper and Row, 1965), p. 132.

12. Philip Booth, *Social Security in America* (Ann Arbor: Institute of Labor and Industrial Relations, 1973), p. 11.

13. Theron F. Schlabach, *Edwin E. Witte, Cautious Reformer* (Madison: State Historical Society of Wisconsin, 1969), p. 19.

14. Edwin E. Witte, *The Development of the Social Security Act* (Madison: University of Wisconsin Press, 1963), p. 24.

15. For a detailed description of the creation of the SSB, see Charles McKinley and Robert W. Frase, *Launching Social Security: A Capture-and-Record Account, 1935–1937* (Madison: University of Wisconsin Press, 1970).

16. Ibid., p. 18.

17. Lubove, *Struggle for Social Security*, p. 176.

18. U.S., Congress, Senate, Committee on Finance, *H.R. 6000, An Act to Extend and Improve the Federal Old-Age and Survivors Insurance System, Hearings before the Senate Committee on Finance*. 81st Cong., 2d sess., 1950, p. 2144

19. Arthur J. Altmeyer, "Speech to the Annual Meeting of National Conferences of Catholic Charities, 1938," File Folder 062, "October-December, 1938," Central Files of the Social Security Board (1935–47), Record Group 47, National Archives, Washington, D.C.

20. Informal Minutes of the Social Security Board, July 22, 1936, Social Security Administration, Woodlawn, Maryland.

21. Robert Huse to John Corson, December 15, 1936, File Folder 317.1, "Nov.-Dec. 1936," Central Files of the Social Security Board (1935–47), Record Group 47, National Archives, Washington, D.C.

22. Arthur J. Altmeyer, "Speech to Catholic Charities."

23. Arthur J. Altmeyer, quoted in U.S., Congress, House, Committee on Ways and Means, *Analysis of the Social Security System: Hearings before a Subcommittee of the Committee on Ways and Means*, 83d Cong., 1st sess., 1953, p. 435.

24. Ibid.

25. Arthur J. Altmeyer to Alan Wilcox, December 2, 1936, File Folder, "Memorandum–Wilcox, Alan," Records of the Chairman of the Social Security Board (1935–40), Record Group 47, National Archives, Washington, D.C.

26. Arthur J. Altmeyer, "Speech to Catholic Charities."

27. Altmeyer to Wilcox, December 2, 1936.

28. J. Douglas Brown, "The Birth of Old-Age Insurance, 1934–35," undated, File Folder 011, "Terminology," Records of the Chairman of the Social Security Board, (1935–40), Record Group 47, National Archives, Washington, D.C.

29. Frances Perkins, *The Roosevelt I Knew* (New York: Viking Press, 1946), p. 286.

30. U.S., Congress, House, Committee on Ways and Means, *Minority Views*, H. Rept. 615, 74th Cong., 1st sess., 1935.

31. Altmeyer, press release, May 24, 1937, quoted in U.S., Congress, House, Committee on Ways and Means, *Analysis of Social Security*, p. 882.

32. Social Security Board, "Security in Your Old Age" (Washington, D.C.: Government Printing Office, 1937).

33. Social Security Board, "The Social Security Act: Who Gets the Benefits?" (Washington, D.C.: Government Printing Office, 1937).

34. Social Security Board, "Old-Age Insurance: Safe as the U.S.A." (Washington, D.C.: Government Printing Office, 1938).

35. Social Security Board, "Your Social Security Card: Why You Have It—What You Do With It" (Washington, D.C.: Government Printing Office, 1940).

36. Louis Resnick to Frank Bane, July 26, 1937, File Folder 011, Central Files of the Social Security Board (1935–47), Record Group 47, National Archives, Washington, D.C.

37. W. R. Williamson to Mr. Altmeyer, September 1, 1937, File Folder 011, "Terminology," Records of the Chairman of the Social Security Board (1935–40), Record Group 47, National Archives, Washington, D.C.

38. Mr. Wilcox to Mr. Eliot, June 21, 1937, File Folder 011, "Terminology," Records of the Chairman of the Social Security Board (1935–40), Record Group 47, National Archives, Washington, D.C.

39. Ibid.

40. Ewan Clague to A. J. Altmeyer, July 1, 1937, File Folder 011, "June-Dec. 1937," Central Files of the Social Security Board (1935–47), Record Group 47, National Archives, Washington, D.C.

41. Ibid.

42. Wilbur J. Cohen to Ewan Clague, May 15, 1937, File Folder 700, "General," Records of the Chairman of the Social Security Board (1935–40), Record Group 47, National Archives, Washington, D.C.

43. W. R. Williamson to Wilbur Cohen, May 19, 1937, File Folder 700, "General," Records of the Chairman of the Social Security Board (1935–40), Record Group 47, National Archives, Washington, D.C.

44. Thomas I. Emerson to Wilbur Cohen, May 19, 1937, File Folder 700, "General," Records of the Chairman of the Social Security Board (1935–40), Record Group 47, National Archives, Washington, D.C.

45. Herbert Kaufman, *Are Government Organizations Immortal?* (Washington, D.C.: Brookings Institution, 1976), p. 3.

46. Wilbur J. Cohen and Milton Friedman, *Social Security: Universal or Selective?* (Washington, D.C.: American Enterprise Institute for Public Policy Research, 1972), pp. 54–57.

47. Arthur J. Altmeyer, testimony before U.S., Congress, House, Committee on Ways and Means, *Analysis of Social Security*, p. 887.

48. Jack B. Tate to Wilbur J. Cohen, December 19, 1944, File Folder 056, General Decimal Files of the Federal Security Administration 1944–50, Record Group 235, National Archives, Washington, D.C.

49. The primary insurance amount is the basic old-age benefit paid to a retiring worker at sixty-five; it may be supplemented by dependents' allowances or reduced by early retirement at sixty-two. For a history of the social security benefit formula, see Joseph A. Pechman, Henry J. Aaron, and Michael K. Taussig, *Social Security: Perspectives for Reform* (Washington, D.C.: Brookings Institution, 1968), p. 269.

50. Arthur J. Altmeyer, "Social Insurance for Permanently Disabled Workers," *Social Security Bulletin* 5 (March, 1941):3–10.

51. Robert Harkins to Arthur J. Altmeyer, March 13, 1949, File Folder 011.1, "House Bills 2000–2999," Actuarial and Office of the Commissioner Records, Accession no. 64a-751, Record Group 47, National Records Center, Suitland, Maryland.

52. Arthur J. Altmeyer to Robert Harkins, March 25, 1949, File Folder 011.1, "House Bills 2000–2999," Actuarial and Office of the Commissioner Records, Accession no. 64a-751, Record Group 47, National Records Center, Suitland, Maryland.

53. Arthur J. Altmeyer to Robert Harkins, April 28, 1949, File Folder 011.1, "House Bills 2000–2999," Actuarial and Office of the Commissioner Records, Accession no. 64a-751, Record Group 47, National Records Center, Suitland, Maryland.

54. Jacob Perlman to I. S. Falk, May 5, 1948, File Folder 011.1, "H.R. 6000–6999," Actuarial and Office of the Commissioner Records, Accession no. 64a-751, Record Group 47, National Records Center, Suitland, Maryland.

55. O. C. Pogge to Wilbur J. Cohen, January 4, 1949, File Folder 011.1, "H.R. 6000, 1949," Actuarial and Office of the Commissioner Records, Accession no. 64a-751, Record Group 47, National Records Center, Suitland, Maryland.

56. Theron F. Schlabach, *Edwin E. Witte, Cautious Reformer* (Madison: State Historical Society of Wisconsin, 1969), pp. 126–28.

57. Ibid., p. 168.

58. Ibid.

59. Ibid., p. 127.

60. Ibid., pp. 127–28.

61. Ibid., pp. 176–77.

62. *Congressional Record*, January 19, 1944, p. 374.

63. E. J. McCormack to H. P. Seideman, October 22, 1936, File Folder 011.4, "December, 1936," Records of the Executive Director, Social Security Board (1935–40), Record Group 47, National Archives, Washington, D.C.

64. Rulon Williamson to Mr. Cohen, August 2, 1940, File Folder 013, "Taxation through 1939," Records of the Chairman of the Social Security Board (1935–40), Record Group 47, National Archives, Washington, D.C.

65. Ibid.

66. Ibid.

67. Dorothy Thompson, "Real Reasoning Absent in Campaign: Social Security Dispute Shows Fireworks But No Light," *Washington Evening Star*, May 12, 1936.

68. Arthur J. Altmeyer to Frances Perkins, May 19, 1936, File Folder 011.3, "Protest, Opposition, and Criticism," Records of the Chairman of the Social Security Board (1935–40), Record Group 47, National Archives, Washington, D.C.

69. Arthur J. Altmeyer to Alan Wilcox, December 2, 1936, File Folder "Memoranda–Wilcox, Alan," Records of the Chairman of the Social Security Board (1935–40), Record Group 47, National Archives, Washington, D.C.

70. H. P. Mulford, *Incidence and Effects of the Pay-Roll Tax*, (Washington, D.C.: Social Security Board, 1936).

71. Ibid.

72. W. R. Williamson to Winant, Altmeyer, Miles, Bane, and Seidemann, November 21, 1936, File Folder 013, "Taxation," Records of the Chairman of the Social Security Board (1935–40), Record Group 47, National Archives, Washington, D.C.

73. Arthur J. Altmeyer to Mr. Hamilton, November 16, 1936, File Folder 013, "Taxation," Records of the Chairman of the Social Security Board (1935–40), Record Group 47, National Archives, Washington, D.C.

74. Ibid.

75. John Brittain, *The Payroll Tax for Social Security* (Washington, D.C.: Brookings Institution, 1972).

76. Arthur J. Altmeyer to Representative McKeough, April 30, 1940, File Folder 604, "Substitute Old-Age Plans," Records of the Chairman of the Social Security Board (1935–40), Record Group 47, National Archives, Washington, D.C.

77. Wilbur J. Cohen to Arthur J. Altmeyer, November 19, 1936, File Folder 013, "Taxation through 1939," Records of the Chairman of the Social Security Board (1935–40), Record Group 47, National Archives, Washington, D.C.

78. Theodore R. Marmor, *The Politics of Medicare* (Chicago: Aldine Publishing Co., 1970), p. 22.

79. Cohen and Friedman, *Social Security: Universal or Selective?*, pp. 68–69.

Chapter 3

1. Frances Fox Piven and Richard A. Cloward, *Regulating the Poor: The Functions of Public Welfare* (New York: Random House, 1971), pp. 100–104. Also see: Sheldon L. Messinger, "Organizational Transformation: A Case Study of a Declining Social Movement," *American Sociological Review* 20 (1955): 3–10; Abraham Holtzman, *The Townsend Movement: A Political Study* (New York: Bookman and Associates, 1963).

2. Charles McKinley and Robert W. Frase, *Launching Social Security, a Capture-and-Record Account 1935–1937* (Madison: University of Wisconsin Press, 1970), p. 454.

3. Ibid.

4. Leonard Calhoun to Frank Bane, Executive Director, Social Security Board,

December 20, 1935, File Folder 604, Records of the Executive Director of the Social Security Board (1935–40), Record Group 47, National Archives, Washington, D.C.

5. Arthur J. Altmeyer to Congressman Doughton, File Folder 604, "Substitute Old-Age Assistance Plans," Records of the Chairman of the Social Security Board (1935–42), Record Group 47, National Archives, Washington, D.C.

6. Ibid.

7. Ibid.

8. Ibid.

9. Quoted in Robert J. Myers to Robert Ball, October 6, 1950, File Folder 011.1, "S. 1–99.9, 1950–46," Actuarial Records (1946–50), Record Group 47, National Records Center, Suitland, Maryland.

10. W. R. Williamson, September 24, 1946, File Folder 321-01, 1947, Actuarial Records (1946–50), Record Group 47, National Records Center, Suitland, Maryland, p. 10.

11. Thomas I. Stokes, "Spenders Hope to Prime the Pump with Pension," *Washington Daily News,* May 12, 1939.

12. Arthur J. Altmeyer, *The Formative Years of Social Security* (Madison: University of Wisconsin Press, 1966), p. 110.

13. Ibid., p. 114.

14. Paul V. McNutt, "Undelivered Speech to the National Industrial Conference Board," New York, New York, March 28, 1940, in Federal Security Agency press release, File Folder 062, "McNutt, Paul V., 1940," Records of the Executive Director of the Social Security Board (1935–40), Record Group 47, National Archives, Washington, D.C.

15. Ibid.

16. Ibid.

17. A clear articulation of this distinction is provided by Wilensky and Lebeaux. Residual conception of social welfare: "Social Welfare institutions should come into play only when the normal structures of supply, the family, and the market, break down." Institutional conception: "Welfare services are normal, first line functions of modern industrial society" and the "inability of the individual to provide fully for himself . . . is considered a normal condition." See Harold L. Wilensky and Charles N. Lebeaux, *Industrial Society and Social Welfare* (New York: Free Press, 1965), pp. 138–40.

18. McNutt, "Undelivered Speech to the Conference Board."

19. Arthur J. Altmeyer to Stephen Early, secretary to the president, March 28, 1940, File Folder 062, "McNutt, Paul V., 1940," Records of the Executive Director of the Social Security Board (1935–40), Record Group 47, National Archives, Washington, D.C.

20. Paul V. McNutt, "Undelivered Speech to the Conference Board."

21. Ibid.

22. Ibid.

23. "Widened Pensions Urged by McNutt," *New York Times*, March 29, 1940.

24. Altmeyer to Early, March 28, 1940.

25. Arthur J. Altmeyer to the president, September 11, 1937, File Folder 221.6,

"Expert Appointments," Records of the Chairman of the Social Security Board (1935–42), Record Group 47, National Archives, Washington, D.C.

26. U.S., Congress, Senate, Committee on Finance, *Hearings before the Senate on S. 1932*, 77th Cong., 1st sess., pt. 2 (1941), p. 85.

27. "Legislative Summary, 1954," Actuarial and Office of the Commissioner Records, Accession no. 64a-751, Record Group 47, National Records Center, Suitland, Maryland.

28. Martha Derthick, *Policymaking for Social Security* (Washington, D.C.: Brookings Institution, 1979), Chapter 5.

29. Ibid., p. 114.

30. Ibid., pp. 128–31.

31. U.S., Congress, Senate, Special Committee to Investigate the Old-Age Pension System, *Old-Age Pension System: Preliminary Report*, S. Rept. 666, 77th Cong., 1st sess., 1941, p. 3.

32. *New York Times*, September 13, 1940, p. 14.

33. Altmeyer, *Formative Years*, p. 128.

34. U.S., Congress, Senate, Committee on Finance, *Old-Age Pensions: Hearings before the Committee on Finance*, 77th Cong., 1st sess., 1941, p. 6.

35. Ibid., p. 6.

36. Ibid., p. 32.

37. Ibid., p. 47.

38. U.S. Congress, Senate, Committee on Finance, *Old-Age Pension System: Hearings before the Special Committee to Investigate the Old-Age Pension System*, 77th Cong., 1st sess., 1941.

39. Ibid.

40. Ibid.

41. Ibid., p. 73.

42. Ibid.

43. Ibid.

44. I. S. Falk to Wilbur J. Cohen, August 9, 1941, File Folder 032.2, "August, 1941," Records of the Executive Director of the Social Security Board (1941–48), Record Group 47, Accession no. 56a-533, National Records Center, Suitland, Maryland.

45. Marjorie Shearon to I. S. Falk, February 3, 1941, File Folder 032.2, "August, 1941," Records of the Executive Director of the Social Security Board (1941–48), Record Group 47, Accession no. 56a-533, National Records Center, Suitland, Maryland.

46. Marjorie Shearon to Arthur J. Altmeyer, July 25, 1941, File Folder 032.2, "August, 1941," Records of the Executive Director of the Social Security Board (1941–48), Record Group 47, Accession no. 56a-533, National Records Center, Suitland, Maryland.

47. Ibid.

48. Falk to Cohen, August 9, 1941.

49. Ibid.

50. Marjorie Shearon to I. S. Falk, April 14, 1941, File Folder 032.2, "August,

1941," Records of the Executive Director of the Social Security Board (1941–48), Record Group 47, Accession no. 54a-533, National Records Center, Suitland, Maryland.

51. W. S. Woytinsky, L. L. Schmitter, and B. S. Sanders to I. S. Falk, March 19, 1941, File Folder 032.3, "August, 1941," Records of the Executive Director of the Social Security Board (1941–48), Record Group 47, Accession no. 56a-533, National Records Center, Suitland, Maryland.

52. Ibid.

53. Ibid.

54. Falk to Cohen, August 9, 1941.

55. Shearon to Altmeyer, July 25, 1941.

56. Falk to Cohen, August 9, 1941.

57. Committee on Finance, *Old-Age Pension System Hearings*, p. 42.

58. Ibid.

59. Ibid.

60. Ibid.

61. Ibid., p. 10.

62. Ibid., p. 75.

63. Ibid., p. 197.

64. Ibid., p. 200.

65. U.S., Congress, Senate, Special Committee to Investigate the Old-Age Pension System, *Old-Age Pension System: Preliminary Report*, S. Rept. 666; 77th Cong., 1st sess., 1941, p. 3.

66. Arthur J. Altmeyer to Stephen Early, secretary to the president, March 28, 1940, File Folder 062, "McNutt, Paul V., 1940," Records of the Executive Director of the Social Security Board (1935–40), Record Group 47, National Archives, Washington, D.C.

67. Arthur Larson, "The American Social Insurance System: Structure, Coverage, and Current Problems," in ed. Harry Willmer Jones, *Economic Security for Americans* (New York: Columbia Graduate School of Business, 1953), p. 59.

68. Altmeyer, *Formative Years*, p. 205.

69. I. S. Falk to A. J. Altmeyer, November 15, 1939, File Folder 720, "Coverage," Records of the Chairman of the Social Security Board (1935–42), Record Group 47, National Archives, Washington, D.C.

70. Robert M. Ball, March 13, 1953, File Folder 750, "Disability, (1958–57)," Actuarial and Office of the Commissioner Subject Files (1936–59), Accession no. 64a-751, National Records Center, Suitland, Maryland.

71. Wilbur J. Cohen to Robert M. Ball, March 13, 1953, File Folder 011.1, "H.R. 9366," Actuarial and Office of the Commissioner Subject Files (1936–59), Accession no. 64a-751, National Records Center, Suitland, Maryland.

72. "Report of the Task Force to Review Proposals for Maturing the OASDI System," File Folder 720, "1956–1954," Actuarial and Office of the Commissioner Subject Files (1936–59), Accession no. 64a-751, National Records Center, Suitland, Maryland, p. 3.

73. Arthur J. Altmeyer to Robert Ball, October 13, 1950, File Folder 720, Actu-

arial and Office of the Commissioner Subject Files (1936–59), no. 64a-751, National Records Center, Suitland, Maryland.

74. Falk to Altmeyer, November 15, 1939.

75. Ibid.

76. Ibid.

77. Ida C. Merriam to Working Group on Double-Decker and Related Plans, November 3, 1950, File Folder 740, Actuarial and Office of the Commissioner Subject Files (1936–59), Accession no. 64a-751, National Records Center, Suitland, Maryland.

78. Ida C. Merriam to A. J. Altmeyer March 23, 1949, File Folder 750, Actuarial and Office of the Commissioner Subject Files (1936–59), Accession no. 64a-751, National Records Center, Suitland, Maryland, p. 2.

79. Ibid., p. 3.

80. Ibid.

81. Ibid., p. 6.

82. Merriam to Working Group on Double-Decker Plans, November 3, 1950, p. 1.

83. Ibid., p. 7.

84. Ibid., p. 9.

85. I. S. Falk to A. J. Altmeyer, January 11, 1950, File Folder 750, "Double-Decker," Actuarial and Office of the Commissioner Subject Files (1936–59), Accession no. 64a-751, National Records Center, Suitland, Maryland.

86. Paul V. McNutt, "Undelivered Speech to the Conference Board."

87. Falk to Altmeyer, January 11, 1950.

88. Robert J. Myers to A. J. Altmeyer, December 23, 1952, File Folder 750, "1952," Actuarial and Office of the Commissioner Records, Accession no. 64a-571, Record Group 47, National Records Center, Suitland, Maryland.

89. Altmeyer, *Formative Years*, p. 204.

90. U.S., Congress, Senate, Committee on Finance, *Social Security Act Amendments of 1950*, S. Rept. 1669, 81st Cong., 2d sess., 1950; and U.S., Congress, House, Committee on Ways and Means, *Social Security Act Amendments of 1949*, H. Rept. 1300, 81st Cong., 1st sess., 1949.

91. Altmeyer, *Formative Years*, p. 209.

92. Elizabeth Wickenden, December 9, 1952, File Folder 720, "1952–51," Actuarial and Office of the Commissioner Records, Accession no. 64a-751, Record Group 47, National Records Center, Suitland, Maryland.

93. Ibid.

94. Ibid.

95. Ibid.

96. Altmeyer, *Formative Years*, p. 216.

97. Ibid., p. 224.

98. Ibid.

99. Ibid., p. 235.

100. Ibid., p. 238.

101. Arthur J. Altmeyer to Congressman Curtis, quoted in: U.S., Congress, House, Subcommittee of the Committee on Ways and Means, *Analysis of Social Se-*

curity System: Hearings before a Subcommittee of the Committee on Ways and Means, 83d Cong., 1st sess., 1953, pp. 892–93.

102. House, Committee on Ways and Means, *Analysis of Social Security System*, pp. 891–92.

103. Ibid., p. 921.

104. Ibid., p. 957.

105. Ibid., p. 958.

106. Ibid., p. 993.

107. Ibid., p. 1012.

108. W. L. Mitchell to Victor Christgau, October 6, 1959, File Folder 011.1, Actuarial and Office of the Commissioner Records, Accession no. 64a-751, Record Group 47, National Records Center, Suitland, Maryland.

109. Lottie R. Lisle, to Robert J. Myers, October 13, 1959, File Folder 011.1, Actuarial and Office of the Commissioner Records, Accession no. 64a-751, Record Group 47, National Records Center, Suitland, Maryland.

110. Charles I. Schottland to HEW Secretary, December 12, 1956, File Folder 720, Actuarial and Office of the Commissioner Records, Accession no. 64a-751, Record Group 47, National Records Center, Suitland, Maryland.

111. "Broadening the Protection of OASDI and PA [Public Assistance]," October 6, 1959, File Folder 011.1, Actuarial and Office of the Commissioner Records, Accession no. 64a-751, Record Group 47, National Records Center, Suitland, Maryland.

112. Lisle to Myers, October 13, 1959.

113. Wilbur J. Cohen to Robert Myers, July 13, 1959, File Folder 042.2, Actuarial and Office of the Commissioner Records, Accession no. 64a-751, Record Group 47, National Records Center, Suitland, Maryland.

114. Ibid.

115. Philip Booth, *Social Security in America* (Ann Arbor: Institute of Labor and Industrial Relations, 1973), p. 39.

116. Joseph A. Pechman, Henry J. Aaron, and Michael K. Taussig, *Social Security: Perspectives for Reform* (Washington, D.C.: Brookings Institution, 1968), pp. 108–9.

Chapter 4

1. Arthur J. Altmeyer to W. R. Williamson, June 22, 1936, File Folder, "Memoranda: W. R. Williamson," Records of the Chairman of the Social Security Board (1935–42), Record Group 47, National Archives, Washington, D.C.

2. Ibid.

3. W. R. Williamson to Seidemann, October 22, 1936, File Folder 011.4, Records of the Executive Director of the Social Security Board (1935–40), Record Group 47, National Archives, Washington, D.C.

4. W. R. Williamson, Memorandum of April 16, 1949, File Folder 056, "1950–46," Actuarial and Office of the Commissioner Subject Files (1936–59), Accession no. 64a-751, National Records Center, Suitland, Maryland.

5. W. R. Williamson, Memorandum of September 12, 1946, File Folder 056,

"1950–46," Actuarial and Office of the Commissioner Subject Files (1936–59), Accession no. 64a-751, National Records Center, Suitland, Maryland.

6. W. R. Williamson, Memorandum of November 15, 1946, File Folder 056, "1950–46," Actuarial and Office of the Commissioner Subject Files (1936–59), Accession no. 64a-751, National Records Center, Suitland, Maryland.

7. W. R. Williamson, Memorandum of November 7, 1946, File Folder 056, "1950–46," Actuarial and Office of the Commissioner Subject Files (1936–59), Accession no. 64a-751, National Records Center, Suitland, Maryland.

8. Ibid.

9. W. R. Williamson, Memorandum of January 8, 1947, File Folder 056, "1950–46," Actuarial and Office of the Commissioner Subject Files (1936–59), Accession no. 64a-751, National Records Center, Suitland, Maryland.

10. Ibid.

11. W. R. Williamson to Bronson, Kendrick, and Myers, May 8, 1948, Box 33, Actuarial and Office of the Commissioner Subject Files (1936–59), Accession no. 64a-751, National Records Center, Suitland, Maryland.

12. Ibid.

13. Ibid.

14. Ibid.

15. Ibid.

16. Ibid.

17. W. R. Williamson, Memorandum of September 24, 1946, File Folder 056, Actuarial and Office of the Commissioner Subject Files (1936–59), Accession no. 64a-751, National Records Center, Suitland, Maryland.

18. W. R. Williamson to Winant, November 20, 1936, File Folder 056, Actuarial and Office of the Commissioner Subject Files (1936–59), Accession no. 64a-751, National Records Center, Suitland, Maryland.

19. W. R. Williamson, Memorandum of May 8, 1948, File Folder 056, Actuarial and Office of the Commissioner Subject Files (1936–59), Accession no. 64a-751, National Records Center, Suitland, Maryland.

20. W. R. Williamson, Memorandum of November 15, 1946.

21. W. R. Williamson, Memorandum of September 24, 1946.

22. Ibid.

23. W. R. Williamson, Memorandum of October 14, 1946, File Folder 321.01, Actuarial and Office of the Commissioner Subject Files (1936–59), Accession no. 64a-751, National Records Center, Suitland, Maryland.

24. W. R. Williamson, "Speech to Insurance Librarians," May 17, 1948, Box 33, Actuarial and Office of the Commissioner Subject Files (1936–59), Accession no. 64a-751, National Records Center, Suitland, Maryland.

25. W. R. Williamson to Wilbur Cohen (not sent), May 17, 1946, File Folder 721.1, Actuarial and Office of the Commissioner Subject Files (1936–59), Accession no. 64a-751, National Records Center, Suitland, Maryland.

26. U.S., Congress, House, Committee on Ways and Means, *Social Security Act Amendments of 1949: Hearings before the Committee on Ways and Means*, 81st Cong., 1st sess., 1949, pp. 1484-1502.

27. Robert J. Myers to McAndless, January 23, 1948, File Folder 042.2, Actuarial and Office of the Commissioner Subject Files (1939–59), Accession no. 64a-751, National Records Center, Suitland, Maryland.

28. Robert J. Myers, "Is Social Security Really Insurance?" *Journal of the Chartered Life Underwriters* 22 (July, 1974):33–58.

29. Myers to McAndless, January 23, 1948.

30. Robert J. Myers to W. R. Williamson, October 31, 1946, File Folder 042.4, Actuarial and Office of the Commissioner Subject Files (1939–59), Accession no. 64a-751, National Records Center, Suitland, Maryland.

31. Robert J. Myers to Wilbur Cohen, November 22, 1958, File Folder 042.4, Actuarial and Office of the Commissioner Subject Files (1939–59), Accession no. 64a-751, National Records Center, Suitland, Maryland.

32. Ibid.

33. Arthur J. Altmeyer to Robert Ball, March 11, 1948, File Folder 025, Actuarial and Office of the Commissioner Subject Files (1939–59), Accession no, 64a-751, National Records Center, Suitland, Maryland.

34. Arthur J. Altmeyer, *The Formative Years of Social Security* (Madison: University of Wisconsin Press, 1968), p. 102.

35. "Why the Increment Should be Kept," August, 1949, File Folder 011.1, Actuarial and Office of the Commissioner Subject Files (1939–59), Accession no. 64a-751, National Records Center, Suitland, Maryland.

36. Robert J. Myers to Wilbur Cohen, October 27, 1949, File Folder 011.1, Actuarial and Office of the Commissioner Subject Files (1939–59), Accession no. 64a-751, National Records Center, Suitland, Maryland.

37. O. C. Pogge to Wilbur Cohen, January 4, 1949, File Folder 011.1, "H.R. 6000, 1949," Actuarial and Office of the Commissioner Subject Files (1939–59), Accession no. 64a-751, National Records Center, Suitland, Maryland.

38. U.S., Congress, House, Subcommittee of the Committee on Ways and Means, *Analysis of the Social Security System: Hearings before a Subcommittee of the Committee on Ways and Means*, 83d Cong., 1st sess., 1953, p. 964.

39. Altmeyer, *Formative Years*, pp. 203–4.

40. Robert J. Myers, Memoranda of February 20, 1953; April 15, 1954; May 10, 1954; File Folder 011.1, "HR 7199," Actuarial and Office of the Commissioner Subject Files (1939–59), Accession no. 64a-751, National Records Center, Suitland, Maryland.

41. Robert M. Ball, Memorandum of December 30, 1953, File Folder 750, Actuarial and Office of the Commissioner Subject Files (1939–59), Accession no. 64a-751, National Records Center, Suitland, Maryland.

42. Robert J. Myers to Schottland, June 22, 1955, File Folder 750, Actuarial and Office of the Commissioner Subject Files (1939–59), Accession no. 64a-751, National Records Center, Suitland, Maryland.

43. Robert J. Myers to Cohen, January 6, 1954, Actuarial and Office of the Commissioner Subject Files (1939–59), Accession no. 64a-751, National Records Center, Suitland, Maryland.

44. Robert J. Myers, Memorandum of March 25, 1955, File Folder 705, Actuarial

and Office of the Commissioner Subject Files (1939–59), Accession no. 64a-751, National Records Center, Suitland, Maryland.

45. Ibid.

46. Ibid.

47. Ibid.

48. Robert J. Myers to Charles Schottland, June 10, 1955, File Folder 750, Actuarial and Office of the Commissioner Subject Files (1939–59), Accession no. 64a-751, National Records Center, Suitland, Maryland.

49. W. L. Mitchell to Charles L. Schottland, June 15, 1955, File Folder 750, "1955," Actuarial and Office of the Commissioner Subject Files (1939–59), Accession no. 64a-751, National Records Center, Suitland, Maryland.

50. Robert Ball to Robert Myers, August 16, 1955, File Folder 750, "1955," Actuarial and Office of the Commissioner Subject Files, (1939–59), Accession no. 64a-751, National Records Center, Suitland, Maryland.

51. Robert Myers to Robert Ball, August 31, 1955, File Folder 750, "1955," Actuarial and Office of the Commissioner Subject Files, (1939–59), Accession no. 64a-751, National Records Center, Suitland, Maryland.

52. Ibid.

53. Robert J. Myers, "Social Security at the Crossroads," *Reader's Digest* 32 (April, 1970):153–58.

54. Willard Edwards, "Career Employee Speaks Out," *Chicago Tribune*, March 19, 1970.

55. Robert J. Myers, "Social Security Taxes: Regression and Subsidies," *Tax Review* 34, no. 12 (December, 1973):45–48.

56. Selma J. Mushkin and Anne DeScitzovsky, "A Formula for Social Insurance Financing," *American Economic Review* 35, no. 4 (September, 1945):646–52; and Selma J. Mushkin, "Comments on 'Social Security in a Stable Prosperity,'" *American Economic Review* 37, no. 2 (May, 1947):355–59.

57. Mushkin and DeScitzovsky, "Formula for Financing," p. 358.

58. Selma J. Mushkin to Daniel S. Gerig, February 25, 1947, File Folder 058.1, Actuarial and Office of the Commissioner Subject Files (1939–59), Accession no. 64a-751, National Records Center, Suitland, Maryland.

59. Ibid.

60. Ibid.

61. Ibid.

62. I. S. Falk to Daniel S. Gerig, March 13, 1947, File Folder 058.1, Actuarial and Office of the Commissioner Subject Files (1939–59), Accession no. 64a-751, National Records Center, Suitland, Maryland.

63. Ibid.

64. Charles McKinley and Robert W. Frase, *Launching Social Security* (Madison: University of Wisconsin Press, 1970), p. 460.

Chapter 5

1. Jane Hoey to Mr. Bane, October 15, 1936, File Folder 011.4, "Sept. 1936,"

Records of the Executive Director of the Social Security Board (1935–40), Record Group 47, National Archives, Washington, D.C.

2. Louis Resnick to Frank Bane, July 26, 1937, File Folder 011, Central Files of the Social Security Board (1935–47), Record Group 47, National Archives, Washington, D.C.

3. Arthur Altmeyer, *The Formative Years of Social Security* (Madison: University of Wisconsin Press, 1968), p. 60.

4. Ruth M. Hester to Mr. L. O. Shudde, July 19, 1946, File Folder 605, Actuarial and Office of the Commissioner Records, Accession no. 64a-751, Record Group 47, National Records Center, Suitland, Maryland.

5. Ibid.

6. Memorandum to Mr. Murphy, February 14, 1949, File Folder 011.1 "1949–1946," Actuarial and Office of the Commissioner Records, Accession no. 64a-751, Record Group 47, National Records Center, Suitland, Maryland.

7. Ibid.

8. Mark P. Hale, "The Process of Developing Policy for a Federal-State Grant-in-Aid Program: As Illustrated by the Work of the Social Security Board, 1935–1946," *Social Service Review* 31 (September, 1957):297.

9. Informal Minutes of the Social Security Board, November 22, 1938, Social Security Administration, Woodlawn, Maryland.

10. General Counsel to Executive Director, May 3, 1937, Carton no. 3, Social Security Commissioner's Action Minutes Documents, Record Group 47, National Archives, Washington, D.C.

11. Ibid.

12. Ibid.

13. Informal Minutes of the Social Security Board, May 4, 1937, Social Security Administration, Woodlawn, Maryland, p. 5.

14. Bureau of Public Assistance to Social Security Board, March 24, 1936, Carton no. 1, Social Security Commissioner's Action Minutes Documents, Record Group 47, National Archives, Washington, D.C.

15. Bureau of Public Assistance to Executive Director, August 17, 1936, Carton no. 1, Social Security Commissioner's Action Minutes Documents, Record Group 47, National Archives, Washington, D.C.

16. Bureau of Public Assistance to Executive Director, December 29, 1936, Carton no. 7, Social Security Commissioner's Action Minutes Documents, Record Group 47, National Archives, Washington, D.C.

17. Bureau of Public Assistance to Executive Director, May 3, 1937, Carton no. 8, Social Security Commissioner Action Minutes Documents, Record Group 47, National Archives, Washington, D.C.

18. Informal Minutes of the Social Security Board, May 4, 1937, p. 6.

19. Informal Minutes of the Social Security Board, November 22, 1938.

20. Ibid.

21. Ibid.

22. Ibid.

23. Ibid.

24. Ibid.

25. Ibid.

26. Jane Hoey to Oscar Powell, June 28, 1943, Carton no. 28, Social Security Commissioner's Action Minutes Documents, Record Group 47, National Archives, Washington, D.C.

27. Ibid.

28. Informal Minutes of the Social Security Board, July 6, 1939, Social Security Administration, Woodlawn, Maryland, p. 6.

29. Altmeyer, *Formative Years*, p. 105.

30. Hale, "Process of Developing Policy," p. 203.

31. Informal Minutes of the Social Security Board, June 29, 1940, Social Security Administration, Woodlawn, Maryland.

32. A. D. Smith to Oscar M. Powell, December 13, 1940, Informal Minutes and Submitted Memoranda, Record Group 363, National Archives, Washington, D.C.

33. Informal Minutes of the Social Security Board, December 13, 1940, and June 29, 1940.

34. Informal Minutes of the Social Security Board, August 30, 1940, Social Security Administration, Woodlawn, Maryland.

35. Ibid.

36. Ibid.

37. Hale, "Process of Developing Policy," p. 302.

38. George Bigge, interview with author, Washington, D.C., August, 1976.

39. Smith to Powell, December 13, 1940.

40. Informal Minutes of the Social Security Board, August 2, 1940, Social Security Administration, Woodlawn, Maryland.

41. Ibid.

42. Ibid.

43. Ibid.

44. Ibid.

45. Ibid.

46. Informal Minutes of the Social Security Board, August 30, 1940.

47. Ibid.

48. Informal Minutes of the Social Security Board, March 24, 1942, Social Security Administration, Woodlawn, Maryland.

49. Ibid.

50. Ibid.

51. Ibid.

52. Ibid.

53. Ibid.

54. Ibid.

55. Ibid.

56. Ibid.

57. Ibid.

58. Ibid.

59. Jane Hoey to Oscar Powell, October 15, 1943, Social Security Board Infor-

mal Minutes and Submitted Memoranda, Record Group 363, National Archives, Washington, D.C.

60. Ibid.

61. Informal Minutes of the Social Security Board, October 15, 1943, Social Security Administration, Woodlawn, Maryland.

62. Informal Minutes of the Social Security Board, December 3, 1943, Social Security Administration, Woodlawn, Maryland.

63. Informal Minutes of the Social Security Board, May 2, 1944.

64. Informal Minutes of the Social Security Board, October 15, 1943.

65. Ibid.

66. Ibid.

67. Altmeyer, *Formative Years*, p. 53.

68. Informal Minutes of the Social Security Board, October 15, 1943.

69. Ibid.

70. Ibid.

71. Bureau of Public Assistance to Executive Director, April 5, 1944, Social Security Board Informal Minutes and Submitted Memoranda, Record Group 363, National Archives, Washington, D.C.

72. Informal Minutes of the Social Security Board, April 14, 1944, Social Security Administration, Woodlawn, Maryland.

73. Bureau of Public Assistance to Executive Director, April 5, 1944.

74. Ibid.

75. Informal Minutes of the Social Security Board, April 14, 1944.

76. Informal Minutes of the Social Security Board, February 12, 1943, Social Security Administration, Woodlawn, Maryland.

77. Wilbur J. Cohen to John J. Corson, October 10, 1937, File Folder 317.1 "Oct.-Dec., 1937," Central Files of the Social Security Board, Record Group 47, National Archives, Washington, D.C.

78. Arthur J. Altmeyer to D. W. Bell, March 23, 1939, File Folder 011.1, "March–April, 1939," Central Files of the Social Security Board, Record Group 47, National Archives, Washington, D.C.

79. Wilbur J. Cohen to Mr. Bragman, February 23, 1950, File Folder 011.1, "February, 1950," Actuarial and Office of the Commissioner Records, Accession no. 64a-751, Record Group 47, National Records Center, Suitland, Maryland.

80. "Douglas Old-Age Assistance Income Exemption," File Folder 011.1, "H.R. 7225," Actuarial and Office of the Commissioner Records, Accession no. 64a-751, Record Group 47, National Records Center, Suitland, Maryland.

81. Gilbert Steiner, *Social Insecurity: The Politics of Welfare* (Chicago: Rand McNally and Co., 1966), p. 25.

Chapter 6

1. U.S., Congress, Senate, Senate Committee on Finance, *Social Security Revision: Hearings before the Senate Committee on Finance.* 81st Cong., 2d sess., 1950, p. 1953.

2. Mark P. Hale, "The Process of Developing Policy for a Federal-State Grant-in-Aid Program: As Illustrated by the Work of the Social Security Board, 1935–1946," *Social Service Review* 31 (September, 1957):290.

3. Ibid., p. 302.

4. Ibid.

5. Hale's missing of this point is attributable to two factors. First, he considered public assistance policy in isolation, failing to study it in relation to social insurance and missing the fact that for the board, the overriding concern was social insurance's protection. More importantly, perhaps, Hale did not have access to the Informal Minutes of the board which contain the important intention data.

6. Martha Derthick, *Policymaking for Social Security* (Washington, D.C.: Brookings Institution, 1979), p. 22.

7. Ibid.

8. Ibid., p. 218.

9. Arthur J. Altmeyer, *The Formative Years of Social Security* (Madison: University of Wisconsin Press, 1966), p. 205.

10. Derthick, *Policymaking for Social Security*, p. 22.

11. Ibid., p. 23.

12. Ibid., p. 171.

13. Marjorie Shearon to Arthur J. Altmeyer, July 25, 1941, File Folder 032.2, "August, 1941," Records of the Executive Director of the Social Security Board (1941–48), Record Group 47, Accession no. 56a-533, Washington National Records Center, Suitland, Maryland.

14. Ibid.

15. Ibid.

16. Marjorie O'Connell Shearon, *Wilbur J. Cohen: The Pursuit of Power* (Washington, D.C.: Gray Printing Co., 1967).

Epilogue

1. Peter J. Ferrara, *Social Security: The Inherent Contradiction* (San Francisco: Cato Institute, 1980).

2. Bruno Stein, *Social Security and Pensions in Transition* (New York: Free Press, 1980).

3. Ibid., pp. 224–25.

4. Mass mailing from Charles T. Manatt, Chairman, Democratic National Committee, January, 1982.

5. John A. Brittain, *The Payroll Tax for Social Security* (Washington, D.C.: Brookings Institution, 1972).

6. Wilbur J. Cohen, "Social Security: Current Myths and Reality: The Need for its Preservation and Reform," in *New Strategic Perspectives on Social Policy*, eds., John E. Tropman, Milan J. Dluhy, and Roger M. Lind (New York: Pergamon Press, 1981), p. 452.

7. Alvin Schorr, "Income Maintenance and the Social Security Ideology," in *The Social Welfare Forum*, ed. Arthur Katz (New York: Columbia University Press, 1970).

8. Frances Fox Piven and Richard A. Cloward, *Regulating the Poor: The Functions of Public Welfare* (New York: Random House, 1971).

9. John A. Menefee, Bea Edwards, and Sylvester J. Scheiber, "Analysis of Nonparticipation in the SSI Program," *Social Security Bulletin* 44 (1981):3–21.

10. Ibid., p. 18.

11. Ibid.

12. Ibid., p. 19.

13. *Congressional Quarterly Weekly*, September 26, 1981, p. 1839.

14. Alicia Munnell, *The Future of Social Security* (Washington, D.C.: Brookings Institution, 1977), p. 52.

15. Ibid., p. 92.

16. Cohen, "Social Security: Myths and Reality," p. 454.

Selected Bibliography

Altmeyer, Arthur J. *The Formative Years of Social Security*. Madison: University of Wisconsin Press, 1968.

————. "Social Insurance for Permanently Disabled Workers." *Social Security Bulletin* 5 (March, 1941);3–10

Bendix, Richard. *Work and Authority in Industry*. New York: John Wiley and Sons, 1956.

Booth, Philip. *Social Security in America*. Ann Arbor: Institute of Labor and Industrial Relations, 1973.

Bortz, Abe. *Social Security Sources in Federal Records, 1934–1950*. Washington, D.C.: Government Printing Office, 1969.

Brittain, John. *The Payroll Tax for Social Security*. Washington, D.C.: Brookings Institution, 1972.

Burns, Eveline. *Social Security and Public Policy*. New York: McGraw-Hill, 1956.

Cohen, Wilbur J. "Social Security: Current Myths and Reality: The Need for its Preservation and Reform." In *New Strategic Perspectives on Social Policy*, edited by John E. Tropman, Milan J. Dluhy, and Roger M. Lind. New York: Pergamon Press, 1981.

Cyert, Richard M., and March, James G. *The Behavioral Theory of the Firm*. Englewood Cliffs, N.J.: Prentice-Hall, 1963.

Derthick, Martha. *Policymaking for Social Security*. Washington, D.C.: Brookings Institution, 1979.

Ferrara, Peter J. *Social Security: The Inherent Contradiction*. San Francisco: Cato Institute, 1980.

Hale, Mark P. "The Process of Developing Policy for a Federal-State Grant-in-Aid Program, as Illustrated by the Work of the Social Security Board, 1935–1946." *Social Service Review* 31 (September, 1957):290–310.

Holtzman, Abraham. *The Townsend Movement: A Political Study*. New York: Bookman Associates, 1963.

Kaufman, Herbert. *Are Government Organizations Immortal?* Washington, D.C.: Brookings Institution, 1976.

Larson, Arthur. "The American Social Insurance System: Structure, Coverage, and Current Problems." In *Economic Security for Americans*, edited by Willmer Jones, pp. 52–62. New York: Columbia University Graduate School of Business, 1953.

Lawrence, Paul and Lorsch, Jay. *Organization and Environment*. Cambridge, Mass.: Harvard University Press, 1967.

Leuchtenberg, William E. *Franklin D. Roosevelt and the New Deal*. New York: Harper and Row, 1965.

Lubove, Roy. *The Struggle for Social Security, 1900–1935*. Cambridge, Mass.: Harvard University Press, 1968.

March, James G., and Simon, Herbert A. *Organizations*. New York: John Wiley and Sons, 1958.

Marmor, Theodore R. *The Politics of Medicare*. Chicago: Aldine Publishing Co., 1970.

McKinley, Charles, and Frase, Robert W. *Launching Social Security: a Capture-and-Record Account, 1935–1937*. Madison: University of Wisconsin Press, 1970.

Menefee, John A.; Edwards, Bea; and Scheiber, Sylvester J. "Analysis of Nonparticipation in the SSI Program." *Social Security Bulletin* 44 (1981):3–21.

Messinger, Sheldon L. "Organizational Transformation: A Case Study of a Declining Social Movement." *American Sociological Review* 20 (May, 1955):3–10.

Munnell, Alicia. *The Future of Social Security*. Washington, D.C.: Brookings Institution, 1977.

Mushkin, Selma J. "Comments on 'Social Security in a Stable Prosperity.'" *American Economic Review* 37 (May, 1947):355–59.

Mushkin, Selma J., and DeScitzovsky, Anne. "A Formula for Social Insurance Financing." *American Economic Review* 35 (September, 1945):646–52.

Myers, Robert J. "Social Security at the Crossroads." *Reader's Digest* 32 (April, 1970):153–58.

———. "Is Social Security Really Insurance?" *Journal of the Chartered Life Underwriters* 22 (July, 1974):33–58.

———. "Social Security Taxes: Regressivity and Subsidies." *Tax Review* 34 (December, 1973):45–48.

Ozawa, Martha N. "Income Redistribution and Social Security." *Social Service Review* 50 (June, 1976):210–35.

Pechman, Joseph A., Aaron, Henry J., and Taussig, Michael K. *Social Security: Perspectives for Reform*. Washington, D.C.: Brookings Institution, 1968.

Perkins, Frances. *The Roosevelt I Knew*. New York: Viking Press, 1946.

Piven, Frances Fox, and Cloward, Richard A. *Regulating the Poor: The Functions of Public Welfare*. New York: Random House, 1971.

President's Commission on Income Maintenance Programs. *Poverty Amid Plenty: The American Paradox*. Washington, D.C.: Government Printing Office, 1969.

Schlaback, Theron F. *Edwin E. Witte, Cautious Reformer*. Madison: State Historical Society of Wisconsin, 1969.

Schorr, Alvin. "Income Maintenance and the Social Security Ideology." In *The Social Welfare Forum*, edited by Arthur Katz, pp. 200–214. New York: Columbia University Press, 1970.

Selznick, Philip. *Leadership in Administration*. Evanston, Ill.: Row, Peterson, 1957.

Stein, Bruno. *Social Security and Pensions in Transition*. New York: Free Press, 1980.

Steiner, Gilbert. *Social Insecurity: The Politics of Welfare*. Chicago: Rand McNally and Co., 1966.

Strauss, Anselm; Schatzman, Leonard; Bucher, Rue; Erlich, Dannte; and Sabsin, Melvin. *Psychiatric Ideologies and Institutions*. New York: Free Press, 1964.

U.S., Congress, House, Committee on Ways and Means. *Social Security Amendments of 1949*. H. Rept. 1330, 81st Cong., 1st sess., 1949.

―――. *Social Security Act Amendments of 1949: Hearings before the Committee on Ways and Means*, 81st Cong., 1st sess., 1949.

U.S., Congress, House, Subcommittee of the Committee on Ways and Means. *Analysis of the Social Security System: Hearings before a Subcommittee of the Committee on Ways and Means*. 83d Cong., 1st sess., 1953.

U.S., Congress, Senate, Committee on Finance. *Social Security Act Amendments of 1950*. S. Rept. 1669, 81st Cong., 2d sess., 1950.

U.S., Congress, Senate, Committee on Finance. *Old-Age Pensions: Hearings before the Committee on Finance*. 77th Cong., 1st sess., 1941.

U.S., Congress, Senate, Committee on Finance. *Social Security Revision: Hearings before the Senate Committee on Finance* 81st Cong., 2d sess., 1930.

Wilensky, Harold L., and Lebeaux, Charles N. *Industrial Society and Social Welfare*. New York: Free Press, 1965.

Witte, Edwin E. *The Development of the Social Security Act*. Madison: University of Wisconsin Press, 1963.

Index